IFAD Studies in Rural Poverty No. 2

GHANA UNDER STRUCTURAL ADJUSTMENT:

THE IMPACT ON AGRICULTURE AND THE RURAL POOR

GHANA UNDER STRUCTURAL ADJUSTMENT:

THE IMPACT ON AGRICULTURE AND THE RURAL POOR

Alexander Sarris
and
Hadi Shams

With a Foreword by Idriss Jazairy

Published for the
International Fund for Agricultural Development
by New York University Press

The opinions expressed in this volume are those of the authors and do not necessarily reflect official views or policies of the International Fund for Agricultural Development, except as explicitly stated.

The designations employed and the presentation of material in this publication do not imply the expression of any opinion whatsoever on the part of the International Fund for Agricultural Development of the United Nations concerning the legal status of any country, territory, city or area or of its authorities, or concerning the delimitation of its frontiers or boundaries.

Library of Congress Cataloging-in-Publication Data

Sarris, Alexander.
    Ghana under structural adjustment: the poverty impact / Alexander Sarris and Hadi Shams.
       p.   cm. — (IFAD studies in poverty alleviation: v. 2)
    Includes index.
    ISBN 0-8147-7932-8 (alk. paper)
    ISBN 92-9072-001-8
    1. Agriculture—Economic aspects—Ghana. 2. Agriculture and state—Ghana. 3. Rural poor—Ghana. 4. Farms, Small—Ghana. 5. Economic stabilization—Ghana. 6. Ghana—Rural conditions. I. Shams, Hadi. II. Title. III. Series.
HD2146.G4S48   1991
338.1'8667—dc20   91-17007
                                                     CIP

New York University Press books are printed on acid-free paper, and their binding materials are chosen for strength and durability.

Manufactured in the United States of America

Contents

Weights and Measures xiii
Official Currency Equivalents xiii
Map of Ghana: Administrative and Infrastructure xv
Acknowledgements xvii
List of Acronyms and Abbreviations xix
Foreword by Idriss Jazairy xxi
Editor's Note xxiii
Introduction xxv

1 Recent Economic Developments 1
   The Circumstances Leading to Adjustment 1
   The Economic Recovery Programme 4
   Macro-economic Performance Under the ERP 8
   The Public Investment Programme 11
   Agricultural Policy 12
   National Food Security 14

2 Agricultural Sector Structure and Performance 20
   Role of Agriculture in the Economy 20
   Land Distribution, Land Use and Land Suitability .. 21
   Resource Base 23
   Ecological Zones, Soils and Vegetation 24
   Farm Size and Distribution 27
   Farming Systems and Crop Rotations 27
   Crop Production Methods and Technology 28
   Labour Use 31
   Crop Production and Yield 31
   Crop Budgets 32
   Post-harvest Handling and Storage 33
   Irrigation 35
   Livestock 37
   Fisheries 38
   Forestry 40
   Environmental Implications of Current Practices 41
   Environmental Action Plan 42

Stability of Farming Systems Under Environmental
Stress   43
Technology Availability   44

3   **Profile of Rural Poverty: Economic Dimensions**   46
Rural Income and Assets   46
Livestock Ownership   51
Regional Crop Pattern of Smallholders   52
Farmer Use of Labour   56
Sources of Income of Rural Smallholders   56
Smallholder Consumption Patterns and Expenditures   59
Demography and Migration   61
Estimates of Rural Poverty   62
Other Rural Poor Groups   67

4   **Social Dimensions of Rural Poverty**   71
Land Tenure   71
Health and Nutrition   79
Education   82
Rural Water   83
Rural Sanitation   85
Mechanisms and Process of Socio-economic
Differentiation   86

5   **Women and Rural Development**   92
General Aspects   92
Women-headed Households   93
Women's Workload Responsibilities   94
Women's Role in Agriculture   96
Women in Off-farm Activities   100
Women's Access to Resources   106
Women's Development Organizations and Institutions   113

6   **Government Support Services**   118
The Ministry of Agriculture   118
Agricultural Research   120
Agricultural Extension   124
Input Supply   125

7   **Agricultural Credit**   127
Formal Credit System   127
Financing of Small Farmers   128

	Informal Credit	130
	Agricultural Credit Policy	131
8	**Agricultural Marketing**	133
	Private Sector Marketing	139
	Marketing System Performance	141
9	**Grassroots Institutions and Non-governmental and Social Service Organizations**	147
	Grassroots Institutions	147
	Cooperatives	151
	Non-governmental Organizations	152
	Social Service Organizations	157
	Linkages Between Grassroots and Other Institutions	158
10	**Initial Impact of Structural Adjustment on Smallholders and the Rural Poor**	161
	The Setting Before and After the SAP	161
	Smallholder Linkages with the Money Economy	163
	Devaluation	163
	Agricultural Price Changes	164
	Input Costs	173
	Impact on Labour Markets	174
	Consumer Goods	178
	Impact of Fiscal Restraint on Agriculture	179
	Administrative and Institutional Reform and Farmer Services	183
	Private Sector Input Supply	184
	Fertilizer Subsidies and Privatization	185
	Land Tenure	186
	Interest Rates and Credit Demand	186
	Social Services and the SAP	187
	Block Farming	190
	Overall Impact on Smallholders and the Rural Poor	192
11	**Structural Problems and Constraints in Smallholder Development**	193
	Incentive Framework and Comparative Advantage	193
	Food Aid and Disincentives	199
	Technological Constraints	203
	Institutional Weaknesses	204
	Extension	205

	Road Communication System	206
	Rural Credit	206
	Input Supply	207

12	**A Framework for Agricultural Assistance to Rural Smallholders**	209
	Regional and National Food Security	211
	Targetting the Smallholder	212
	Collaboration with NGOs	213
	Support for Rural Women	214
	Flexibility Under a Changing Economic Environment	214
	The SAP and the Policy Dialogue	215
	The Response of the Government	216
	The General Nature of Proposals Under the PAMSCAD	217

Annexes

A	Supplementary Tables	219
B	Smallholder Food Production and Consumption Patterns	233
C	Methodology Note for Calculation of the Number of Smallholders Below the Poverty Line	241

| **Bibliography** | | 247 |
| **Index** | | 259 |

Tables and Figures

Tables

1.1   Average Annual Growth Rates of Main Economic Indicators, 1950-70 (percent)   3

1.2   Average Annual Growth Rates of Selected Basic Indicators, 1965-83 (percent)   4

1.3   Recent Performance of Selected Production Indicators, 1982-86 (thousand metric tons unless otherwise stated)   10

1.4   Cereal Production-Demand, 1970-88 (thousand metric tons)   16

1.5   Cost of Cereal and Other Food Imports, 1975-87   19

2.1   Recent Performance of Non-traditional Agricultural Export   22

2.2   Land Use by Area   22

2.3   Land Suitability by Categories of Crops - Area of Suitable Land (thousand ha)   23

3.1   National and Regional Size Distribution of Holdings, 1970   47

3.2   National Size Distribution of Holdings, 1970 and 1984   49

3.3   Number of Holdings of all Sizes (in parentheses those under 0.8 ha (2 acres)) in 1970 and 1984   50

3.4   Number of Small and Total Holdings, 1984 and 1986   50

3.5   Crop Pattern of Smallholders, 1986   53

3.6   Types of Labour and Their Relative Contributions to Major Operations on Farms in Otinibi and Sekesua Villages of the Eastern Region   57

3.7   Ratio of Gross Crop Income to Staple Food Consumption Expenditure for Representative Smallholder Households by Region, 1970-86 (percent)   60

3.8   Estimation of Numbers of Smallholders Below Poverty Line, 1986   63

3.9   Estimation of Numbers of Smallholders Below Poverty Line, 1984   64

3.10   Estimation of Numbers of Smallholders Below Poverty Line, 1970   65

4.1   Land Tenure by Regions, 1970, 1974, 1986 (thousand
      farms)   76
4.2   Farms Under Different Tenancies, 1987   78
4.3   Selected Educational Statistics in 1980   84

5.1   Heads of Household by Gender, 1970 and 1984   94
5.2   Female Working Population, 1984 (thousands)   95
5.3   Persons Aged 15 Years and Over Employed in
      Agriculture, by Region and by Sex, 1984 (thousands)   98
5.4   Estimated Person-days Required to Headload Various
      Crops from Farm to Village   98
5.5   Persons Aged 15 Years and Over Employed in
      Commerce, by Region and by Sex, 1984 (thousands)   101
5.6   Regional Coverage of Women Farmers' Extension
      Services (as of June 1987)   111

6.1   Funding of Research by Commodity   123

8.1   Produce Prices for Maize and Rice, 1979-87 (cedis per
      mt)   138
8.2   Percentage Differences of Monthly Wholesale Prices
      Between Major Urban Consuming and Rural Producing
      Centres (1982-86)   142
8.3   Intra-seasonal Variation of Monthly National
      Wholesale Prices of Maize and Rice, 1975-86 (prices in
      cedis per bag)   145

10.1 Selected Economic Indicators Before and After the
      ERP   162
10.2 Official and Parallel Exchange Rates, 1975-89
      (cedis/US dollars)   164
10.3 Incentives for Cocoa Farmers, 1975-89   165
10.4 Index of Real Wholesale Prices of Major Food Crops
      and Cocoa, 1970-86 (1970 = 100)   167
10.5 Price Indices for Traded and Non-traded Staple Foods
      and Cocoa, 1970-86 (Index 1970 = 100)   168
10.6 Index of Typical Smallholder Gross Food Crop Income
      by Region 1970-86 (1970 = 100)   171
10.7 Index of Gross Food Crop Income per Hectare of a
      Representative Smallholder by Region, 1970-86
      (Ghana = 100)   172
10.8 Input Costs, 1983, 1987, 1989 (cedis)   174

10.9 Cost of Purchased Inputs for Staple Food Production, 1981-87 (cedis/ha)   175
10.10 Trends in Nominal and Real Wages: 1970-87   176
10.11 Returns per Man-day of Family Labour in Various Crops 1981-87 (cedis/day)   177
10.12 Rural Consumer Price Indices, 1978-87 (1977=100)   180
10.13 Public Expenditure on Agriculture, 1981-87 (₵ million, except where noted)   181
10.14 Components of the Recurrent Expenditure Budget of the Ministry of Agriculture   182

11.1 Annual Changes in Real Wholesale Prices of Staple Food Crops, 1971-86 (figures are percent changes from previous years)   195
11.2 Returns to Smallholders for Maize and Rice Production (Traditional and Improved Technologies) Under Alternative Marketing Strategies (cedis per man-day of family labour except as noted)   196
11.3 Comparative Advantage in Staple Foods   200
11.4 Food Aid Imports, 1981-87 (in metric tons)   201
11.5 Cereal Food Aid as Proportion of Domestic Cereal Marketed Production, 1981-86   202

Figures

1.1 Cereal and Starchy Staple Production, 1970-87   18

2.1 Ghana and its Regions: Staple Food and Tree-Crop Production   25

4.1 Malnutrition Among Children Under Five Years Old, 1980-84   81

Weights and Measures

1 metric ton (mt)	=	0.98 long ton
1 long ton	=	2 240 lbs = 1 016 metric tons
1 hectare (ha)	=	2.47 acres
1 acre	=	0.405 ha
1 kilometre (km)	=	0.62 miles
1 mile	=	1.609 km

Official Currency Equivalents

Note: Official monetary unit is the cedi (₡)

February 1973 to June 18, 1978	US$ 1 = ₡ 1.15
As of August 26, 1978	US$ 1 = ₡ 2.75
As of April 21, 1983	US$ 1 = ₡ 24.69
As of October 19, 1983	US$ 1 = ₡ 30.00
As of March 25, 1984	US$ 1 = ₡ 35.00
As of August 25, 1984	US$ 1 = ₡ 38.50
As of December 3, 1984	US$ 1 = ₡ 50.00
As of April 19, 1985	US$ 1 = ₡ 53.00
As of August 12, 1985	US$ 1 = ₡ 57.00
As of October 7, 1985	US$ 1 = ₡ 60.00
As of January 11, 1986	US$ 1 = ₡ 90.00
As of September 19, 1986 (Second Window Auction)	US$ 1 = ₡ 128-170
October, 1987 (Second Window Auction)	US$ 1 = ₡ 170-175

Ghana's Fiscal Year
1 January to 31 December

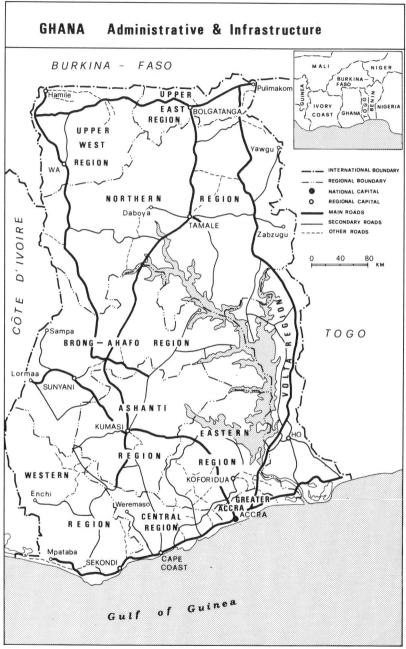

GHANA Administrative & Infrastructure

BURKINA - FASO

Hamile

UPPER
EAST
REGION

Pulimakom

BOLGATANGA

UPPER
WEST
REGION

WA

Yawgu

NORTHERN   REGION

Daboya

TAMALE

Zabzugu

CÔTE D'IVOIRE

Sampa

BRONG — AHAFO REGION

TOGO

Lormaa

SUNYANI

ASHANTI

KUMASI

EASTERN

HO

REGION

VOLTA REGION

WESTERN

REGION

Enchi

Weremaso

KOFORIDUA

CENTRAL
REGION

GREATER
ACCRA

ACCRA

Mpataba

SEKONDI

CAPE
COAST

Gulf of Guinea

MALI   NIGER

BURKINA—
FASO

GUINEA

IVORY
COAST

GHANA

TOGO

BENIN

NIGERIA

INTERNATIONAL BOUNDARY
REGIONAL BOUNDARY
NATIONAL CAPITAL
REGIONAL CAPITAL
MAIN ROADS
SECONDARY ROADS
OTHER ROADS

0   40   80
KM

Source : The World Bank

Author's Preface and Acknowledgements

In July 1987, IFAD participated in the inter-agency mission to Ghana, along with the World Bank, ILO, UNDP, UNICEF, WFP, WHO and the UK Overseas Development Administration, to assist the Government in the preparation of a Programme of Action to Mitigate the Social Costs of Adjustment (PAMSCAD). This was followed by a full IFAD Special Programming Mission (SPM), which visited Ghana in October 1987. The purpose of the SPM was to trace the developments of the agricultural, especially the smallholder rural, sector over the recent years; to identify systemic problems confronting rural Ghana; to draw the profile and process of rural poverty; to review the consequences of the structural adjustment programme on smallholders and the rural poor; and to propose a framework and strategy for future IFAD involvement in Ghana, taking into account the concerns of the Government of Ghana as reflected in the PAMSCAD document. This report is largely based on the findings of the SPM members who were: Professor Alexander Sarris (Economist, Mission Leader, Consultant), Vineet Raswant (Institutions and Credit Specialist, Consultant), John Newton (Agronomist, Consultant), Ian Jones (Sociologist, Consultant), Esmail Aghazadeh (Economist, Consultant), Theresa Panuccio (Women's Expert, Economist, Policy and Planning Division, IFAD). Radcliffe Williams, Project Controller, Africa Division, IFAD, joined the mission during its last week in Ghana. Hadi Shams, at the time Senior Economist for the Africa region of the Policy and Planning Division, IFAD, (currently on secondment to UNDP/Office of Project Services) coordinated and supervised the work of the mission during its field work and report writing. Most figures in the text refer to the period when the IFAD mission visited Ghana. However, some effort was made to update certain factual information through contacts with the Ministry of Agriculture, after the first draft of the report was produced. The original report was revised and edited for this publication by the authors although a large part of the analysis is based on the work of the individual mission members.

Since the time of the mission and the end of the research for this volume, there has been a considerable amount of further work on Ghana, most of which is in the form of official reports and unpublished. In particular, the massive World Bank-sponsored Ghana Living Standard Survey (GLSS), which at the time of the mission was in the process of data collection, has been analysed. Having had the chance to examine some of these later reports it is comforting to note that most of the findings and conclusions of this volume have been broadly confirmed by more intensive subsequent research.

The IFAD mission, whose work formed the basis of this volume, received extensive support in the field from a large number of people, the list too long to mention here, but our special thanks go to the Ministry of Agriculture for all their assistance.

Alexander Sarris and
Hadi Shams
November 1991

List of Acronyms and Abbreviations

ADB	Agricultural Development Bank
AGDP	Agricultural Gross Domestic Product
ASRP	Agricultural Services Rehabilitation Project
BNI	Basic Needs Income
BOG	Bank of Ghana
₵	Cedi
CIDA	Canadian International Development Agency
c.i.f.	cost, insurance, freight
CIMMYT	International Centre for Maize and Wheat Improvement
CPI	Consumer Price Index
CRI	Crops Research Institute (Kwadaso, Ghana)
DANIDA	Danish International Development Agency
EEC	European Economic Community
ERP	Economic Recovery Programme
FAO	Food and Agriculture Organization of the United Nations
f.o.b.	free on board
GCB	Ghana Commercial Bank
GCMB	Ghana Cocoa Marketing Board (COCOBOD)
GDP	Gross Domestic Product
GFDC	Ghana Food Distribution Corporation
GIDA	Ghana Irrigation Development Authority
GSC	Ghana Seed Company
IDA	International Development Association
IFAD	International Fund for Agricultural Development
IITA	International Institute of Tropical Agriculture
ILO	International Labour Organisation
IMF	International Monetary Fund
ISSER	Institute of Statistical, Social and Economic Research
MOA	Ministry of Agriculture
MOH	Ministry of Health
mt	metric ton
MTADP	Medium-term Agricultural Development Plan
NCWD	National Council on Women and Development
NGO	non-governmental organization
PAMSCAD	Programme of Action to Mitigate the Social Costs of Adjustment

PIP	Public Investment Programme
PNDC	Provisional National Defence Council
PPMED	Policy Planning, Monitoring and Evaluation Department
RB	Rural Bank
RIC	Reconstruction Import Credit
SAL	Structural Adjustment Lending
SAP	Structural Adjustment Programme
SOE	state-owned enterprise
SPM	Special Programming Mission
T&V	Training and Visit
UNDP	United Nations Development Programme
UNICEF	United Nations Children's Fund
USAID	United States Agency for International Development
VORADEP	Volta Region Agricultural Development Project
WARDA	West African Rice Development Association
WCARRD	World Conference on Agrarian Reform and Rural Development
WFP	World Food Programme
WHO	World Health Organization

Foreword

Rural smallholders figure among Ghana's poorest social groups. These same smallholders, however, are also one of Ghana's richest resources. With their potential to increase food production, smallholders can make the difference between national food security and self-sufficiency or continued food dependency. In Ghana, as in many developing countries, recognition of this fact is refocussing attention on the role smallholders can play in economic development.

In 1983, the Government of Ghana began implementing an Economic Recovery Programme (ERP) which attempted to reverse more than a decade of decline in most sectors of the economy. An integral part of the ERP was the adoption of measures that would increase revenues from key export crops, especially cocoa - traditionally the mainstay of Ghana's agricultural export industry.

Despite important successes at the macro-economic level, including growth in GDP, investments and savings, as well as declining inflation and an improving balance of trade, it became clear by 1985 that adequate measures had not been taken to increase agricultural productivity on a sustained basis. Notably, it was recognized that the smallholder sector, which accounts for the majority of those involved in agriculture, had largely been neglected. Based on these observations, a new agricultural policy was adopted placing greater emphasis on small-scale farmers. For the first time, they were expected to be key players in Ghana's attempt to increase food production, particularly in helping to obtain self-sufficiency in food staples such as maize, rice, and cassava. Achieving food security was to be given priority along with promoting agricultural exports.

This new emphasis, however, has created enormous challenges for the Government of Ghana. These challenges include the need to improve agricultural storage, processing and distribution systems; streamline the Ministry of Agriculture, in part by decentralizing activities; improve agricultural research centres, and credit and marketing facilities; and ensure adequate returns to farmers, distributors, and processors in order to promote the efficient production, processing, and distribution of agricultural goods. These challenges require not only substantial financial resources and trained manpower, but also new research to determine how the challenges can best be met. Many national and international organizations have already begun to contribute to this effort.

Within this context, IFAD has taken special interest in the effect on the rural poor of Ghana's structural adjustment efforts. Specifically, the Fund has sought to trace the developments of the agricultural - especially smallholder - sector over recent years; identify systemic problems confronting rural Ghana; delineate rural poverty and its causes; and review the consequences of the structural adjustment programme on smallholders and the rural poor. The ultimate goal of this study was to propose a framework and strategy for future involvement in rural development in Ghana, taking into account the objectives and concerns of the Government.

This study incorporates many of the results of IFAD's research. It represents, in my view, the most detailed and authoritative analysis currently available on the Economic Recovery Programme in Ghana and its effects on smallholders. The study also provides a comprehensive strategy for sustainable agricultural development for Ghanaian smallholders. Among the specific conclusions drawn is the strategic need for broadening popular and private participation in agricultural development, as well as for enhanced retention among smallholders of the value of their output. In this context, grassroots groups and non-governmental organizations should play a greater role in the organization of contacts between small producers and markets for output and inputs (including credit) and be supplemented by private sector operations. Only by including smallholders and the rural poor in all stages of the development process can meaningful progress be made towards rural poverty eradication and sustainable development. This study provides a solid framework for further action.

Idriss Jazairy
President of IFAD,
Rome, November 1991

Editor's Note

This study of Ghana under Structural Adjustment is the second volume in the series of IFAD Studies in Rural Poverty undertaken in collaboration with New York University Press. The first study, *Providing Food Security for All*, by Mohiuddin Alamgir and Poonam Arora, sought to identify the food security status of the world's rural poor, who constitute more than 80 percent of global poverty, and focussed on strategies designed to enhance food security at the household level, in particular.

This volume looks at rural poverty and food security at the household level in one country - Ghana - in terms of the impact of the Government's major structural adjustment programme on smallholder farmers. Like all the volumes in this series, it seeks to illuminate the problems and possibilities facing the rural poor from a micro-economic perspective, but within the overall framework of a particular macro-economic setting. In the case of Ghana, the setting is one of painful economic restructuring, and the volume's special value lies in tracing the impact of these macro-economic adjustments on those who live in poverty.

We are again indebted to New York University Press for their support and assistance in helping to fill a major gap in micro-economic studies of the development process.

William P. Lineberry
Theresa Panuccio
Editors

Introduction

Agriculture is the mainstay of the Ghanaian economy, providing food for its population and accounting for a large part of the country's foreign exchange earnings. The sector has many aspects - economic, social and institutional - conditioned both by historical and by more recent economic events. The general purpose of this study is to examine these various aspects, particularly as they pertain to rural smallholders. The study identifies structural problems confronting the rural economy of Ghana, draws a profile of the rural poor, outlines the dynamics of rural poverty, analyses the initial impact of the Government's Economic Recovery Programme (ERP) on smallholders and the rural poor and proposes a framework and strategy for future rural development projects in Ghana.

The main study is organized around six major themes. The first concerns macro-economy as it conditions the agricultural sector, the events leading to adjustment, the nature of the ERP and the relationship between the Government's agricultural policy and the country's food security. This is covered in Chapter 1.

The next theme concerns the structure and performance of the agricultural sector, focussing in particular on the technical aspects of production. Chapter 2 presents this overview and lists the technological possibilities available to Ghana for agricultural development.

The third main subject of the study is the economic and social profile of smallholders and the rural poor. Three chapters are devoted to this theme. Chapter 3 analyses the type and economic structure of rural smallholders in terms of land ownership and other assets and estimates the number of rural households below the poverty line. Chapter 4 examines several other aspects of rural poverty, particularly the land tenure system, health and nutrition, education, water and sanitation. The chapter also analyses the historical and economic forces behind rural poverty in Ghana. Chapter 5 is devoted to the important role of women in rural development. Both economic and social aspects are reviewed to assess the potential for targetting women in specific project activities.

The fourth theme of the study focusses on the structure of rural institutions. It is organized in five chapters. Chapter 6 analyses the performance of various government support services, particularly research and extension, as well as the role of the Ministry of Agriculture in coordinating input supply and in planning. Chapter 7 analyses the institutions and sources of rural credit. Formal banking institutions as well as informal sources are assessed in terms of the extent to which they reach smallholders. Chapter 8 analyses the public and private agricultural marketing systems, from both an institutional and economic perspective. The aim is to assess whether the current structure is appropriate to or hampers smallholder agricultural growth. Chapter 9 assesses the role of grassroots institutions in rural Ghana and that of non-governmental organizations. The chapter identifies the potential linkages these institutions offer between smallholders and the rural poor on the one hand and the more formal rural and non-rural institutions on the other.

The fifth theme of the study concerns the initial impact of the structural adjustment programme on smallholders and the rural poor. Chapter 10 analyses the many aspects of the problem, especially as they impinge on rural smallholders. Changes in the markets for agricultural outputs and inputs turn out to be quite important and are given particular attention. Attendant changes in public institutions and social services are also fully examined. An overall first evaluation of the impact of the ERP is provided and many unclear aspects are highlighted.

Finally, the study outlines a strategy for rural development operations in Ghana consistent with the major constraints that face the rural economy and the Government's overall objectives. Chapter 11 summarizes the major hurdles to smallholder development, while the strategy presented in Chapter 12 is directed at alleviating the most binding of these constraints.

Chapter 1

Recent Economic Developments

Ghana has swung sharply between prosperity and decline since
independence in 1957. As agriculture has been an integral part of
these macro-developments, the economic and policy context within
which agricultural development has taken place in the last three
decades and the recent changes that have occurred, as they affect
future prospects, need to be reviewed. After briefly reviewing the past
30 years, this chapter will highlight some of the important recent
developments, with the aim of making a detailed analysis of the
agricultural sector.

The Circumstances Leading to Adjustment

A brief account of Ghana's economic performance during the
nineteen-fifties and the nineteen-sixties illustrates the problems which
led to adjustment. At independence in 1957, Ghana was one of the
most prosperous countries in sub-Saharan Africa, with the highest per
caput income in the region and very low inflation. Agriculture in 1955
was the major source of income and wealth, contributing about half of
GDP and supporting a much larger proportion of the population than it
does today. A single crop, cocoa, provided about three-fifths of total
export earnings (Bequele 1983). The foreign reserve situation was
very healthy as a result of booming cocoa exports and an abundant
supply of labour, which included migrants from neighbouring
countries (Tabatabai 1986). During 1950-60, GDP grew annually by
4.1 percent and agricultural output by 4.3 percent. During 1955-60 the
economy in general, and agriculture in particular, enjoyed even higher
annual growth rates: GDP grew by 5.1 percent, agricultural output by
5.7 percent and cocoa output by 9 percent. High growth in the output
of the major export crop, cocoa, provided the basis for rising
investment via increased foreign exchange availability. With export
earnings rising at 3.2 percent *per annum* during the nineteen-fifties,

both imports and gross domestic investment grew at 8.9 percent *per annum* during the decade.

There was no reason to doubt that this prosperity would continue. Certain warning signs, however, emerged in the nineteen-sixties. Even though industrial output rose at 6.7 percent *per annum* during the decade, cocoa output declined at an average annual rate of 0.2 percent. Thus the growth rate of exports fell to 0.1 percent *per annum*, leading to a decline in gross domestic investment of 3.2 percent *per annum*. Imports also fell by 1.6 percent *per annum* (Table 1.1).

Although worse was to come in the nineteen-seventies, it is important to understand that the economic crisis then was due to relative neglect of the agricultural sector in the nineteen-sixties (see Bequele 1983; Tabatabai 1986). Ghana's post-independence economic strategy emphasized rapid industrialization by state-owned enterprises (SOEs) at the expense of agriculture. This resulted in lower export production and export earnings. Industrialization strategy opted for self-reliance, and established import-substitution industries behind highly protective trade and non-trade barriers. This caused further economic deterioration during 1973-83: GDP fell by 1.3 percent *per annum*, industrial output by 7 percent, exports by 6.4 percent, imports by 8 percent, cocoa output by 7.1 percent and food production by 2.7 percent. The annual rate of inflation rose from about 6 percent during 1965-73 to 50 percent overall in the following decade. During the period 1973-83 annual inflation rates of 53.2 percent for food prices and 46.5 percent for non-food prices were registered (Table 1.2). In 1970-81, cereal output fell by 2.3 percent *per annum* and that of starchy staples by 3.7 percent (Tabatabai 1986). The decline in agricultural output was the result of policy choices based on incorrect signals in both factor and produce markets, resulting in domestic distortions inimical to growth, equity and poverty alleviation.

Under public sector management the import, production and distribution of inputs grew increasingly inefficient. Agricultural producers, especially smallholders, had to cope with a deteriorating incentive structure as agriculture, and in particular non-food crops, became heavily taxed. For example, cocoa farmers in 1983 received only 21 percent (in real terms) of the producer price in 1970, cotton farmers in 1982 received 9 percent of 1970 prices, while tobacco farmers in 1984 received 38 percent. Because of high elasticity of production for these commodities, by 1983 cotton production was lown to 25 percent of its average in 1975-77, while tobacco

Table 1.1:   Average Annual Growth Rates of Main Economic Indicators, 1950-70 (percent)

Indicator	1950-60	1955-60	1960-70
GDP	4.1	5.1	2.1
Agriculture	4.3	5.7	3.7
Food production	-	-	1.8
Cocoa production	-	9.0	-0.2
Industrial production	4.6	6.3	6.7
Services	-	3.0	-1.4
Population	2.2	-	2.4
GDP per head	1.9	2.9	-0.3
Food production per head	-	-	-0.6
Gross domestic investment	8.9	-	-3.2
Total imports	8.9	-	-1.6
Total exports	3.2	-	0.1
Cocoa exports	-	5.4	-1.2

Source: Based on Bequele 1983, Tables 78 and 81.

production was 20 percent of its average level in 1974-76. Cocoa producers responded by smuggling output into neighbouring countries.

By 1982 *per caput* income had fallen by 30 percent, export earnings were halved, and import volumes fell to one-third of their 1970 levels (World Bank 1985c). The production base of the economy was generally eroded as a result of emigration of skilled labour; lack of private capital formation as a result of widespread dissavings; and deterioration of the national infrastructure. Consequently, production, savings and investment declined. At the same time, import volumes and retailing activities increased substantially, leading to widespread "Kalabuleism" or underground production and marketing activities. External factors worsened the economic situation. The collapse of primary commodity prices for cocoa, coffee and timber in particular, sharp rises in world interest rates and the oil price shocks in 1973 and 1979 played a part in the nation's economic decline. The external debt, at the end of 1982, stood at 105.7 percent of GDP (translated to US dollars at parallel market rates). The deterioration was so severe that in April 1983, against considerable internal opposition, the Government adopted an Economic Recovery Programme (ERP), considered to be one of the severest adjustment programmes the IMF and World Bank have ever persuaded a developing country to accept.

Table 1.2: Average Annual Growth Rates of Selected Basic Indicators, 1965-83 (percent)

Item	1965-73	1973-83
1. Population	2.2	3.1
2. Domestic production		
(a) GDP	3.4	-1.3
(b) GDP per capita	1.2	-4.4
(c) Agriculture	4.5	0.0
(d) Industry	4.3	-7.0
(e) Services	1.1	-0.3
3. Merchandise trade		
(a) Exports	3.5	-6.4
(b) Imports	-3.3	-8.0
(c) Terms of trade		-6.5
4. Cocoa production	-1.2	-7.1
5. Food sector		
(a) Food production	2.0	-2.7
(b) Food production per capita	-0.3	-5.9
(c) Calorie availability per capita	1.3	-3.9
(i) from cereals	3.8	-3.3
(ii) from roots and tubers	-2.0	-1.8
(d) Protein availability per capita	4.1	-4.0
6. Inflation		
(a) Consumer prices	6.3	49.9
(b) Food (local and imported) prices	6.6	53.2
(c) Non-food prices	5.8	46.5

Source: Tabatabai 1986, Table 1.

The Economic Recovery Programme

The Economic Recovery Programme (ERP) started in April 1983 with the first cedi devaluation; thereafter, a progressive movement towards a realistic and flexible exchange rate was sought. The periodic adjustment of the exchange rate made it possible to improve price incentives in the economy. The policy package under the programme, *inter alia*, sought to:

- realign the exchange rates;
- arrest hyperflation;
- realign interest rates;
- reform prices and restore production incentives: i.e., restore relative price increases for key export crops such as cocoa, timber, and minerals to favour production;
- reduce the cumulative budget deficit;
- rehabilitate the country's economic and social infrastructure;
- encourage private savings and investments;
- restore fiscal and monetary discipline; and
- establish workable priorities for the allocation of scarce foreign exchange resources.

The IMF supported the programme with three successive stand-by arrangements totalling SDR 611 million, or 229 percent of quota. Total assistance from members and observers of the Consultative Group for Ghana rose sharply with commitments rising from the 1980-83 low of US$ 198 million to US$ 430 million during 1984-86, including two World Bank Reconstruction Import Credits amounting to US$ 127 million.

In November 1985 the Government of Ghana presented to the Third Meeting of the Consultative Group for Ghana in Paris the policy framework for 1986-88, which consisted of the second phase of the ERP. The funding for the second phase included the World Bank's US$ 130-million Structural Adjustment Programme (SAP) for 1987-89, and the IMF's US$ 245.4-million Extended Fund Facility for 1987-90. The main objectives of this programme were, on the one hand, to consolidate gains made throughout the first three years of the ERP and, on the other, to institute a gradual process of structural adjustment aimed at accelerating growth, improving incentives, strengthening the capabilities of the ministries in policy planning and implementing monitoring and evaluation programmes so as to remove the remaining barriers to efficiency and growth. Meanwhile, the Extended Fund Facility set annual macro-economic targets as additional conditionalities, growth rates in real GDP, domestic inflation, rate of velocity and growth of broad money supply.

The main instruments and policies under the two phases of the ERP, including the SAP and the Extended Fund Facility, were the following:

Trade and exchange rate policy reform. Between April 1983 and October 1985, the cedi was officially devalued from ₵ 2.75 = US$ 1.00 (a rate that had been kept constant for four years

prior to that, despite cumulative inflation of more than 400 percent) to
₵ 60 = US$ 1.00. In January 1986 the rate was further adjusted to
₵ 90 = US$ 1.00. In September 1986, the Government established a
second window foreign exchange auction, covering most transactions
but excluding cocoa, petroleum, debt service for official debts
contracted before the beginning of 1986, and some essential drugs.
Consumer goods continued to be imported under Special Import (or
Unnumbered) Licences. However, by February 1987, about 50 percent
(in value terms) of goods and services imported under Special Import
Licences became eligible for funding through the auction for foreign
exchange. This allowed more goods, especially spare parts, to be
imported, alleviating some of the supply constraints responsible for
strangling developments in the industrial and agricultural sectors. In
February 1987 the Government unified the official and the auction
foreign exchange markets. Currently all foreign exchange transactions
are conducted at a floating rate based on the weekly auction of foreign
exchange. In October 1987 the rate was around ₵ 175 = US$ 1.00. By
the end of November 1989, the cedi was valued at ₵ 280 = US$ 1.00,
although the Bureaux de Change had priced transactions between
₵ 330 and ₵ 360.

   Administered price reform. The main reform has been the
adjustment of the price paid to cocoa farmers by the Ghana Cocoa
Marketing Board. Prices rose from ₵ 12 000/mt in 1982/83, to
₵ 30 000/mt in 1984/85, to ₵ 56 600/mt in May 1985, and to
₵ 85 500/mt for the 1985/86 season. In 1989, the price was raised
even further to ₵ 165 000/mt. Cotton, tobacco and coffee prices have
also been raised substantially. Other administered prices, such as
petroleum products, have increased following exchange rate
devaluations. In mid-1986, fertilizer prices were raised by about
80 percent on average and have been raised since then to reflect the
declining value of the cedi. By the end of 1986, however, a subsidy
element remained to cover handling and distribution costs. Tariffs and
utility charges had increased substantially and price controls had also
been dismantled for most essential goods. Only a handful of goods
remained under price controls to fulfil the conditionality requirements
of the World Bank's Reconstruction Import Credit (II) Facility.

   Public sector reforms. At the end of 1984, public sector wages and
salaries were raised by an average of 89 percent. In January 1986 the
Government began implementing management reform programmes in
the public sector, with the object of raising public service productivity
through redeployment, salary rationalization and improvement in civil

service management. Public sector wages and salaries were raised by another 29 percent in January 1986. Salary scales have been restructured to increase the differential between the highest and lowest paid civil servants from 2:1 to 6:1. In February 1987 the minimum wage was raised by 25 percent for all workers. Reorganization of several ministries was expected to lead to retrenchment of several thousand employees. The minimum wage was equal to US$ 180 per month by October 1989.

Interest rates. Interest rates were gradually raised so that by 1985 they were positive in real terms. The nominal deposit and lending rates have more than doubled since 1982. On 18 September 1987, a liberalized system to determine borrowing and lending interest rates for all commercial and secondary banks was introduced by the Central Bank. This was followed in November 1987 by the introduction of a new treasury bill discounting scheme by the Bank of Ghana.

Fiscal policy. Reforms were introduced, centred on the elimination of various subsidies and mobilization of new resources through improved tax collection. Restructuring of key public sector budgets (such as agriculture) was undertaken to increase capital as well as operations and maintenance expenditures. In order to promote economic development and production capacity without setting off inflationary spirals, a rolling three-year Public Investment Programme (PIP) was launched in 1986. Careful budgetting procedures and the use of proper guidelines provided by the Ministry of Finance and Economic Planning ensure that it meshes with the growth targets and other objectives of the SAP.

State enterprises reform. The Government's programme to restructure the public sector aims at allowing state-owned enterprises (SOEs) to stand on their own feet and operate as commercial units. With the help of the World Bank, a review of all SOEs took place in 1986/87. Under the restructuring programme some of the SOEs were to be privatized, merged, diversified, turned into joint ventures or liquidated. Although substantial employment cuts took place in some of the SOEs, including the Ghana Cocoa Marketing Board, the State Fishing Corporation, the State Farms Corporation, and the Food Production Corporation, little progress was made by the high-powered National Implementation Committee in implementing the programme. Meanwhile, guidelines for the use of budgetary funds by SOEs were put in place to restore financial discipline. Substantial progress was made in providing the country with a core of skilled SOE managers through a comprehensive management training programme.

Sector rehabilitation. Programmes were undertaken in several areas such as roads, railways, health and education, with the PIP playing a key role.

Social sector management. The Government sought to address the plight of groups severely hit by the economic decline of the previous 20 years. Assistance to these groups, mostly women, rural youngsters and urban poor, was in the form of programmes designed to increase employment and raise incomes. Components of this programme were nutritional support projects and food-for-work schemes for selected target groups in Northern Ghana; improved water supplies, sanitation, schools, clinics, feeder roads and rural electrification to make the rural areas habitable for the rural poor; rehabilitation of health and educational services to make them more easily accessible; and income-generating activities for small-scale farmers including women.

Macro-economic Performance Under the ERP

Macro-economic performance during the period of the ERP was quite satisfactory. After a disastrous drought in 1983 that cut food production by about 50 percent, and ensuing bush fires that destroyed tree crop plantations as well as food in the fields and in storage, GDP and *per caput* GDP grew at a quite healthy rate. Investment and savings as proportions of GDP both improved. Money supply as a proportion of GDP increased considerably and financing of the public sector declined in favour of cocoa and the private sector. Inflation declined drastically and the balance of trade improved.

In 1987, agriculture contributed about 75 percent of total foreign exchange earnings, derived mainly from cocoa and timber. With increased output, cocoa foreign exchange earning capacity increased from US$ 269 million in 1983 to US$ 465 million in 1987, with corresponding index numbers of unit of value of cocoa exports increasing from 280 (1980 = 100) and 390 (1980 = 100) to 3 676 and 2 616 for cocoa beans and cocoa products respectively. The income from non-cocoa items (gold, diamonds, manganese, bauxite, timber) also went up from US$ 171 million in 1973 to US$ 322 million in 1987. On the other hand total imports in value terms increased from US$ 535 million in 1983 to US$ 827 million in 1987. Analysis of trade balances, unrequited transfers, long-term loans, medium-term loans and net private capital transfers and grants shows that the balance of payments position improved steadily from a deficit of 3.3 percent of GDP in 1983 to a surplus of 3.3 percent of GDP in 1987.

While the current account deficit does not occupy an alarming proportion of GDP (at either official or parallel exchange rates), the major burden on the economy remains external debt. In 1986, principal amortisation was US$ 248 million, interest payments were US$ 99 million (US$ 55 million constituting IMF charges), and IMF repurchases, trust fund repayments and arrears payments amounted to US$ 37 million. Thus in 1986, the total outflow was US$ 384 million or 50.3 percent of export earnings. This figure rose to US$ 568 million or 70.7 percent of export earnings of goods and services in 1987 (Annex A, Table A.1).

The objective of increasing net export earnings from agriculture to alleviate the foreign exchange situation is closely linked to the issues of agricultural export diversification, import substitution and export promotion in general. The pressure to generate more export earnings from agriculture to lessen the debt burden has been heightened by the trend towards declining international cocoa prices, and the subsequent strain on the balance of payments. Despite the modest increase in foreign exchange earnings from non-traditional exports of US$ 27.07 million in 1988, the total agricultural exports declined in value to US$ 264.62 million. Cocoa contributed US$ 233.05 million, substantially less than the low figure of US$ 269 million in 1983. The world price index for cocoa (1979-81 = 100) has shown consistent decline since 1986. It was 83.9 in 1986, 79.5 in 1987 and 72.3 in 1988. This trend is likely to put a severe strain on the balance of payments and the capacity of Ghana to meet external debt obligations.

Production in several key sectors has recovered substantially since 1983. There appears, however, to be substantial variation in growth rates. While macro-economic indicators manifested a steady growth after 1983, more detailed production indicators highlight a significant instability that starts to taper off in 1986 (Table 1.3). From an examination of the annual growth rates from 1983 to 1986 it is apparent that output in almost all sectors has fluctuated quite violently. It is not clear whether this instability is due to the ERP or is connected with the aftermath of the massive repatriation of about 1.2 million Ghanaian workers from Nigeria in 1983, and another 150 000 in 1985, and the results of the disastrous drought of 1983.

The government budget has continued to serve as an instrument not only for rehabilitating run-down infrastructure but also for financing high-priority investments. The public finances have shown substantial improvement since 1983. Due to fiscal stringency, increased revenue collection and sales tax reform, total revenue increased by 153 percent and grants by 125 percent during the 1983-87 period. Revenues as a

Table 1.3: Recent Performance of Selected Production Indicators, 1982-86 (thousand metric tons unless otherwise stated)

	1982	1983	1984	1985	1986[1]	Percentage Changes			
						1983/82	1984/83	1985/84	1986/85
Agriculture									
Cereals	543	308	965	780	905	-43.3	213.3	-19.2	16.0
Starchy staples	2 470	1 729	4 065	3 075	3 040	-30.0	135.1	-24.4	-1.1
Cocoa[2]	179	159	174	219	230	-1.2	9.4	25.9	5.0
Forestry									
Logs (thousand m^3)	410	560	578	620	890	36.6	3.2	7.3	43.5
Sawn timber (thousand m^3)	150	189	180	223	232	26.0	-4.8	23.9	4.0
Mining									
Index of mineral production (1977=100)	59.9	50.2	57.9	66.3	62.6[3]	-16.2	15.3	14.5	-5.6
Gold (thousand fine troy ounces)	331	277	287	299	288	-16.3	3.6	4.2	-3.7
Diamonds (thousand carats)	684	339	346	636	556	-50.4	2.1	83.8	-12.6
Manganese ore	160	175	267	357	333	9.4	52.6	33.7	-6.7
Bauxite	64	70	49	170	204	9.4	-30.0	246.9	20.0
Electricity Generation (million KWh)	4 982	2 575	1 819	3 020	3 599[3]	-48.3	-29.4	66.0	19.2
Crude Oil Refinery Throughput	1 040	481	747	958	985	-53.8	55.3	28.2	2.8

1 Estimated.
2 Ghana Cocoa Marketing Board purchases beginning in year stated.
3 January-October 1986.

Source: World Bank 1987b, and mission computations.

percentage of GDP grew from 5.5 percent in 1983 to 13.9 percent in 1987. The money was used to rehabilitate social and economic infrastructure such as clinics, hospitals, roads and school buildings and abandoned public buildings. Recurrent expenditures increased from 7.3 percent of GDP in 1983 to 10.7 percent in 1987, after reaching a high of 11.2 percent in 1985. Development expenditures also increased from a level of 0.7 percent of GDP in 1983 to 2.5 percent of GDP in 1987. Deficit financing of development expenditure was reversed by more closely monitoring government expenditure and by monetary and fiscal stringency (excluding development expenditure financed through external project aid). While in 1983 the deficit was about 2.7 percent of GDP, in 1987 a surplus equivalent to 0.6 percent was registered. Thus in 1987 the budget surplus, together with high domestic non-bank borrowing, enabled the Government to return as much as ₡ 7.4 billion of debt owed to the banking system. This increased the liquidity position of the banks by the equivalent of 1.0 percent of GDP (Annex A, Tables A.2, A.3).

Under the ERP, the Government committed itself to cutting down Civil Service employment, which had grown by 14 percent *per annum* between 1975 and 1982. During 1986-88 a retrenchment of the Civil Service by 5 percent per annum (about 15 000) was due to take place. It is not known whether this target has been achieved.

The Public Investment Programme

The Public Investment Programme (PIP) was the centrepiece of the Government's effort to plan and organize investment priorities and seek donor assistance effectively. The PIP for 1986-88 consisted of 201 projects, of which 78 were in productive sectors (50 in agriculture), 96 dealt with economic infrastructure such as roads and highways, communications, energy and water supply, and 27 were in the health and education sectors.

The total PIP cost for the three-year period is estimated at ₡ 184.9 billion, of which ₡ 139.0 billion, or 75 percent, is the foreign exchange component. The total public cost (including cost beyond 1988) is ₡ 337.7 billion. This constitutes 81 percent of the total envisioned cost of the projects. Investment in agriculture accounted for 13.6 percent of the total. The selection of projects for the PIP was based on the economic rate of return and the cost-effectiveness criterion. A relatively low share of investment went to education and health (less than 6 percent in total) (Annex A, Table A.4).

Large projects, namely those costing more than US$ 5.0 million, were required to have a minimum economic rate of return of 15 percent to qualify for inclusion in the "core" PIP. The core consisted of 155 projects, of which 43 were in agriculture, with three cocoa projects accounting for a quarter of their total value.

Agricultural Policy

Ghana's agricultural policy has a long history. As early as 1948, the Watson Commission report, which investigated the causes of urban riots that year, noted that, while the life of the colony depended on its food supply, there was much more interest displayed in export crops (mainly cocoa) at the expense of crops grown for home consumption. By 1950 the then Gold Coast had a 50-year-old agricultural policy which emphasized export crops, neglected food production but encouraged food imports and neglected the needs of the countryside while financing urban development by extracting rural-based wealth.

The policies of the first post-colonial Government emphasized urban development and large-scale farms. By the early nineteen-sixties, large-scale agriculture had proved a failure. Nevertheless, the Government shifted emphasis to promoting state and cooperative agriculture and paid relatively little attention to small-scale farming. In fact, the Ministry of Agriculture (MOA) no longer had responsibility for helping small-scale farmers. Between 1961 and 1965 the bulk of development expenditure went to the socialized sector even though its contribution to aggregate production was less than 1 percent. The policy was to deal with urban employment and avoid political dependence on small-scale private farmers.

Over the next 15 years (1966-81) all governments tended to favour large-scale, capital-intensive modes of agricultural production over small-scale farm units. All regimes during this period tended to give higher priority to industrialization.

While this policy of support to industry generally still continues, the emphasis within agriculture has recently shifted. The period 1983-85 initiated a number of *ad hoc* programmes designed to overcome the neglect of agriculture and the food shortages caused by the 1982/83 drought and the exodus of over one million Ghanaians from Nigeria. The principal objectives were: to mobilize all available human resources (returnees and the rural and urban unemployed) and other resources to increase the production of the major staples (maize, cassava, cocoyam, rice); to reclaim abandoned cocoa farms; and to replant cocoa farms devastated by the 1983 bushfires. At the same time MOA organized a national debate on agricultural policy from 1984 to 1986. The debate resulted in the publication of a policy document emphasizing food crops. Maize, rice and cassava were selected for production support through farm inputs and services. The farmers selected for support were expected to sell 30 percent of their harvest to the Food Distribution Corporation. While in 1984 production figures were well above those planned, in the next two years actual production fell well short of expectations. For example, maize production, which fell to an all-time low of 141 000 mt in 1983, increased to 574 000 in 1984 but dropped to 411 000 mt in 1985. The decline was due mainly to the adverse effect of the 1984 low prices (prices fell from an average of ₵ 10 000/100 kg to ₵ 6 000 in 1984).

By 1985, the absence of a national agricultural policy to increase agricultural productivity on a sustained basis was clearly evident. The bumper harvest of 1984 led to a sharp decline in output prices due to the absence of viable post-harvest handling facilities. Farmers responded to the low output prices by reducing their production in 1985. In January 1986, a new agricultural policy document, "Ghana Agricultural Policy: Action Plans and Strategies, 1986-88," (Rep. of Ghana 1986a) was approved. Its objectives were:

- self-sufficiency in production of cereals, starchy staples and animal protein foods, with priority for maize, rice, and cassava in the crop subsector in the short term;
- maintenance of adequate buffer stocks for price stabilization and food security during periods of seasonal shortfalls and major crop failures;
- self-sufficiency in production of industrial raw materials - cotton, oil-palm, tobacco, groundnut, etc. - for agro-based industries;
- increased production of exportable crops - cocoa, pineapple, coffee, shea-nuts, ginger and kola;
- improvement in storage, processing and distribution systems to minimize post-harvest losses;
- strengthening MOA, including the decentralization of its activities by shifting operational responsibility from headquarters to the regions;
- improving existing institutions and facilities, such as the agricultural research centres, credit facilities, marketing facilities, etc; and

- ensuring adequate returns to farmers, fishermen, distributors and processors in order to promote efficient production, processing and distribution of agricultural and other food items. Incomes must be high enough to raise productivity in Ghanaian agriculture to levels comparable to those prevailing internationally.

While many of the above objectives were not new, greater emphasis was placed on small-scale farmers for the desired increases in production.

During the implementation of the first phase of the ERP, it was realized that MOA and its supporting institutions were ineffective because of the neglect of past governments. A programme to tackle short-term adjustment issues was put in place and was to be supported by a Structural Adjustment Loan. As part of the programme, the World Bank undertook an Agriculture Sector Review (World Bank 1985a and World Bank 1985b) which identified the main elements of a strategy to promote agricultural development on a sustainable basis. This led to the launching of a US$ 53.5-million Agricultural Services Rehabilitation Project (ASRP) in 1987. The aim now became to strengthen the capacity of the public sector to support research and extension services, irrigation and policy planning, and monitoring, evaluation and coordination; and to make the investments necessary to expand agricultural production. The basic objective of the project was to initiate a self-sustaining process of rehabilitation so that MOA could give more effective support to agriculture through an improved implementation capacity. Specifically, it had three inter-linked objectives:

- to strengthen the institutional framework for the formulation and implementation of agricultural policies and programmes;
- to improve the delivery of public sector services to agriculture; i.e., extension, research, irrigation, and veterinary services; and
- to improve the procurement and distribution of agricultural inputs by privatizing them.

National Food Security

Since the 1983 drought, the Government has focussed increasingly on national food security. Conceptually, food security at the national level denotes the ability of the nation to feed its inhabitants adequately from its own resources at all times. This includes both domestic food production as well as export-generated foreign exchange with which food can be purchased on the world market. The question posed here is whether Ghana can feed its population adequately from its own production and whether the gap or surplus has been growing or not over time. While in the early nineteen-seventies the domestic cereal situation appears to have been in balance, since 1975 it seems to have moved to a permanent and growing deficit situation (Table 1.4). The cereal food deficit is not covered by the production of the other starchy staples. Figure 1.1 indicates that the production peaks and troughs of cereals and starchy staples largely coincide. If this is an accurate picture, then Ghana is currently facing a substantial food gap. It is not clear if the substantial increase in maize production in 1988, which covered all of the projected domestic deficit, will continue into the nineties. If not, then the cereal gap is likely to increase, since the population is growing at about 2.5 percent annually while cereal and other staple food crop production has declined considerably from the peak year of 1984, except in 1988.

Data on the imports of various types of cereals in the period 1975-87 shows that in most years the total cereal imports covered the deficit and in some years might have surpassed it (Annex A, Table A.5). Besides cereals, Ghana has been importing a large variety of other food products. Table 1.5 indicates the value of food and live animal imports and compares it with the value of cereal imports. The data indicate that food and live animal imports in the last few years, as a proportion of total imports, have approximately doubled to about 17 percent.

Cereal imports do not appear to be a large proportion of total food imports. The breakdown of official external trade statistics by individual products, however, is not available for any years except 1983, which was an exceptionally bad production year. For that year, if the cedi figure for cereal imports is translated to US dollars at the official exchange rates, then cereal imports accounted for US$ 138.4 million, as compared to the figure of US$ 31.2 million, which is computed using separate quantity and price figures. Even if the implicit value of food aid is included in the figure of US$ 138.4 million, that alone could not account for more than about US$ 20 million of the total. This still leaves a figure for commercial cereal imports in excess of US$ 100 million. For years other than 1983, cereal imports were estimated to have reached as much as 18 percent of total imports.

The ability of Ghana to finance an increasing amount of cereal and other food imports will depend on the growth of foreign exchange

Table 1.4: Cereal Production-Demand, 1970-88 (thousand metric tons)

Year	Pop. (millions)	Demand					Production					Production for Consumption [2]	Surplus(+) Deficit (-)	Surplus/ Deficit as % of Demand
		Wheat	Maize	Rice [1]	Sorghum/ Millet	Total	Wheat	Maize	Rice [1]	Sorghum/ Millet	Total			
(1)		(2)	(3)	(4)	(5)	(6)	(7)	(8)	(9)	(10)	(11)	(12) [3]	(13) [4]	(14) [5]
1970	8.56	51.4	291.0	68.5	136.9	547.8	0	482.0	49.0	327.0	858.0	605.5	57.7	10.5
1971	8.79	52.7	298.9	70.3	140.6	562.6	0	465.0	55.0	303.0	823.0	581.6	19.0	3.4
1972	9.02	54.1	306.7	72.2	144.3	577.3	0	402.0	70.0	259.0	724.0	518.7	-58.6	-10.2
1973	9.26	55.6	314.8	74.1	148.2	592.6	0	427.0	62.0	276.0	764.0	541.7	-50.9	-8.6
1974	9.51	57.1	323.3	76.1	152.2	608.6	0	486.0	73.0	331.0	890.0	630.3	21.7	3.6
1975	9.63	57.8	327.4	77.0	154.1	616.3	0	343.4	69.8	257.0	670.2	476.1	-140.2	-22.7
1976	9.75	58.5	331.5	78.0	156.0	624.0	0	286.0	69.6	333.4	689.0	489.3	-134.7	-21.6
1977	9.85	59.1	334.9	78.8	157.6	630.4	0	312.2	62.9	272.6	647.7	459.7	-170.7	-27.1
1978	9.99	59.9	339.7	79.9	159.8	639.3	0	269.3	60.8	258.2	588.3	417.9	-221.4	-34.6
1979	10.12	60.7	344.1	81.0	161.9	647.7	0	308.6	63.0	307.2	678.8	481.5	-166.2	-25.7
1980	10.24	61.4	348.2	81.9	163.8	655.3	0	354.0	64.1	292.6	710.7	503.9	-151.4	-23.1
1981	10.37	62.2	352.6	83.0	165.9	663.7	0	334.2	43.6	301.2	679.0	479.7	-184.0	-27.7
1982	10.50	63.0	357.0	84.0	168.0	672.0	0	264.3	37.1	246.3	547.7	387.1	-284.9	-42.4
1983	11.99	71.9	407.7	95.9	191.8	767.3	0	140.8	26.9	220.2	387.9	274.2	-493.1	-64.3

Table 1.4: Cereal Production-Demand, 1970-88 (thousand metric tons) (Cont'd)

Year	Pop. (millions)	Demand					Production					Production for Consumption[2]	Surplus(+) Deficit (-)[4]	Surplus/ Deficit as % of Demand[5]
		Wheat	Maize	Rice[1]	Sorghum/Millet	Total	Wheat	Maize	Rice[1]	Sorghum/Millet	Total			
	(1)	(2)	(3)	(4)	(5)	(6)	(7)	(8)	(9)	(10)	(11)	(12)[3]	(13)[4]	(14)[5]
1984	12.29	73.7	417.9	98.3	196.6	786.5	0	574.4	76.0	315.0	965.4	683.4	-103.1	-13.1
1985	12.60	75.6	428.4	100.8	201.6	806.4	0	395.0	80.0	305.0	780.0	554.0	-252.4	-31.3
1986	12.92	77.5	439.3	103.4	206.7	826.9	0	576.0	62.7	290.8	936.7	662.0	-164.9	-19.9
1987	13.24	79.4	450.2	105.9	211.8	847.3	0	452.0	62.5	298.0	812.5	575.0	-272.3	-32.1
1988	13.62	75.79	456.6	89.0	213.5	824.6	0	751.0	95.0	300.0	1146.0	821.2	-3.4	-0.04
Per Capita Demand (kg 1987)		6	4	8	16	4								

[1] Paddy rice

[2] Physical production is reduced by 30% for maize, sorghum and millet and 20% for rice to allow for seed, feed, wastage, etc. Proportions supplied by MOA.

[3] $(12) = 0.7 \times (8) + 0.8 \times (9) + 0.7 \times (10)$

[4] $(13) = (12) - (6)$

[5] $(14) = ((13) \times 100)/(6)$

Source: Computed from figures provided by Ministry of Agriculture.

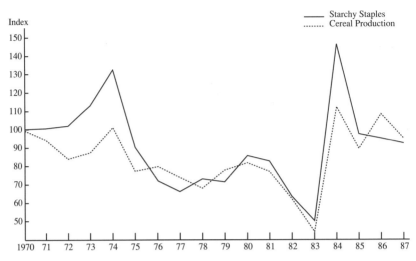

Figure 1.1: Cereal & Starchy Staple Production, 1970-87; 1970=100

Source: IFAD

earnings compared to the growth of the food import bill. Food imports are taking an increasing share of the total merchandise export earnings which, apart from grants and loans, are the main source of foreign exchange for Ghana. This problem is compounded by the fluctuations in the world price of cocoa, Ghana's major export. Cocoa prices swing fairly widely from year to year. Given the relative stability in the importation of manufactured goods, this translates into large instability in the international purchasing power of cocoa exports. The purchasing power of cocoa in 1983, the year when large food imports were necessary, was less than half of what it had been in 1977 and 1978.

Table 1.5: Cost of Cereal and Other Food Imports, 1975-87

Year	Imports of food and live animals (¢ mill.)	Imports of food and live animals (US$ mill. at off. exchange rate)	Value of cereal imports[1] (US$ mill.)	Value of total merchandise imports[2] (US$ mill.)	Proportion of food imports to total imports (%)	Value of total merchandise exports f.o.b. (US$ mill.)	Proportion of food imports to total merchandise exports (%)
	(1)	(2)	(3)	(4)	(5)	(6)	(7)
1975	105.0	91.3	29.8	791	11.5	728	1.5
1976	118.8	103.3	15.1	862	12.0	779	12.0
1977	95.6	83.1	14.6	1 038	8.0	891	8.0
1978	143.5	95.0	44.8	1 114	8.5	895	8.5
1979	178.4	64.9	18.3	882	7.4	1 066	7.4
1980	241.5	87.8	40.7	972	9.0	1 104	9.0
1981	247.3	89.9	32.8	1 021	8.8	711	8.8
1982	276.3	100.5	19.9	631	15.9	641	15.9
1983	1 220.0	353.7	31.2[3] (138.4[4])	539	65.6	439	65.6
1984	NA	123.0[2]	26.4[3]	681	18.1	566	18.1
1985	NA	123.0[2]	16.0[3]	727	16.9	632	16.9
1986	NA	133.0[2]	10.1[5]	780	17.1	773	17.1
1987	NA	NA	37.7[6]	NA	NA	NA	NA

[1] Computed by multiplying official quantity figures for commercial imports of wheat, maize and rice (see Annex A, Table A.4) by world cereal prices augmented by 15% to account for transport, freight and insurance.

[2] World Bank estimates from World Bank 1985c, Vol. I.

[3] Computed using marketing year world prices; e.g., 1983/84 prices used for 1983 figures, etc.

[4] Figure for cereal imports (translated at official exchange rates) reported in Republic of Ghana 1984b.

[5] Computed using 1985/86 world prices.

[6] Based on provisional estimates and using 1985/86 world prices.

Sources: Columns (1), (4) and (6) from World Bank 1987b and Republic of Ghana 1984b.

Chapter 2

Agricultural Sector Structure and Performance

Agriculture is the mainstay of the Ghanaian economy, providing employment and income to the majority of the population. Hence economic development is closely tied with, and dependent on, agricultural growth. The first aspects of agriculture examined in this study are its physical and technical characteristics.

Role of Agriculture in the Economy

Agriculture, including livestock, forestry and fisheries, accounted for 55 percent of GDP (¢ 27.2 billion) in 1984. This sector had shown negative growth rates up to 1983 when the situation became even worse owing to severe drought followed by numerous bush fires. GDP that year was substantially lower than levels attained in the nineteen-sixties. Since 1983, the Government has launched a number of policy reforms and, with the resumption of more or less normal weather patterns and aided by an inflow of repatriated Ghanaians, agricultural GDP achieved a positive growth of 10.2 percent in 1984, 5.1 percent in 1985, and 5.3 percent in 1986.

Cereals and root crops account for 62 percent of agricultural GDP, cocoa for about 18 percent, forestry for 10 percent, livestock for 7 percent, and fishing for 3 percent. Agricultural products make up some 74 percent of exports, of which cocoa comprises 70 percent and forestry products 4 percent. About 57 percent of the total labour force is employed in agriculture.

The series of exchange rate alignments of the cedi and the improved incentive prices of agricultural products have had a favourable impact on the comparative advantage of Ghanaian agriculture, including export and food crops as well as import-substituting crops. Non-traditional agricultural commodity exports represent 64 percent of the total non-traditional exports for 1988

(Table 2.1). In 1988, for instance, the number of different, non-traditional, agricultural commodities exported increased to 65 from 49 in 1986. This is a clear indication that the expansion of non-traditional export crops can help reduce the vulnerability that comes with dependency on cocoa. Export diversification within the agricultural sector would contribute to reducing this dependency. The still high concentration of non-traditional agricultural exports (Table 2.1) suggests that there is a need to expand the small base of these exports in order to increase their contribution to the GDP.

Land Distribution, Land Use and Land Suitability

The total land area of Ghana is 23.9 million ha. Five regions, Ashanti, Western, Central, Eastern and Brong-Ahafo, lie in the forest zone. Sixty percent of this geographical area is considered available for cultivation. The corresponding figure for cultivable land in the Upper West, Northern and Volta Regions is 50 percent and in the densely populated Upper East, which lies in the Sudan Savannah, and the densely populated Greater Accra it is about 75 percent. Based on these assumptions, approximately 13.58 million ha in Ghana are cultivable, of which 7 percent is allotted to tree crops, and 5 percent to annual crops (Table 2.2). Of the cultivable land only about 50 percent is actually cultivated (Annex A, Table A.6).

As part of the Medium-Term Agricultural Development Plan (MTADP), a land suitability assessment has been undertaken using FAO principles (FAO 1976). These make a distinction between land that is highly suitable (S1) for a given use, land that is moderately suitable (S2) and land that is only marginally suitable (S3). By implication other land is classified as unsuitable for the specified use. The taxonomy of land suitability is based on the factors limiting its use for a particular crop, such as nutrient status, erosion, depth or moisture availability. Table 2.3 summarizes land suitability for the various crops by categories.

Generally speaking, land availability for food crop production is not a constraint. However, in localized, highly populated districts of the more forested and transitional zones, pressure is increasing and the bush-fallow period is being reduced. Also, in the Upper East Region, owing to a combination of adverse weather conditions and the recent migration of families from disease-prone districts in Northern and Upper West Regions (sleeping sickness and river blindness), environmental degradation, including reduced vegetative cover, loss of soil fertility and soil erosion, is a serious and increasing hazard.

Table 2.1: Recent Performance of Non-traditional Agricultural Exports

	1986	1987	1988
Non-traditional products, agricultural:			
Number of products	49.0	55.0	65.0
Number of exporters	197.0	377.0	708.0
Value US$ million	17.8	18.7	27.1
Non-traditional exports total:	23.8	27.9	42.3
Value US$ million			
Total exports:			
(Value US$ million)	749.3	826.2	838.0
Product concentration, non-traditional			
agricultural exports, percent of total			
non-traditional exports			
- Top 1		59	33
- Top 5		96	94
- Top 8		99	98

Source: MTADP, PPMED, and Export Promotion Council, Ministry of Agriculture, 1989.

Table 2.2: Land Use by Area

Land Use	Area (thousand km²)	% of total
Forest reserves	26	11
Wildlife reserves	12	5
Unreserved forests	5	2
Savannah woodland	71	30
Tree crops	17	7
Annual (arable)	12	5
Unimproved pasture	36	15
Bush-fallow and other uses	60	25
Total	239	100

Source: MTADP, PPMED, Ministry of Agriculture, 1989.

Table 2.3: Land Suitability by Categories of Crops - Area of Suitable
Land (thousand ha)

Crop	S1	S2	S3
I. Cereals			
Maize	3 900	4 220	3 730
Sorghum/millet	3 820	2 660	730
Rice upland	300	3 080	760
Rice lowland	2 390	300	2 250
II. Roots, Tubers/Plantain			
Yam	320	210	800
Cassava	3 900	4 020	760
Cocoyam/plantain	200	4 020	760
III. Legumes			
Groundnuts/cowpeas	3 900	6 160	1 320
IV. Industrial Crops/Export			
Cotton	3 820	2 660	730
Tobacco	3 820	1 020	1 710
Cocoa	2 890	690	530
Oil-palm	3 320	760	650
Rubber	3 320	760	650
Coffee	3 320	760	650
Coconut	430	110	-

Source: Ministry of Agriculture, 1989, Accra.

Resource Base

Climate

The climate of Ghana is tropical and monthly temperatures range from
24°C to 35°C in the north of the country and from 26°C to 30°C in the
south. The hottest months are March and April; August is the coolest.
Relative humidity during the rainy season rises to 70-80 percent in the
south and to over 90 percent in the north. During the dry season,
under the influence of the dry harmattan winds from the Sahara, which
begin in November and last until April or May, relative humidity drops
to 60-70 percent in the south and as low as 20 percent in the north.

Rainfall is the predominant climatic factor and agriculture is very
dependent on its pattern. Seasonal fluctuations in the onset of the

rains dictate both planting dates and levels of inputs used by farmers. Rainfall is highest and most reliable in the extreme southwest of the country (over 2 000 mm) but decreases to less than 1 000 mm in the extreme northeast and in the southeastern coastal areas. In addition, the wet season begins later in the north than in the south.

The rainforest and southern coastal savannah regions have a bimodal rainfall pattern. Most rain falls in May/June with a second but minor peak in September/October allowing two growing periods: the major season from March/April to late July and the minor season from September to early December. The northern savannah is divided into Guinea savannah and the drier Sudan savannah. The areas are characterized by one rainy season commencing in April/May, reaching a peak at the end of August or early September and ending in October. Drought is a frequent cause of crop failure in these zones.

Ecological Zones, Soils and Vegetation

Ghana can be divided into three main zones on the basis of soils, climate and vegetation: the rainforest, transitional, and savannah zones. The rainforest zone can be sub-divided into high-rainfall forest evergreen and semi-deciduous forest; the savannah zone into coastal savannah and northern savannah (Figure 2.1).

(i) *High-rainfall forest (4 percent of total land area).* Located in the southwest corner of Ghana. This area occupies one-third of the Western Region, and has bi-modal rainfall of 1 700 mm to 2 100 mm per annum. Soils are relatively poor and acidic, owing to heavy leaching by high rainfall, and are easily erodible owing to the mainly undulating topography. The principal agricultural use is for acid-tolerating tree crops (oil-palm, rubber, coconut, plantain), and rice in valley bottomlands, with cocoyam and cassava on the uplands. The soil loses fertility rapidly under annual cropping.

(ii) *Semi-deciduous forest (21 percent).* This area includes the main cocoa belt covering the remainder of the Western Region, most of Ashanti, Central and Eastern Regions and the southern part of the Brong-Ahafo Region, which have a bimodal rainfall distribution in the range of 1 200 mm to 1 600 mm per annum. Soils are richer than in the high-rainfall forest, less acid, gravelly and with good permeability. The main agricultural use is for cocoa, oil-palm, plantain and the rootcrops cocoyam and cassava. Maize is increasingly grown as a cash crop.

FIGURE 2.1

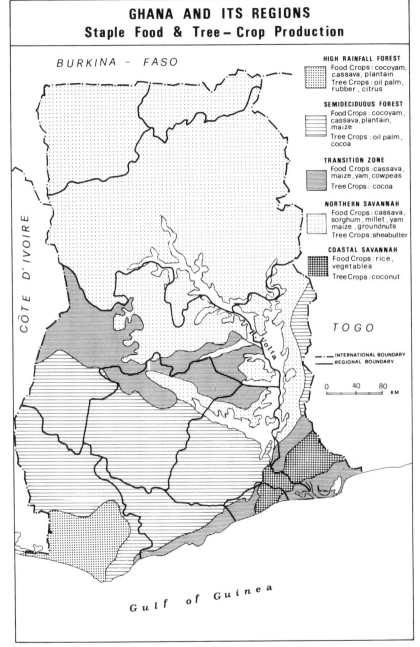

GHANA AND ITS REGIONS
Staple Food & Tree – Crop Production

BURKINA - FASO

CÔTE D'IVOIRE

R. Volta

TOGO

Gulf of Guinea

HIGH RAINFALL FOREST
Food Crops: cocoyam, cassava, plantain
Tree Crops : oil palm, rubber , citrus

SEMIDECIDUOUS FOREST
Food Crops : cocoyam, cassava, plantain, maize
Tree Crops : oil palm, cocoa

TRANSITION ZONE
Food Crops : cassava, maize, yam, cowpeas
Tree Crops : cocoa

NORTHERN SAVANNAH
Food Crops : cassava, sorghum, millet , yam maize , groundnuts
Tree Crops : sheabutter

COASTAL SAVANNAH
Food Crops : rice, vegetables
Tree Crops : coconut

— · — INTERNATIONAL BOUNDARY
——— REGIONAL BOUNDARY

0   40   80
|___|___|___|___| KM

Source: IFAD on the basis of a map produced by the World Bank

Preservation of soil fertility relies on the bush-fallow period being maintained.

(iii) *Transitional zone (11 percent).* This area includes northern Ashanti, southern Brong-Ahafo and parts of Eastern and Volta Regions, which have a bi-modal annual rainfall of 1 300 mm to 1 800 mm. Soils are gravelly on gently sloping topography and easily erodible. The main agricultural use is for food crops, including maize, cassava, plantain, cocoyam, yam and groundnut, and the industrial crops cotton, tobacco and kenaf. Although the trend in this zone is towards continuous cropping associated with increased mechanization, there are problems of soil management, including loss of soil structure, pan formation and soil capping which can only be cured by the introduction of crop rotations and fallow periods.

(iv) *Coastal savannah (7 percent).* Located in the southern coastal plains of Central, Eastern and Volta Regions, this area has a more erratic, bi-modal annual rainfall of 600 mm to 1 000 mm. Soils are a combination of sandier, which are easy to cultivate and seasonally waterlogged, mixed with the heavier, which are more fertile and suitable for irrigation. The main crops are maize, cassava, groundnuts, vegetables and shallots on the coastal sands with rice and sugar-cane on the heavier, irrigated soils. The erratic rainfall can make rainfed cropping of the annual food crops marginal with wide yield fluctuations.

(v) *Northern savannah (57 percent).* This area covers northern Brong-Ahafo and all of Northern, Upper East and Upper West Regions, and has a monomodal annual rainfall of 800 mm to 1 200 mm. Vegetation is predominantly fire-resistant trees and bushes mixed with grassland. Soils are generally less fertile and can be divided into three groups: reddish-brown, gravelly, well-drained soils of relatively low fertility, producing yam, maize, millet, sorghum, cotton, groundnuts and tobacco, and requiring either long fallow periods or constant addition of fertilizer under continuous cropping; groundwater laterites, with frequent iron pans and manganese concretions, which are either shallow soils subject to erosion when cultivated, or heavier soils along flood plains (fadamas), suitable for mechanized rice cultivation; and eroded shallow soils (lithosols) of low fertility, supporting unimproved pasture and only good for extensive grazing.

Apart from the clayey, alluvial, bottom-land soils, most Ghanaian soils are old and have been leached of all nutrients derived from the rocks from which they were formed. In addition, the predominant clay minerals have limited ability to retain nutrients, while the organic matter content of the soils is low, particularly in the savannah. These soils have very low nitrogen and phosphorus reserves.

Farm Size and Distribution

Agriculture in Ghana is predominantly on a smallholder basis although there are some large farms and plantations for rubber, oil-palm, coconut and rice, and to a lesser extent maize and pineapple.

Information available on the number of farm holdings from the 1970 and 1984 Sample Censuses of Agriculture (Rep. of Ghana 1972, 1986b) indicates that the total of 805 000 farm holdings in 1970 had increased to 1 849 800 by 1984. Holdings with less than 1.6 ha (4 acres) comprised 55 percent of all holdings in 1970 but only 12.7 percent of total cultivated land. In 1984 these comprised 84 percent of total holdings and accounted for 47.1 percent of cultivated land.

In 1970 it was estimated that the 805 000 holders cropped approximately 2 829 million ha (6 988 million acres); but by 1984 1 849 800 holders cultivated only 1 878 million ha (4 639 million acres) according to the 1984 census. The total area under bush-fallow was estimated at around 12 million ha in 1984 suggesting that, overall, the theoretical average regeneration period for shifting cultivation has been reduced from nine years in 1970 to about 6.5 years in 1984. Actual figures vary widely by region, since in some areas of Ashanti, Brong-Ahafo and Upper Regions semi-permanent cropping is practised, while in other regions a bush-fallow period of 8-12 years is followed.

Farming Systems and Crop Rotations

The main system of farming is traditional, dependent on simple hand tools such as the axe, hoe and cutlass. Intercropping is practised extensively and is combined with the bush-fallow system of shifting cultivation. Mixed cropping reduces the risks associated with variations in seasonal rainfall, reduces the weeding requirements and makes optimal use of soil moisture and nutrients. Input use in this traditional system is low except where cash crops such as rice and maize are grown. With these crops, fertilizer use is increasing, subject to availability, particularly in Brong-Ahafo, northern Ashanti and Northern Regions where soil fertility has been reduced by shortened bush-fallows or continuous cropping.

Mechanized farming using more inputs (fertilizer, herbicides, pesticides) is found on medium and larger-scale holdings which mono-crop food crops (maize and rice) and industrial crops (cotton and tobacco). Despite the higher level of inputs combined with tractor-based land preparation, output from these farms is often disappointing owing to both poor management and little attention to more intensive methods of crop production.

The main crop associations and rotations vary from the dry savannah north of the country to the south. Farmers in the north have traditionally based their staple food crop production on millet and sorghum, with yam grown as a cash crop, and maize (short season varieties) increasing in popularity. Since the 1983 drought, cassava production has also increased in the north as a famine reserve crop. In the transitional zone, maize is the main cash crop, with cassava, yam and plantain grown for home use. Farmers in the wetter forest belt have centred their food crop production around cocoyam and plantain, with maize, cassava and vegetables. Cocoa is the main cash crop. Oil-palm and rubber are becoming the dominant crops in the wetter southwest. Apart from cocoyam, which grows wild in the rainforest, and cassava, which can tolerate a wide range of soils and climate, arable cropping has been less successful in the rainforest area because of low soil fertility, excessive weed growth and, in the case of maize, extended rains. A combination of low cocoa prices in the early eighties and relatively higher farm-gate food crop prices caused an increase in food crop production (mainly maize and cassava) in the forest zone, particularly where bush fires had destroyed former cocoa farms. In terms of the contribution of different crops to the total value product, the ranking of the first ten is as follows: cassava (19.16 percent); yam (16.66 percent); cocoa (13.3 percent); plantain (12.98 percent); cocoyam (10.16 percent); maize (4.8 percent); groundnut (3.83 percent); pepper (3.16 percent); okra (2.79 percent); and tomato (1.83 percent).

Crop Production Methods and Technology

Agricultural production in Ghana is still mostly undertaken by smallholder farmers on relatively small plots of land and is very labour-intensive. Use of draught power is largely confined to the northern regions, which are free from the tsetse fly. Shifting cultivation in both the forest and savannah zones is practised; a new parcel of land is opened up each year for cereal production, followed usually by root crops and plantains in the forest zone, or groundnuts in the savannah zone. This method of cultivation is open to risks such as fluctuations in seasonal rainfall and soil fertility and unreliable access to inputs. By adopting a low-input method of production, risk is reduced. Yields, however, are also reduced, while the ability to respond to factors such as good rainfall patterns is further limited by the unavailability and cost of inputs such as seed, fertilizer and simple farm tools.

Prior to its reorganization, the field extension staff of MOA were responsible for input supply to farmers, including crop chemicals and fertilizer. Although this reduced the transfer of improved technology to farmers, one benefit was that they had access to implements, fertilizer, seed and some chemicals. With the recent breakdown in field extension (see Chapter 6) and the privatization of input supply, subsistence farmers' access to these inputs has been reduced. The result has been a reduction in fertilizer use despite its increased availability, and a slower uptake of improved seed for crops such as maize and rice. Farmers are using their own seed for longer periods, rather than replacing it with new seed. Indications are that plant populations are now lower in maize than when seed was more freely available, and, while planted area may have increased, yields have gone down.

The farmers are aware of the benefits of new technology, particularly for maize, and to a lesser extent for rice and cowpeas. The problem in recent years has been guaranteeing farmers access to inputs. A Grains Development Project, begun in 1979 with assistance from the Canadian International Development Agency (CIDA), recently undertook a survey of adoption of new maize production practices in Brong-Ahafo (1986 major season for maize) in eight villages where extension had been active and verification-demonstration trials had been carried out (Grains Development Project 1987). The survey found that the adoption of recommended practices had been high, especially with the farmers who monocropped maize. About half of the area was planted with improved maize varieties and the majority of farmers had experience in buying commercial seed. Row planting had been adopted with the result that plant spacing and populations were better than in traditional fields. Despite supply shortages and increased costs, almost half of the farmers used fertilizer on their crop in 1986. Rates varied, and there was a tendency to apply the fertilizer later than recommended, since farmers were cautious about applying an expensive input before it was clear that other factors, such as rainfall, would not prevent yield benefits from being achieved.

The pattern of adoption revealed careful step-by-step testing of recommended alternatives rather than a sudden switch to the complete set of recommended practices. Most farmers surveyed had attended verification-demonstration field days. Extension activities were the most important source of information, and advice from fellow farmers also played an important role. There was no evidence that the message was not reaching either female farmers or those with little or no education. Patterns of adoption also reflected the farmers' understanding with regard to their individual requirements. The recognition that fertilizer gave its greatest response on fields that had been continuously cropped, and on fields where plant populations were adequate, was clear since it was those fields which received the most fertilizer.

Other results of surveys undertaken by the Grains Development Project (1985, 1986) indicate that most farmers who try a new maize variety continue planting it in subsequent years, devoting more and more of their area to the improved variety. Farmers rated the improved varieties as superior in yield, with or without the addition of fertilizer. Use of fertilizer depends on availability, price and cropping history. In a survey conducted when fertilizer was in short supply, of the 78 percent who did not use any, 24 percent said they had tried to buy it but could not find any, 21 percent said they lacked the cash to buy it, and 33 percent said their land was fertile and did not need fertilizer. In a survey in the Ejura District of the Ashanti Region, it was noted that access to marketing also affected the crop production method and level of technology adopted. Farmers were reluctant to adopt new technologies if the marketing of the crop was unstable or risky. Low prices for agricultural produce acted as a constraint on increasing production and on the adoption of improved farming techniques.

In conclusion, it should be noted that, although the present overall crop production methods and technology used are tradition-based, the smallholder farmers' awareness of the benefits of improved techniques is high. Uptake of these techniques would be high if regular access were provided. Under the World Bank-financed ASRP, with substantial improvement made in delivery mechanisms (input supply, extension, credit and marketing), uptake and yields have increased.

Labour Use

Both hired and family labour are used on farms. The actual percentage of hired labour in use varies from district to district with averages ranging from 30 to 50 percent of total labour. Generally, hired labour is used for land clearance, preparation and weeding; family labour is used for planting, harvesting, shelling (maize) and transport from farm to household or market. Much of this labour use pattern reflects traditional use of hired labour rather than actual shortages of family labour. In some villages, even during high-labour-demand activities such as weeding, all labour is supplied by the family. The use of female labour also varies from region to region but averages 50 percent for planting and harvesting. In addition, women have their own crops, for example, groundnuts in the north and vegetables in the forest zone, which they produce completely by themselves.

In the case of female-headed households, labour for land clearance and land preparation is hired, which may account for the smaller parcels of land farmed by these families. With the recent rapid increases in the cost of hired labour, there is a suggestion that subsistence farmers are using less hired labour than in previous years; however, substantive evidence for this is lacking. Owing to increases in the cocoa producer price, it is inevitable that the cocoa producers will be using more hired labour (already the price of hired labour in the cocoa-producing regions of Ashanti has reached ¢ 500 per day compared to an average for non-cocoa labour for 1987 of ¢ 250). The effects of this increased labour demand on food production should be closely monitored.

In a recent survey of labour use in the Northern Region, widely differing levels in use of hired labour were found, depending on the cropping patterns of the farmers. In general, hired labour contributed about 30 percent of monthly labour, with peaks during land clearing, soil preparation and weeding. Where farmers have access to bullocks for land preparation, use of hired labour dropped and farm size increased, suggesting a more efficient use of labour.

Crop Production and Yield

From 1980 to 1983, production of all food crops decreased in line with the gradual breakdown of agricultural input supply services and marketing of crops. This reduction culminated in 1983 with the catastrophic drought which reduced maize yields to only 40 percent of 1980 levels. The impact of the drought and the simultaneous repatriation of many rural males from Nigeria, led farmers to increase by more than double the planted area of food crops in 1984. Coupled with normal rains, this resulted in a quadrupling of maize production and a national surplus for the first time since the early nineteen-seventies. Similar increases were seen in other crops; root crops and plantain more than tripled from 3 million mt to over 10 million mt. In general, however, the market was unable to absorb these amounts and prices collapsed to below production costs in some cases. Predictably, in 1985 and later years, production was lower than in 1984, although it stayed well above pre-1983 levels, with maize production averaging between 450 000 mt and 550 000 mt *per annum,* which is 70-80 percent of total maize requirements (Annex A, Table A.7).

In general, present yields show considerable potential for increase. In the case of maize, the Grains Development Project trials on farmers' fields showed dramatic increases in yield when the recommended package was tested next to traditional methods. In the forest zone, improved practices gave 3.88 mt/ha compared to 1.20 mt/ha using traditional methods, and in the transitional zone the improved package gave 4.42 mt/ha compared to 1.62 mt/ha. According to the Grains Development Project analysis, 21 percent of yield increases were attributed to using an improved variety alone, 7 percent to adopting the recommended weeding regime, 18 percent to planting at the recommended spacing, and 54 percent to fertilizer use. With these potential yield gains available for maize and, to a lesser extent, for other crops, it is evident that cereal and root crop production in Ghana could be increased considerably without an increase in planted area (see also Annex A, Table A.8).

Crop Budgets

The main input cost of the traditional farmer is hired labour. For example, in the case of maize, hired labour is 90 percent of total input cost. To cover this amount at the 1988 maize price of ₵ 4 200 per 100 kg, the yield must be 500 kg/ha. At 700 kg/ha, the return per man-day of family labour is estimated to be ₵ 130, which is considerably below the present daily cost of hired labour of about ₵ 200-250 per day. If the maize yield is increased to 900 kg/ha, the return per man-day under the traditional methods of production would be increased to ₵ 270 per man-day of family labour. This large fluctuation in returns underscores the considerable risk faced by smallholder farmers in Ghana with regard to seasonal fluctuations in rainfall (particularly the planting rains). The farmer can reduce this risk by increasing family labour inputs, but this would restrict both the area planted and the flexibility in choice of crop pattern and rotations. Mixed cropping of maize with cassava reduces the farmer's risk of complete crop failure and increases overall return per man-day. Combining maize with cocoyam and plantain spreads risk even further and increases average return per man-day to ₡ 307 over a four-year period. Even with the total failure of a farmer's maize crop, returns under mixed cropping would be adequate (₡ 201 per man-day of family labour).

Post-harvest Handling and Storage

Post-harvest handling of cereals and root crops in Ghana is based on traditional methods which vary from one ecoclimatic zone to another. In the dry, northern savannah, storage of sorghum and millet is in clay containers attached to dwellings. Storage losses are relatively low as the crops are harvested with low moisture contents and the storage containers are secure against rodent and insect attack. Rice harvested in the north has a moisture content of less than 12.5 percent which necessitates parboiling the rice prior to milling if a high percentage of broken grains is to be avoided.

In the wetter transitional and forest zones, maize is stored on the cob for two or three months after harvesting before being shelled and stored in bags. Maize harvested at the end of the major crop season has a moisture content of between 18 percent and 21 percent, which is too high for immediate shelling. With the introduction of improved varieties of maize, traditional storage methods are slowly undergoing change, partly because new varieties require slightly earlier harvesting to avoid field insect infestation. This requires a two-phase approach to maize storage: drying and storage (up to three months), followed by shelling, chemical insect control and bag storage.

In recognition of the importance of post-harvest handling and storage, the Post-Harvest Development Unit of MOA is being strengthened with the assistance of FAO. Initially, this support is aimed at training MOA central and regional staff in post-harvest technology. Improved storage technology is available in the form of drying cribs and recommendations for insecticide use. Ultimately the staff of the Post-Harvest Unit will assist in annual crop loss assessment to enable more accurate crop forecasting to be undertaken.

In response to the severe drought and associated food shortages of 1983, the Government places increased emphasis on the bulk storage of grains as part of a food security policy. The Government, through the Ghana Food Distribution Corporation, has instituted a major three-phase programme for the establishment of grain storage and handling facilities. Under Phase I, completed in 1986, 17 500 mt capacity of bulk storage was installed in the principal maize-producing areas of the Ashanti, Brong-Ahafo, Central and Western Regions. The offshore costs of this phase (US$ 3.75 million) were financed under an export guarantee credit from the United Kingdom. Phase II was to add a further 33 000 mt capacity of bulk and bagged storage, financed by the Saudi Fund and Danish International Development Agency (DANIDA). Phase III makes provision for an extra 100 000 mt, including the rehabilitation of the Drevicci silos and construction of facilities in the Northern and Upper Regions.

The only starchy staple crops which can be stored for any length of time after harvesting are yam and cocoyam, the latter for a relatively shorter period. Yam can be stored in purpose-built yam barns or heaps for three to six months, but since yam stored for longer than three months can be reduced 30-50 percent due to moisture loss, the normal practice is not to store it beyond two months. Cassava has a very short life after harvesting, only one to three days, and therefore, must undergo some form of processing to allow storage. In Ghana several methods are used, the most common of which is drying the peeled tuber to make a flour, or fermenting it to form "gari". Once dried, the product has a storage life of three to six months, depending on the quality of the product. Similarly, plantain can be peeled and dried to make the flour used in preparing a popular dish, "kokonte".

Post-harvest handling of industrial crops (cotton, tobacco, bast fibres, oil-palm, coconut, rubber, groundnuts, fruits and sugar-cane) is done through processing by using a variety of techniques. Production and marketing of some of these crops are organized by the processors. The Ghana Cotton Company Ltd., a quasi-governmental organization owned by the Government and the textile mills, provides technical advice and production inputs to the farmers, who in return sell their cotton seed to the company for processing. The tobacco manufacturers (Pioneer Tobacco Company and International Tobacco Ghana Ltd.) and the Bast Fibre Development Board have responsibility for the production and post-harvest handling of tobacco and of kenaf respectively. Under these arrangements, the processors organize buying teams which mop up the produce from the producing centres and transport it to the processing plant. Large oil-palm nucleus estates purchase fresh fruits from smallholders and outgrowers for processing. Independent smallholder oil-palm producers sell their fruits to the nearest private industrial mill or to traditional processors, mostly women. There are a large number of small-scale processors of groundnuts using traditional methods. However, industrial processing of the produce into oil and cake is undertaken by the Vegetable Oil Mill Division of Ghana Industrial Holding Company Canneries in Tamale and Atebubu, Achimota Oil Mill, Crystal Oil Mill in Tema and Tema Food Complex Corporation. Coconut or copra is also processed into oil and the oil mills compete with traditional processors, who, because of their better prices, tend to have a competitive edge over the large-scale wholesalers and are able to absorb a large proportion of the market. Sugar-cane processing is limited to small presses - mechanized or manual - that extract the syrup for distilling into alcohol, a favourite local drink which in the pre-independence period was a contraband good. The two sugar factories at Asutsuare and Komenda have broken down and the debate as to whether to rehabilitate or install a new plant is still going on. On the whole, there is a market for chewing cane grown in bottom lands and it is dominated by market women who buy the produce from the farmers' fields or from the roadside. Latex processed into rubber from plantations operated by the Ghana Rubber Estate Ltd., the State Farms Corporation, is generally of low grade (Grade TSR 20), which is partly sold to the state-owned Bonsa Tyre Co. Ltd. and exported to Romania under a barter arrangement. The Leader Rubber Company and Ghana Export Company also absorb a significant proportion of the higher-grade rubber, mostly the ribbed smoked sheets (RSS grades 3 and 4). The low producer price for rubber and poor road infrastructure in the producing areas are disincentives to harvesting of the latex. Fruits and vegetables, including pineapples, oranges, limes, lemons, mangoes, grapefruits, tomatoes, garden eggs and peppers, are generally traded on the domestic fresh fruit markets but some are exported fresh or processed. Appropriate storage devices, especially cold storage, and an efficient marketing and pricing system would increase the production of horticultural crops. Improved road infrastructure, processing and port handling facilities for storage and marketing would stimulate demand and production. There is a wide range of fruit and vegetable processing plants but capacity utilization is low, resulting in a high average cost of production and difficulties in meeting the processing needs of the fruit and vegetable sub-sector.

Irrigation

According to FAO estimates, corroborated by the World Bank in its Ghana Irrigation Sub-sector Review of 1986, Ghana has an irrigation potential of 120 000 ha (World Bank 1986b). On the other hand, MOA has estimated the irrigation potential to be substantially higher and had earlier set an irrigation target for 1990 of 180 000 ha. The target proved to be unachievable. The total area of the irrigation programme and the irrigable areas of projects actually implemented are 346 000 ha and 17 000 ha respectively. MOA has been the main institution involved, and in 1975 the Ghana Irrigation Development Authority (GIDA) was established within MOA to promote the development of irrigation. Over the past 18 years, about 18 irrigation schemes of varying sizes, with a potential irrigated area of over 10 000 ha, have been initiated in Ghana. By 1989, about 8 850 ha had been completed by GIDA and handed over to farmers. Many still remain uncompleted, owing in part to a shortage of funding. The economic and financial performance of the projects actually realized has fallen significantly short of design expectations. Despite substantial budgetary allocations (37 percent of non-cocoa public investment programme funds in agriculture during 1984-86), progress has been slow and costs of development, when measured on a per hectare basis, extremely high (US$ 10 000 to US$ 50 000 per hectare). Some of the factors contributing to the very high capital costs of irrigation are:

- inadequate local expertise in planning, design and construction of irrigation projects and, hence, involvement of expensive expatriate expertise at all stages;
- inadequate initial design planning leading to costly design changes during construction;
- costly involvement in on-farm works which could have been handled by farmers;
- delays in obtaining imported inputs owing to shortage of foreign exchange; and
- unsuitable and avoidable use of mechanization for construction.

Consequently, on the basis of an irrigation sub-sector review (World Bank 1986b), the ASRP recommended postponing major irrigation development and instead addressing the institutional weaknesses undermining efficient operation of the irrigation sub-sector (World Bank 1987c). The recommendations proposed and agreed to under the Credit Agreement for implementation included:

- strengthening the capacity of GIDA;
- establishing incentives for farmers to make full use of investments in irrigation;

- ensuring that necessary input supplies and services are readily available;
- training farmers in irrigation management skills;
- organizing research to determine the most appropriate technologies for efficient water use; and
- developing technologies for swamp rice production in wet valley bottom areas.

Direct assistance proposed under the ASRP included technological improvement of irrigation farming by "on-farm" testing of techniques proven elsewhere and modified where necessary for application to existing schemes. In addition, about six pilot, small-scale, irrigation schemes of about 50 ha were proposed, involving simple watercourse diversions or low head pumping, which would be constructed and managed by farming groups. GIDA would give technical advice in planning and implementation. Expenditure for materials and equipment would be recovered from production of irrigated crops over a reasonable period of time, e.g. seven to ten years.

The role of GIDA with respect to project management is now limited to the operation and maintenance of the irrigation system and the distribution of irrigation water. The many paternalistic features of irrigation agriculture have been transferred to the Extension Services Department of MOA. Action has also been taken to ensure that future irrigation projects guarantee the sustainability of irrigation development. An important aspect is the ability of farmers to repay capital and maintenance costs. Consequently, a cost-effective scheme for irrigation was set up by MOA in 1989. The overall purpose is to recover operational and maintenance costs for all goods and services rendered except those for extension services.

Livestock

The livestock sector contributed about 9 percent of agricultural GDP between 1977 and 1987. Meat was the predominant livestock product, amounting to about 45 000 mt in 1986, of which 35 percent was beef, 34 percent poultry, and the remainder mutton and goat. Egg production made a significant contribution (58 million in 1986). The dairy industry is undeveloped and is of minor significance. If one takes into consideration that "bush meat" - game, rabbits, snails, etc. - amounts to about 20 000 mt a year, domestic production of meat closely approximates national consumption, but there is a large and growing gap between supply and demand for animal products.

The West African shorthorn is the predominant cattle breed in Ghana and, together with its crosses, the Sanys, accounts for about 80 percent of the national cattle herd. Three-quarters of all cattle are in the Upper Regions (East and West) and the Northern Region. Sheep and goats are more evenly distributed throughout the country, being the main source of domestic meat supply for the rural farming community. They are mostly kept in small units of one to ten. Most sheep and goats are of the West African dwarf breeds with no more than 10 percent of crosses with the Sahelian sheep. The pig population has shown consistent growth during the nineteen-eighties, reflecting the increasing acceptability of pork. The importation of large white and land-race breeding stock has proved successful. Local breeding stock was established following crossing of the imported breeds with indigenous pigs. Poultry farming is the most developed and popular animal industry in Ghana yet, while the country reached self-sufficiency in 1976, shortages and high prices of grains in recent years have considerably reduced the poultry populations (Annex A, Table A.9).

The Government Animal Health and Production Department, formerly the Ghana Veterinary Service, has been one of the most effective in West Africa. Over the last ten years, however, as with other government services, there has been a marked deterioration. As a result, outbreaks of serious animal diseases have occurred including rinderpest, anthrax, African horse sickness, contagious pleuro-pneumonia, rabies and Newcastle disease, which have caused considerable losses in livestock. The generally low productivity of sheep and goats stems from a combination of poor nutrition, especially in the dry season, plus endemic diseases such as pneumonia, worms and other small ruminant diseases. Private companies are now allowed to procure, distribute and sell veterinary drugs and chemicals, including anthelmintics, coccidostats, disinfectants, feed additives, water-soluble powders, dressings and acaricides.

Fisheries

The fishing industry in Ghana is both inland and marine, with inland fishing mainly concentrated on Lake Volta. A smaller and less well-developed level of fish production comes from brackish and freshwater aquaculture and fish farming. The marine fisheries can be sub-divided into three: the artisanal, canoe fishery which operates from approximately 270 landing beaches; the inshore vessels and small trawlers, which fish between the 25-fathom and 100-fathom lines; and the distant-water and tuna vessels which operate from the main ports located on the coast.

Very little research has been done on the fishery sector. The main source of data is the Fisheries Department of MOA, and available information is in the form of general fish catches with statistics covering mainly canoes and motor vessels. The Fisheries Department collects data on fish catches by sampling canoes in a few places along the coast, usually four to six fishing villages, and then extrapolating this data to cover the whole coast.

Based on the above data, the 1986 catch increased by 12 percent over 1985 with marine fish contributing 84 percent of the total catch. Small-scale, artisanal marine and lake fishermen, operating mainly from canoes, contributed over 75 percent of the total fish catch in 1986. Part of the increase can be attributed to improvements in input supply (outboard motors, spares and nets) funded under bilateral aid from the EC. Prior to 1986, outboard motors were in short supply. However, 3 700 units were imported that year and a further 1 300 units were expected in 1987.

Government strategy and objectives are to increase the marine and lake fish catches to meet 50 percent of national requirements, estimated at 655 000 mt in total. Fishing on the continental shelf is by privately owned, wooden-hulled inshore vessels and canoes, some powered by outboard motors. It is estimated that there are some 8 200 canoes operating from the coastal villages, of which half are motorized. Thus the Government's strategy to increase the marine and lake fish catches places a great deal of emphasis on modernizing the canoe-based fishery. Since the introduction of commercial aquaculture in the nineteen-fifties, the Government has been promoting its development, and encouraging the production and exploitation of specific species for export, especially lobsters, shrimps, and prawns. According to a 1982/83 survey by the Fisheries Department, between 1 100 and 1 400 ponds with an average size of about 600 m² have been set up. These ponds are being developed by cocoa farmers, poultry farmers, timber contractors and private businessmen. The strategies for implementing the programme include combining aquaculture support for commercial and household fish ponds; establishing pilot fish farms and hatcheries in all regions; and formulating appropriate fish feed.

At present, 65 percent of all fish landed is smoked prior to being transported inland. This is mainly undertaken as a small-scale business, mostly by women. The quality of smoked fish is extremely variable because of poor handling facilities at the landing stages and inefficient smoking methods. An improved smoker called the "Chorker" is being popularized by UNICEF and the National Council on Women and Development (NCWD) with limited success. One of the main constraints to increasing the landed amounts and quality of the fish caught on Lake Volta are the poor facilities at the main landing ports.

Forestry

The forestry and logging sector in Ghana has historically accounted for about 5-6 percent of total GDP and ranks third next to cocoa and minerals for commodity exports. The industry employs an estimated 70 000 persons and supplies all of the country's basic timber and fuelwood requirements. Managed properly, the forestry sector has an important environmental role to play through controlling water runoff and soil erosion and providing a habitat for wildlife.

The forestry sector and associated forest industries have been in a state of decline since the mid-nineteen-seventies; production of logs dropped from 1.9 million m³ in 1975 to 0.6 million m³ in 1982. The value of timber exports also declined during the same period, from US$ 91.4 million to US$ 15.3 million. The main causes of this decline were the artificial cedi-dollar exchange rate; the poor state of logging, transportation and sawmilling equipment; the non-availability of spare parts; deteriorating road infrastructure; government control of export marketing; and the export ban on 14 primary species. Overland smuggling of timber to neighbouring countries also confused official production statistics.

Since 1983, reforms within the Government have revived the forestry industry. Specific actions included the abolition of the Ghana Timber Marketing Board, the removal of government controls on timber exports, and the introduction of a policy of allowing timber exporters to retain 20 percent of foreign exchange for the import of spare parts and materials. Immediate physical constraints (mainly shortages of equipment, transportation, materials and spare parts) have been alleviated with the help of the IDA-funded Export Rehabilitation Project and with credits from the United Kingdom and Canada.

These measures have gradually revitalized the forestry industry. The annual out-turn of logs and export receipts rose steadily reaching 0.9 million m³ and US$ 30 million by 1985, and US$ 48 million in 1986. This represented a 300 percent increase over the 1983 export earnings of US$ 16 million.

Now, with increased, almost uncontrolled exploitation of forests by loggers, and encroachment by cocoa and food crop farmers, action is needed to protect the sector as well as the environment. Burning has been singled out as the greatest threat to the existence of forests, especially the dry, marginal forests that appear to be losing their ability to regenerate from successive fires. However, it is evident that a single management strategy cannot be applied to the whole of Ghana. Rather each reserve must be treated as unique and appropriate management options formulated.

Environmental Implications of Current Practices

The well-established, traditional method of shifting cultivation, by which land is cropped for two to three years with food crops and then left to return to a bush-fallow for eight to ten years or more, is a farming system which causes no lasting damage to the environment. In the rainforest zone, provided that tree stumps are not removed when the land is cleared, regeneration of secondary bush takes place rapidly following the return to bush-fallow, allowing the soil to recover its fertility and organic levels gradually. In the drier savannah zone, the fewer tree species are mainly fire-resistant and, under the traditional methods of agriculture, are left *in situ* during the cropping phase and, in combination with the savannah grasses, provide a reasonably stable environment for the recovery of fertility during the fallow period.

Problems of environmental degradation became apparent when the bush-fallow cycle is altered, either by shortening the regeneration phase or by changes in land-clearing methods, such as clear-felling of forest areas for mechanized crop production. When this occurs, the soil's regenerative capacity is reduced as a result of the removal of secondary bush stumps and the tendency of grasses and other weeds to dominate the vegetation cover. These provide a much lower regenerative capacity for soil fertility and require more labour in land clearing compared to the more traditional secondary bush regeneration. An additional hazard created by clear-felling is change in soil structure due to rapid loss of organic matter. Initial manifestations are soil capping and a more rapid runoff of surface water which, in the long term, result in permanent changes in the seasonal flow rates of streams and rivers. Perennial rivers become seasonal and dry up during the dry season. This phenomenon can cause serious hardship in areas where perennial rivers are the sole source of drinking water and is already being observed in parts of the Ashanti, Brong-Ahafo and Eastern Regions.

On savannah soils the results can be more destructive due to sheet-erosion occurring in heavy rainfall. There is evidence that this is becoming more common in the densely populated areas of the Upper Region (East) where continuous cropping of some of the soils is becoming a necessity; and in other parts of the northern savannah zone where annual burning of vegetation, coupled with the shortened bush-fallow, is contributing to environmental degradation. During years of normal rainfall these effects are gradual; however, during periods of scarce rainfall, such as the drought years of 1982-83, they become particularly evident.

Some changes in farming practices are inevitable since progress towards increased food targets necessitates the adoption of increased input use and, in some cases, the mechanization of land preparation. While levels of use of fertilizer and chemicals for weed and insect control and concomitant dangers of water pollution and food contamination are currently low, where increased use is advocated, for example in the cocoa sector, care will need to be exercised to avoid the contamination of food crops and potable water sources.

Permanent damage to the environment caused by modifications to farming systems can be reduced and, in many cases, avoided through research programmes combined with education and training in the application of fertilizers and chemicals. Although this is being investigated by international institutes (for example, the International Institute of Tropical Agriculture (IITA) located at Ibadan in Nigeria), little activity in this field of agricultural research is currently being undertaken in Ghana. The exceptions are the Nyankpala Station, located near Tamale in Northern Region, where the savannah-based farming system is being studied, and the root and tuber component of the Smallholder Rehabilitation and Development Programme, supported by IFAD, which commenced in 1988 at the Crops Research Institute near Kumasi in the Ashanti Region. Farming systems research should aim at integrated pest management (IPM) and investigate ways to reduce pesticide dependency, including crop rotation, the use of disease-resistant varieties and the use of natural predators in biological control.

Environmental Action Plan

The Government is seriously concerned that development in general and agricultural development in particular should be consistent with the responsible use of the environment. Consequently, an Environmental Action Plan has been drawn up under the auspices of the Environmental Protection Council. In addition to setting out a national policy for environmental protection, the plan deals with issues of legislation, institutional arrangements, and monitoring and action programmes in a variety of fields. The plan is fundamental to agricultural development, and the strategies for growth set out in MOA's MTADP are consistent with its prime objectives.

The plan contains proposals for the planning and management of land and water resources, for forestry and wildlife, for marine and coastal ecosystems, for mining and industry, for the control of dangerous chemicals and toxic waste and for human settlements. Proposals have been put forward which entail the establishment of a national agency for land use planning. The agency would provide a forum for interaction between technicians and natural scientists, agriculturalists, atomic scientists, engineers, etc.

Stability of Farming Systems Under Environmental Stress

Two main factors determine the environmental stability of the existing farming system: soil fertility and rainfall. Fertilizer application can alleviate the reduction in crop yields associated with reduced soil fertility due to continuous cropping. While the use of animal manures and other sources of organic matter could be a practical solution, currently there appears to be a shortage of the former and farmers lack experience in using the latter, particularly in southern regions. The use of leguminous, nitrogen-fixing trees (alley-cropping) also provides an alternative source of soil fertility. Although this has been extensively demonstrated at the research level (at IITA), it has not proved popular with farmers in Ghana, partly on account of hidden labour requirements and inadequate demonstration.

Inclusion of legume crops, such as cowpeas and groundnuts, in the crop rotation is a good method of maintaining soil fertility. The Grains Development Project has been promoting the inclusion of cowpeas, particularly the short-season (60-day) varieties, in the forest zone, as a minor season crop to follow the major season maize crop. By demonstrating new crop varieties on farms, the Grains Development Project has established a link between research staff, extension staff and the farmer, a link sadly lacking for other crops, with the exception of maize, which is also supported by the Grains Project. In the district where the project staff have been active, farmer response to cowpeas has been good but yields have frequently been disappointing, mainly because effective insect control has been hampered by lack of access to chemicals and sprayers. Farm-gate prices are high (¢ 175-200 per kg for cowpeas). This should maintain farmer interest and, with improvements in input supply, including seed, chemicals and credit, production should increase.

Farmers are well aware of the benefits of compound and ammonium-based fertilizer. The principal problem in recent years however, has been availability, particularly for the major season maize crop and the rice crop in the north. Given regular access and adequate purchasing power, it is evident from field observations that farmers, whether they be subsistence or large-scale commercial, will purchase fertilizer to ensure a certain level of production of maize and rice. With the present price of compound fertilizer at approximately ¢ 27 per kg and the farmgate value of maize at ¢ 42 per kg, the cost-benefit ratio for incremental production due to fertilizer, even at 3.1, is attractive.

The effects of changes in annual and seasonal rainfall on the farming system have not been quantified despite the fact that climatic data from the Meteorological Department are among the most reliable time-series data available in Ghana. Total annual rainfall amounts can be misleading, because what the farmer looks for is the variation above and, more particularly, below the average expected for the planting months. If these rains are more or less normal (and in most years they are), then the farmer proceeds to plant and apply some fertilizer, if available. If rains are less than normal, the farmer may still plant but reduces the amount of fertilizer applied (in the north it is excluded altogether). If, after planting in the north, the rains fall more normally, the farmer will compensate for lack of base dressing by putting on a heavier top dressing at the time of weeding and consequently the demand for sulphate of ammonia and urea increases (as in 1987). At present, a farmer's judgement is based on personal intuition and experience but, if the rainfall data were analysed on a yearly basis, it would be possible to forecast with reasonable accuracy the likelihood of normal or abnormal rains from the early season rains.

Technology Availability

Improved planting material and a field-tested package of practices for maize (plant density, fertilizer, weeding and post-harvest recommendations) have been developed by the Grains and Legumes Development Project. Improved composite varieties have been released for forest, transitional and savannah zones, and hybrid maize varieties, which have a higher yield potential, should now be available.

Improved planting material for sorghum and millet is not available. The Nyankpala Research Station is working on the selection of improved varieties and, in recent years, some of the sorghum area has been replaced by short-season improved maize. Improved varieties and practices have been selected and released for rice grown under irrigated conditions and for valley bottoms. The mechanized schemes in the north have experienced problems with weed control and, after producing low yields, the cultivated area is contracting. Vegetables, in addition to rice, are profitable within the irrigation schemes using imported seed from the USA and Europe. There is a need for the selection of improved tomato seed, adapted to the local conditions of rainfed and irrigated production.

With regard to root crops, a selection of improved cultivars of cassava have been introduced by IITA. They are being tested in the Volta Region. The mini-sett technique for seed-yam multiplication has been introduced under IITA supervision and is also being tested and improved cultivars of sweet potato have been introduced and tested. With the expected commencement of the IFAD-supported National Root and Tuber Research Programme at the Crops Research Institute (CRI), Kwadaso, rootcrop technology should be improved further and emphasis placed on forging strong links between the farmer, research and MOA extension staff.

Chapter 3

Profile of Rural Poverty: Economic Dimensions

Development primarily concerns people. Behind the resource base and structure of agriculture outlined in the previous chapter lies a diversity of people in rural Ghana. This and the following two chapters will focus on them. In particular, attention is given to the profile and potential of rural smallholders and the extent of rural poverty. This chapter examines several areas that illuminate the extent and nature of rural poverty and delineates the numbers and functions of the rural poor. The objective is to uncover economic possibilities as well as constraints to growth among smallholders and the rural poor.

Rural Income and Assets

Size Distribution of Land Holdings

Farmland distribution in Ghana is highly unequal and has changed substantially over the last 15 years. To place the current situation in perspective, it is useful to start with earlier indications of rural poverty. At the national level, in 1970 more than half (55 percent) of total cultivated land comprised large holdings, namely those greater than 6.1 ha (15 acres). These, however, constituted only 11 percent of all holdings. The smallest holdings, less than 1.6 ha (4 acres), 55 percent of all holdings, covered only 13 percent of total land. This gives a Gini coefficient of 0.64 for land distribution in Ghana as a whole (the Gini coefficient is a shorthand measure of the degree of income/asset inequality. It varies between 0 (the case of perfect equality) and 1 (the case of perfect inequality); the smaller this coefficient, the lower the degree of inequality). The corresponding coefficients for the north and the south, respectively 0.52 and 0.67, indicate a greater degree of inequality of land distribution in the south than in the north (Table 3.1).

Table 3.1: National and Regional Size Distribution of Holdings, 1970[1]

Size of holdings (acres)	Ghana			South			North		
	Holdings No.	%	Land within each group (%)	Holdings No.	%	Land within each group (%)	Holdings No.	%	Land within each group (%)
0-1.9	246 100	31	3.7	217 700	35	4.0	28 400	16	2.2
2.0-3.9	194 200	24	9.0	137 100	22	7.9	57 100	32	13.8
4.0-5.9	105 200	13	8.2	71 600	11	6.9	33 600	19	13.7
6.0-7.9	71 800	9	7.8	48 000	8	6.5	23 600	13	13.5
8.0-9.9	42 100	5	5.9	32 300	5	5.6	9 800	5	7.2
10.0-14.9	55 000	7	10.8	42 500	7	10.3	12 500	7	12.8
15.0-19.9	31 600	4	8.7	23 900	4	8.1	7 700	4	11.0
20.0-29.9	27 200	3	10.7	22 600	4	11.0	4 600	3	9.4
30.0-49.9	17 900	2	11.2	16 400	2	12.7	1 500	1	4.9
50 or more	14 100	2	24.0	13 000	2	27.0	1 100	-[2]	11.5

[1] The land within each group was derived by assuming that farm sizes are uniformly distributed within each class and farmers with average size of 50 acres or more are residual. The average size for holdings larger than 50 acres was assumed to be 150 acres (figure suggested by MOA experts).

[2] Less than 0.5%.

Source: Republic of Ghana 1972.

Over the period 1970-82 and especially after the oil boom of 1973-74, many rural Ghanaians, especially from the south, emigrated to Nigeria and other neighbouring countries (the number is estimated at around two million). In 1983 about 1.2 million of these emigrants returned to Ghana. Many of them initially settled in their villages of origin and started cultivating small plots of land. Furthermore, in 1983 a disastrous drought and attendant rural food scarcity created tremendous food insecurity, obliging many urban poor to return to the rural areas to farm for subsistence. These factors, in addition to the natural population growth, contributed to a sharp observed rise in both total holdings and smallholdings in 1984 compared to 1970 (Table 3.2).

The major observed changes between 1970 and 1984 have been, on the one hand, the fourfold increase in the number of holdings under 0.8 ha (2 acres) and, on the other hand, the 70 percent decline in the number of holdings above 2.4 ha (6 acres) from 259 700 in 1970 to 153 200 in 1984. Total land under cultivation declined from 2 830 000 ha (6 987 700 acres) in 1970 to 1 879 000 ha (4 639 440 acres) in 1984. Farmers with holdings larger than 2.4 ha (6 acres) occupied 79.1 percent of the total cultivated land in 1970, while in 1984 the same class of farmers occupied 38.8 percent of the total cultivated land. Whereas in 1984, 84.4 percent of farmers with less than 1.6 ha (4 acres) occupied 47.1 percent of total cultivated land, in 1970 the same class, which constituted 55 percent of all farmers, occupied only 12.7 percent of farmland. Most of the increase in both total holdings as well as those under 0.8 ha (2 acres) occurred in the southern regions, as summarized below in Table 3.3.

The causes of the sharp increase in the numbers of smallholdings started to dissipate after 1984. In 1986 the total number of holdings decreased by 22.6 percent compared to 1984. The decline in holdings occurred in all regions except the Upper East and Upper West Regions, where the number of holdings increased (Table 3.4). The number of larger holdings did not apparently decrease over that period.

The data paint a picture that is not easy to explain. Between 1970 and 1986 a decline in the total cultivated area is observed together with an increase in the number of total holdings and especially smallholdings, mostly in the south. This implies a decrease in the average size of the typical holding. Given that labour is the main factor of production and that land is not a seriously binding constraint in most regions, the implication appears to be a decrease in labour input to agriculture by typical rural households. As will be analysed later, the historically important migratory movements in Ghana have

Table 3.2: National Size Distribution of Holdings, 1970 and 1984

Size of holdings (acres)	1984					1970					% Change in No. of holdings 1970-84
	No. of holdings	% of holdings	Cumulative % of holdings	Land within each group (%)	Cumulative land area (%)	No. of holdings	% of holdings	Cumulative % of holdings	Land within each group (%)	Cumulative land area (%)	
0.1-9	1 223 100	66.1	66.1	25.7	25.7	246 100	31	31	3.7	3.7	397.0
2-3.9	338 700	18.3	84.4	21.4	47.1	194 200	24	55	9.0	12.7	74.4
4-5.9	134 800	7.3	91.7	14.2	61.3	105 200	13	68	8.2	20.9	28.1
6-7.9	61 000	3.3	95.0	9.0	70.3	71 800	9	77	7.8	28.7	-15.0
8-9.9	31 000	1.7	96.7	5.9	76.2	42 100	5	82	5.9	34.6	-26.4
10-14.9	34 100	1.8	98.5	9.0	85.2	55 000	7	89	10.8	45.4	-38.0
15-19.9	14 300	0.8	99.3	5.3	90.5	31 600	4	93	8.7	54.7	-54.7
20-29.9	7 300	0.4	99.7	3.8	94.3	27 200	3	96	10.7	64.8	-73.2
30+	5 500	0.3	100.0	5.8	100.0	32 000	4	100	35.2	100.0	-82.8
Total	1 849 800	100.0		100.0		805 200			100.0		129.8

Source: Computed from Republic of Ghana 1972, 1986b.

Table 3.3:   Number of Holdings of All Sizes (in parentheses those under 0.8 ha (2 acres)) in 1970 and 1984

Region	Number of Holdings		
	1970	1984	% increase
South	625 300	1 557 800	149.2
	(217 700)	(1 139 000)	(423.2)
North	179 900	292 000	62.4
	(28 400)	(84 100)	(196.1)
Total	805 200	1 849 800	129.8
	(246 100)	(1 223 100)	(397.0)

North consists of the Northern and Upper Regions only and the remaining regions are those in the south.
Sources: Republic of Ghana 1972, 1986b.

Table 3.4: Number of Small and Total Holdings, 1984 and 1986

Region	All Holdings			Smallholdings (thousands)[1]		
	1984	1986	% Change 1984-86	1984	1986	% Change 1984-86
Western	206 000	150 510	-27.0	171.0	102.1	-40.3
Central	217 400	146 497	-32.6	205.8	117.3	-43.0
Greater Accra	48 700	29 198	-40.0	46.9	23.0	-51.0
Eastern	244 200	197 810	19.0	238.3	166.6	-30.1
Volta	274 500	147 177	-46.4	261.1	128.5	-50.8
Ashanti	314 200	264 909	-15.7	275.7	219.2	-20.5
Brong-Ahafo	252 800	168 104	-33.5	195.9	118.6	-39.5
Northern	139 800	116 304	-16.9	84.0	72.0	-14.3
Upper West	31 000	56 500	82.5	25.9	20.6	-20.5
Upper East	121 200	154 864	27.7	93.0	99.2	6.7
Total	1 849 800	1 431 873	-22.6	1 597.6	1 067.1	-33.2

[1]   Smallholdings are defined (somewhat arbitrarily) as those of 0-3.9 acres (0-1.6 ha) in all regions except the Northern Region where those up to 5.9 acres (2.4 ha) have been included. For the 1986 figures for the Northern Region, holdings only up to 5 acres were included because it was impossible from the 1986 census classification presented in Giri, Oku, Fukai 1987 to compute the number of holders with holdings between 5 and 6 acres.
Source: Mission calculations based on data in the 1984 and 1986 agricultural census.

been from the northern rural areas to the southern rural and urban areas. Most migrants, in addition to seeking off-farm employment, tried to cultivate a small plot for subsistence. The shrinking of the average size of holding, however, appears to indicate that agriculture stopped being the main source of income for many households, with off-farm income increasing in importance. With the decline of the cocoa industry in the nineteen-seventies, the bulk of off-farm income opportunities probably shifted to the urban areas. If this is true, it would explain why more crowding of smallholdings appears around urban areas, and why environmental problems are becoming more acute there. These explanations are only tentative, but seem consistent with the observations above and the analysis of the rest of this chapter.

In 1986, 51 percent of the landholders in Ghana cultivated one farm (a farm denotes a separate parcel of land, a holding can be composed of several farms), while 34.7 percent cultivated two farms. The weighted average number of farms operated by farmers in Ghana is 1.66 farms. This pattern prevails in most regions. Only in the North and Upper Regions are more than 10 percent of holders operating more than two farms (Annex A, Table A.10). Of the total farms operated in Ghana (2 374 200 in 1986), 26.4 percent are run only for subsistence, where none or only a very small share of output is marketed, 54 percent are operated mainly for subsistence, defined by the census as a situation in which not more than 50 percent of output is sold, and only 19.6 percent are operated mainly for sale of their output. The proportion of farmers operating only for subsistence is much higher in the Northern and Upper Regions (Annex A, Table A.11).

Livestock Ownership

The other assets of rural smallholders in Ghana are mainly livestock. About 30 percent of all holders in Ghana, based on the 1986 survey, hold livestock other than poultry and 37 percent hold poultry. In 1970, by comparison, 8.6 percent of holders owned cattle, 22.9 percent owned sheep, 27.3 percent owned goats and 57 percent owned poultry. Apparently the proportion of holders having livestock has increased since 1970 while the share of those owning poultry has declined. The Greater Accra Region is highly atypical of the rest of Ghana (apparently there are several large cattle and poultry holders there). As for cattle, apart from the Greater Accra Region, they are mostly held by farmers in the North and Upper Regions. Sheep, goats and pigs seem to be fairly evenly distributed in terms of average size of herd in all regions. Ashanti and Brong-Ahafo seem to have relatively large poultry flocks.

The average herd does not appear to be large in any region except Greater Accra and, since only about 30 percent of holders own livestock, it is clear that the level of livestock assets is generally quite small. During droughts or other bad crop years, livestock tend to be sold to raise cash.

Regional Crop Pattern of Smallholders

The major activity of smallholders in Ghana is food production. This conclusion emerges by computing the average crop pattern of growers in a given region in Ghana from the latest census data. The crop pattern computed for all growers is not necessarily representative of smallholders. Since the 1970 and 1984 census data do not distinguish with respect to crops grown by different farm sizes, the 1986 survey, which purported to have surveyed only smallholders, is indicated. In Annex B, which describes the methodology, crop patterns for 1970 and 1984 are also shown. Table 3.5 shows the area cultivated for each crop per unit of total area cultivated by a typical smallholder, the cropping intensity, average size of smallholding, number of smallholdings and percent of total area cultivated by smallholders. Smallholders are defined as those having a holding smaller than 1.6 ha (4 acres) in all regions except in the Northern Region where all holdings of less than 2 ha (5 acres) are included.

The striking observation from this table is the absence of large areas under tree crops in the cropping pattern of smallholders in all regions. Even in those regions presumably rich in export crops, Western, Central, Eastern and Ashanti, the proportion of the typical smallholder's cultivated area allocated to sugar-cane and the five major commercial tree crops, cocoa, oil-palm, coconut, coffee and cola, is less than 4 percent. This accords with evidence from the 1984 census which points out that coconut is grown by only 8 percent of the growers in the Western Region (and less than 1 percent in Central). With mean area per holder at 4.8 ha, this is already larger than the cut-off point used to classify smallholders. Oil-palm, according to that census, is grown by 11.2 percent of the holders in the Western Region, by 5.2 percent in the Central Region, 4.6 percent in the Eastern Region, 3.1 percent in the Volta Region, 4.7 percent in the Ashanti Region, and 2.1 percent in the Brong-Ahafo Region. The mean area per holder in all these regions is 1.66 ha (4.1 acres), again larger than

Table 3.5: Crop Pattern of Smallholders, 1986[1]

	Western	Central	Greater Accra	Eastern	Volta	Ashanti	Brong-Ahafo	Northern	Upper West	Upper East	Total Ghana
Maize	0.178	0.298	0.214	0.396	0.242	0.242	0.364	0.533	0.246	0.031	0.279
Rice	0.024	0.015	0.004	0.022	0.019	0.006	0.056	0.026	0.066	-	0.028
Guinea corn	-	-	-	-	-	-	-	0.492	0.404	0.208	0.129
Millet	-	-	-	-	-	-	-	0.294	0.214	0.323	0.102
Cassava	0.227	0.277	0.183	0.424	0.298	0.257	0.372	0.179	-	-	0.221
Yam	0.052	0.012	0.001	0.091	0.107	0.073	0.213	0.242	0.104	-	0.102
Cocoyam	0.147	0.085	-	0.269	0.034	0.279	0.155	-	-	-	0.111
Groundnuts	-	0.005	0.002	0.004	0.001	0.013	0.045	0.305	0.167	0.168	0.087
Beans/Bambara beans	-	0.001	-	-	0.003	0.006	-	0.216	0.279	0.428	0.110
Plantain	0.117	0.101	0.002	0.217	0.038	0.262	0.161	-	-	-	0.102
Vegetables	0.028	0.044	0.174	-	0.103	0.044	0.134	0.054	-	-	0.047
Cocoa	-	0.016	-	0.017	-	0.004	-	-	-	-	0.003
Oil-palm	0.024	0.006	-	0.008	-	0.019	-	-	-	-	0.004
Coconut	0.020	0.004	-	-	-	-	-	-	-	-	0.002
Sugar-cane	-	0.002	-	-	0.001	0.001	-	-	-	-	0.003
Coffee	-	-	-	-	-	0.001	-	-	-	-	0.000
Cola	-	-	-	-	-	0.001	-	-	-	-	0.000
Cropping intensity	0.817	0.866	0.580	1.448	0.846	1.208	1.500	2.341	1.480	1.158	1.330
Average size of smallholding (ha)	0.796	0.696	0.697	0.677	0.663	0.714	0.791	0.909	1.078	0.809	0.748

Table 3.5: Crop Pattern of Smallholders, 1986[1] (Cont'd)

	Western	Central	Greater Accra	Eastern	Volta	Ashanti	Brong-Ahafo	Northern	Upper West	Upper East	Total Ghana
Smallholders as proportion of total (percent)	67.8	80.5	83.6	88.3	90.7	83.5	71.5	62.1	37.4	64.3	75.8
Total No. of smallholdings[2] (thousands)	102.1	117.3	23.0	166.6	128.5	219.2	118.6	72.0	20.6	99.2	1 067.1
Total area under cultivation (thousand ha)	223.7	168.2	28.5	169.9	118.9	267.8	225.0	273.2	135.4	248.2	1 858.9
Percent of area cultivated by smallholders	38.6	50.1	58.2	68.1	73.1	60.7	44.2	34.7	16.9	34.3	43.9

[1] The figures denote the area cultivated in each crop per unit of total area cultivated. See Annex B for the methodology.

[2] A smallholding is defined as having a size of total cultivated area of less than 1.6 ha (4 acres) in all regions, except the Northern Region where a cut-off of 2 ha (5 acres) was used.

Source: Computed from data in Giri, Oku, Fukai (1987).

the cut-off point. Only 24 500 holders produce sugar-cane, of which 24 percent are in the Volta Region.

The cocoa area is not included in the preliminary 1984 census data. The exact number of cocoa growers is not accurately known. It has been recently determined that cocoa farm owners number about 265 000 (FAO, 1987). The average size of cocoa holdings is 4.02 ha (10.3 acres) which is only slightly smaller than the 4.8 ha (12.3 acres) reported in the 1970 census (from 292 600 holders), and is much larger than the maximum assumed smallholding size. Most cocoa farm owners manage one or two parcels of land themselves and use sharecroppers for the extra farms. There are an estimated 240 000 of these sharecroppers who, in addition to cocoa, grow one or two parcels of food crops. The 1986 survey apparently either does not include these caretaker farmers in the sample or, if it does (which is most likely), it does not include the cocoa farms managed by them in the surveyed area under crops, since the land does not belong to them. Nevertheless, most of these farmers are reported to have 1-2 wives and 7-10 children, which indicates that they are among the better-off crop producers. It is therefore reasonable to conclude that smallholders in Ghana are generally food producers.

The crop pattern illustrated in Table 3.5 is quite different in various regions. In the southern part of the country, the major crops are maize, cassava, cocoyam and plantain. Vegetables are quite important in all southern regions, especially in the Greater Accra and Brong-Ahafo Regions. In the northern regions, besides maize, millet and sorghum are major crops, followed by groundnuts and beans. The cropping intensities (computed as total area planted to crops divided by total area under cultivation), which signify the number of times a given plot of land is cultivated in a year, vary substantially between the regions. They are largest in the Northern, Brong-Ahafo, Upper West, and Eastern Regions. Generally speaking, holders in the northern part of the country seem to practise a lot of mixed cropping, probably as a food security device.

From Table 3.5 it can be seen that smallholders constitute about 76 percent of all holders in Ghana, but cultivate only 44 percent of total cultivated land. Smallholders are a large proportion of total holders in all regions except the Upper West Region. The classification used, however, with a cutoff point of 1.6 ha (4 acres), has excluded many poor farmers with holdings larger than 1.6 ha. This is because the method of cultivation in all the regions of the north is extensive, and hence it takes a larger farm in the north to produce what can be produced in 1.6 ha in the south.

Farmer Use of Labour

Most small-scale food farmers in Ghana use their own labour. A survey of two villages in the Ashanti Region in 1977-78 revealed that for most food crop enterprises more than 90 percent of farm labour is provided by the holder and his family. Nevertheless, some labour is hired during the year by most farmers, whether subsistence or not. In 1970, 63 percent of all farmers hired some labour, while 26 percent of the subsistence farmers did so, according to the 1970 Census of Agriculture.

Among holders with less than 1.6 ha (4 acres), more than 50 percent hire some labour during the year. Most of the hired labour is used for bush clearing and weeding. Household women do much of the sowing and planting and 100 percent of the food marketing. The children are heavily engaged in sowing and planting, crop care and fertilizer use, weeding and harvesting (Table 3.6). About 80 percent of the hired labour was paid in cash while 4 percent was paid in kind, and 16 percent in both. In the Upper Region, however, in 1970 the payments in cash were to only 35 percent of hired labourers. While recent figures are not available, the 1970 Census provided some idea of the numbers of labourers. A total of about 500 000 people were engaged as agricultural labourers in 1970, of which 216 600 were permanent. The large concentration of hired labour in the Eastern, Ashanti and Brong-Ahafo Regions is due to demand by cocoa farms. In all of Ghana, only 97 000 holders employed permanent labour in 1970 out of a total of 508 000 holders employing some kind of labour. The above numbers strengthen the view outlined earlier that small-scale food farmers use mostly temporary labour in small amounts.

Sources of Income of Rural Smallholders

As already outlined, the major occupation of rural smallholders is food crop production. While a large portion of the food is consumed on farm, the marketing of food provides a major source of cash income. About 20 percent of peasant farms in Ghana market more than 50 percent of their produce (Giri, Oku, Fukai 1987). Marketing of food crops is undertaken by farmers with holdings of all sizes in all regions. It has been observed (Atta-Konadu 1974) that in some regions, maize holders with holdings smaller than 0.4 ha (1 acre) market more than 25 percent of their maize.

Of all the holders surveyed in the 1970 Census (Republic of Ghana 1972), 19 percent had additional employment, the proportions being

Table 3.6: Types of Labour and Their Relative Contributions to Major Operations on Farms in Otinibi and Sekesua Villages of the Eastern Region

Type of operation	Types of labour used and proportion of the total labour contributed: Otinibi					Types of labour used and proportion of the total labour contributed: Sekesua				
	Men		Women %	Children %	Total %	Men		Women %	Children %	Total %
	Farmer %	Hired %				Farmer %	Hired %			
Bush clearing	60	33	-	7	100	31	68	1	-	100
Tree felling and chopping of tree trunks	82	18	-	-	100	65	35	-	-	100
Burning and "Apem"	86	3	5	6	100	81	-	10	9	100
Mounding	72	3	25	-	100	11	1	45	44	100
Sowing and planting	31	-	46	23	100	56	-	12	32	100
Crop care and fertilizer spreading	66	-	1	33	100	34	-	28	38	100
Weeding (brushing and hosing)	20	32	5	43	100	49	34	5	12	100
Harvesting, shelling and drying	8	15	48	29	100	45	-	12	43	100
Marketing	-	-	100	-	100	10	-	42	48	100
Other operations	38	18	18	26	100	42	26	10	22	100

Source: S.Y. Atsu and P.M. Owusu, Food Production and Resource Use in the Traditional Food Farms in the Eastern Region of Ghana, 1982, as exhibited in ILO 1985

much higher for subsistence farmers and in the southern part of the country. As already indicated, there were about 500 000 farm labourers in Ghana in 1970. In that year there were 805 000 holdings, of which 440 000 were of 0-1.6 ha and another 105 000 were of 1.6-2 ha. If it is assumed that the households with the smallest land holdings provide the bulk of rural labour, then it is reasonable to suggest that almost every household employs, as part of the extended family, some rural labourers, whether permanent or temporary.

As documented later in this chapter, much rural-urban migration has taken place. Many of the urban migrants send remittances home. The 1974 Household Economic Survey (Republic of Ghana 1979) reported that, of the total income received by all households in Ghana, other than salaries or wages or proceeds from self-employment, 49 percent was due to remittances from relatives and friends in Ghana. A lot of this reflected remittances from urban residents to rural households. Furthermore, migration to other countries, especially Nigeria, also gave rise to remittances from abroad. The size of these, however, is unknown, as the overvaluation of the cedi in the nineteen-seventies led most recipients to change them outside official channels.

Surveys of sources of rural income are lacking in Ghana. Data from a small survey of five villages in the Central and Greater Accra Regions conducted in the late nineteen-seventies indicated that overall about 30 percent of household income in these five villages came from sources other than agriculture or fishing (ILO 1985). Since it is most likely that farmers under-report their income, this proportion is likely to be an underestimate of the proportion of rural income that comes from outside agriculture.

Further evidence on sources of income comes from two villages recently surveyed in Ashanti (Mensah 1986). Information was obtained from several farm households on weekly cash food expenditures, annual expenditures on non-food items, and net cash receipts from farm incomes. When the ratio of total net cash farm income (from the 1984 minor and 1985 major seasons) to total annual cash expenditure was taken (averaged over all surveyed households), for the first village it was 5-8 percent, while for the second it was close to zero. Part of the results can be explained by the low farm incomes deriving from the very low prices in 1984 and 1985, caused by the bumper harvest of 1984. Nevertheless, it appears that a major portion of the total income of rural smallholders does not come from farming. This is further substantiated by what follows.

Smallholder Consumption Patterns and Expenditures

In rural households in Ghana, about half of the cash expenditure is on food. The next largest expenditure is on clothing and footwear. Furthermore, rural consumption patterns are fairly uniform in all regions (Republic of Ghana 1979). Noticeable, nevertheless, are the relatively higher shares spent on beverages and tobacco, and the relatively lower shares spent on medical care, recreation, education, etc. in the northern regions. The relatively large expenditure on food is surprising, given that most farmers in Ghana grow their own food. Many sell much of their produce, however, early in the season for cash, and buy food later in the season; this might account for the large share. If staple food production were roughly equal to staple food consumption by rural smallholders, then they would incur a loss by selling at depressed prices early in the season and buying back later at higher prices. This loss could presumably be reduced by providing incentives and means to store crops for longer periods.

Rural consumers spent 58 percent of their cash food expenditures on cereals and cereal products, starchy staples and starchy products, pulses and fresh vegetables. These are the products which, as was seen earlier, contribute almost all of the peasant farmers' income from staple crops in all regions.

To obtain a better idea of the smallholder's food consumption and how much of it can be covered by his food production, Table 3.7 is presented. The table indicates the ratio of imputed gross crop income to imputed gross staple food consumption expenditure for a representative smallholder household and for average yields computed for all regions in Ghana for years 1970 to 1986. The variations among years are due only to prices as the yields are kept constant to reflect the picture for a "normal" farmer.

The results of the table are quite revealing. In all regions, the imputed gross food crop income of a representative smallholder household is less than its imputed gross staple food expenditures. Except for the Eastern Region, where the ratio is close to 100 percent, the computed ratio, which, as mentioned, is an overestimate of the true ratio, in the other regions ranges from a low of 23 percent for the Upper East Region to a high of 64 percent for the Northern Region. The average for a typical smallholder in Ghana as a whole is near 59 percent. The ratios seem to have stayed fairly constant over the period 1970-86, indicating that relative staple food prices have not changed so as to make the staple food income-expenditure situation any better or worse. The results of this table further support the

Table 3.7: Ratio of Gross Crop Income to Staple Food Consumption Expenditure for Representative Smallholder Households by Region, 1970-86 (percent)[1]

Region	1970	1971	1972	1973	1974	1975	1976	1977	1978	1979	1980	1981	1982	1983	1984	1985	1986
Western	44.1	41.3	42.5	42.0	43.4	43.7	39.3	35.6	38.8	44.6	39.8	37.7	37.9	34.2	38.7	42.7	38.7
Central	53.9	49.8	53.3	53.5	52.0	51.6	50.4	46.9	46.1	54.2	51.5	50.4	49.0	46.3	47.7	54.4	49.4
Greater Accra	70.2	59.1	68.3	73.9	65.5	64.5	59.7	50.9	47.3	73.3	60.3	59.4	57.7	44.6	54.2	79.2	58.4
Eastern	101.3	99.2	100.6	97.7	101.1	101.7	96.3	92.3	95.9	102.6	97.4	94.5	93.0	92.8	94.8	94.4	94.8
Volta	63.8	59.6	61.3	63.6	62.3	62.4	56.3	51.2	56.7	62.3	57.8	53.6	54.3	46.4	57.2	69.6	57.1
Ashanti	57.0	53.3	55.7	54.9	56.3	56.6	51.9	47.5	48.8	61.2	51.7	51.3	51.3	47.0	49.7	53.5	50.5
Brong-Ahafo	46.7	44.2	45.9	46.3	45.7	45.8	43.8	40.6	41.9	46.9	44.1	43.1	43.2	38.8	42.7	48.1	43.4
Northern	62.8	62.3	63.4	62.6	62.8	63.5	63.2	63.4	62.0	64.9	63.6	66.6	64.1	63.3	60.5	64.1	64.2
Upper West	48.2	49.2	49.0	47.4	50.2	54.3	46.3	44.3	49.4	52.1	44.9	47.1	46.3	43.1	45.1	49.5	49.1
Upper East	21.2	20.4	20.4	20.5	22.7	21.2	20.7	19.9	20.3	24.4	22.2	26.0	25.3	21.6	21.7	24.0	23.2
Ghana	63.7	60.4	62.0	62.2	63.5	63.2	58.7	54.2	57.4	66.5	59.6	58.7	59.0	53.6	58.3	63.3	58.7

[1] The quantities produced and consumed of all staple foods (computed as outlined in Annex B) were multiplied by yearly national wholesale prices (indicated in Annex A, Table A.12) and the partial products were summed to obtain the representative smallholder's imputed gross crop income and his representative gross staple food expenditure. The computed gross income figures are overestimates of true gross income because the farmgate prices are much lower than wholesale prices (of course net income is even lower). Also the gross staple food expenditures are underestimates of true staple food expenditure because wholesale rather than retail prices were used. Hence, the ratio of gross food income (which, as was seen, comprises almost all the smallholders' farm income) to gross food expenditure computed by this procedure is most likely an underestimate of the true ratio.

Source: Computed as outlined in Annex B.

assertion that crop income of smallholders, even under the best of circumstances, does not cover their basic food needs and corroborates the results quoted earlier which indicated that for the two Ashanti villages surveyed in 1984 and 1985, the ratio of net cash crop income to total annual cash food outlays was very low.

Demography and Migration

Since independence in 1957, there have been three population censuses in Ghana: in 1960, 1970 and 1984. On the basis of the spatial distribution of population and its changes, the following observations are made. The growth rate of population has slightly accelerated since 1970 compared to the nineteen-sixties, with the average annual growth rate showing a rise from 2.44 percent to 2.57 percent.

This has been accompanied by a slow-down in the rate of urbanization, especially in the three largest cities (Accra, Kumasi and Sekondi-Takoradi), whose share of total population remained unchanged from 1970 to 1984. The population growth rate of the north accelerated above that of the south in the nineteen-seventies and early nineteen-eighties, while in the nineteen-sixties the north was growing less rapidly than the south, because of a relatively higher rate of southward migration.

The average growth rates for 1970-84 hide substantial variations within the observed period. After 1973-74, many Ghanaians, mainly from the rural south and presumably mainly from poorer farm households, migrated to Nigeria and neighbouring countries (the estimates put the number of migrants at two million). This led to substantially lower population growth from 1974 to 1983. It has been estimated that between 1975 and 1982 the total population grew at only 1.2 percent annually (Tabatabai 1986). In 1983, the massive repatriation of about 1.2 million Ghanaians from Nigeria led to a sudden population growth of 14.2 percent that year.

In 1970, about 71 percent of the population in Ghana lived in rural communities. This proportion decreased to 69 percent in 1984. The absolute number of people in the rural communities, however, increased by 37.3 percent within the same period. The most populated rural regions are the Upper West and Upper East where, in 1970 and 1984, over 90 percent of the population lived in rural areas. In Greater Accra only 17 percent of the population were in the rural sector in 1984.

An analysis of the age structure of the population in 1984 indicates that about 50 percent of the population is dependent (children under

15 years and elderly over 64 years). In the rural areas the dependency ratio is higher.

Of the four types of internal migratory movements, urban to urban, urban to rural, rural to urban, and rural to rural, the last named seems to be the most important type of migration. Rural to rural migration, based on the 1960 and 1970 population censuses, is 60 percent of the total migratory movement in the country; rural to urban accounts for about 18 percent; urban to urban for 11 percent; and urban to rural for the remaining 11 percent (Ewusi 1977). The Greater Accra, Western, Brong-Ahafo and Ashanti Regions, in that order, showed positive net gains from migration, while the Volta and the Upper Regions were the ones losing the most people because of net out-migration.

Total employment in Ghana increased on average by 4 percent per annum over 1970-84 and employment in the agricultural sector, including hunting, forestry and fishing, increased by 4.5 percent per annum for the same period. The regions with agriculture employment growth rates above the national average were Western, Greater Accra, Eastern, and Upper Regions. The Central Region had the lowest rate (2.6 percent per annum) with respect to both overall and agricultural employment. The agricultural sector employed 61 percent of the labour force in 1984. Within the sector, 96.5 percent of employment is accounted for by agriculture and hunting, 0.5 percent by forestry and logging, and 3.0 percent by fishing. Only in the Greater Accra Region is over 30 percent of the sector's employment in fishing.

Estimates of Rural Poverty

For the purpose of this section, absolute poverty income is defined as "that income level below which a minimal nutritionally adequate diet plus essential non-food requirements is not affordable" (Tabatabai 1986). By using the regionally computed, imputed food crop income for 1986 for representative smallholders, based on the estimates made by the IFAD research mission, and adjusting for household size and other sources of income, a figure for adjusted smallholder household income that can be compared to the computed Basic Needs Income (BNI) may be obtained (the methodology is outlined in Annex C). The figure is likely to be an overestimate of true income because the gross crop income figure computed is an overestimate of true net crop income.

Tables 3.8 to 3.10 indicate the computed typical smallholder household income figures for 1986, 1984 and 1970 respectively, and estimate the numbers of small peasant households, as well as the

Table 3.8: Estimation of Numbers of Smallholders Below Poverty Line, 1986

Region	Unadjusted average smallholder household income (¢ thousands)	Average rural household size	Adjusted average household poverty line (¢ thousands)	Adjusted smallholder household income (¢ thousands)	Percent of smallholder households under BNI	Number of smallholder households below 1986 BNI (thousands)	Number of rural people below 1986 BNI (thousands)
Western	41.6	4.32	87.9	56.4	72.4	73.9	319.2
Central	35.2	3.82	77.7	65.4	51.8	60.8	232.3
Greater Accra	36.5	4.46	90.8	69.6	65.6	15.1	67.3
Eastern	70.0	5.25	106.8	96.8	50.1	83.5	438.4
Volta	66.9	4.85	98.7	97.6	57.7	74.1	359.4
Ashanti	61.1	4.90	99.7	86.5	80.6	176.7	865.8
Brong-Ahafo	118.5	5.19	105.6	159.8	47.7	56.6	293.8
Northern	129.3	9.27	188.7	142.2	83.9	60.4	561.1
Upper West	60.2	8.74	177.9	66.4	69.4	14.3	125.0
Upper East	25.1	5.81	118.2	28.3	97.5	96.7	562.0
Ghana	69.3	5.27	107.5	98.0	66.8	712.8	3 824.3

Source: Computed from data collected by IFAD mission.

Table 3.9: Estimation of Numbers of Smallholders Below Poverty Line, 1984

Region	Unadjusted average smallholder household income (₵ thousands)	Average rural household size	Adjusted average household poverty line (₵ thousands)	Adjusted smallholder household income (₵ thousands)	Percent of smallholder households under BNI	Number of smallholder households below 1984 BNI (thousands)	Number of rural people below 1984 BNI (thousands)
Western	58.8	4.32	66.7	79.8	63.6	108.8	470.0
Central	22.6	3.82	59.0	42.0	83.0	170.8	652.5
Greater Accra	41.3	4.46	68.9	78.8	59.1	27.7	123.5
Eastern	38.0	5.25	81.1	52.6	87.1	207.4	1 088.9
Volta	34.0	4.85	74.9	49.6	86.1	224.8	1 090.3
Ashanti	34.1	4.90	75.7	48.3	86.9	239.6	1 174.0
Brong-Ahafo	83.6	5.19	80.2	112.7	50.5	98.9	513.3
Northern	112.5	9.27	143.2	123.8	73.3	61.6	571.0
Upper West	59.9	8.74	135.0	66.1	88.0	22.8	199.3
Upper East	33.5	5.81	89.7	37.8	95.2	88.4	513.8
Ghana	45.5	5.27	81.4	64.5	78.3	1 251.3	6 396.6

Source: Computed from data collected by IFAD mission.

Table 3.10: Estimation of Numbers of Smallholders Below Poverty Line, 1970

Region	Unadjusted average smallholder household income (¢)	Average rural household size	Adjusted average household poverty line (¢)	Adjusted smallholder household income (¢)	Percent of smallholder households under BNI	Number of smallholder households below 1970 BNI (thousands)	Number of rural people below 1970 BNI (thousands)
Western	85.0	5.4	316.0	115.3	94.2	26.3	142.0
Central	121.6	5.0	292.6	225.8	81.3	45.1	225.5
Eastern	134.3	4.8	280.9	185.8	86.8	71.9	345.1
Volta	214.6	5.2	304.3	313.0	69.4	54.2	281.8
Ashanti	76.7	5.5	321.9	108.5	93.9	67.2	369.6
Brong-Ahafo	220.7	5.9	345.3	297.8	79.9	23.2	136.9
Northern	551.6	7.1	415.3	606.8	42.5	17.5	124.3
Upper	210.6	6.8	398.0	237.5	85.1	48.2	327.8
Ghana	156.9	5.6	327.7	222.5	80.3	353.6	1 953.0

Source: Computed from data collected by IFAD mission.

number of rural people below BNI in each region and in Ghana as a whole. The results from the tables reveal several facets of the rural poverty problem in Ghana. In 1970, 80.3 percent of all smallholders, or 1.95 million rural people, were below the poverty line. This represented 43.8 percent of all holdings in Ghana and 43.3 percent of the farming population. In 1984 (the year immediately after the drought and the massive repatriation), 78.3 percent of all smallholdings were below the poverty line, and this represented 67.6 percent of all holdings. In terms of people, 6.4 million rural people were estimated to be below the poverty line, or 67.3 percent of the total farming population. This figure is a drastic increase from 1970 and it is influenced by the severe events of 1983. As mentioned earlier, large numbers of people were drawn to rural areas, after the repatriation from Nigeria and the 1983 drought, to farm for subsistence. The observed cropping pattern in 1984, which is the basis for the income calculations and the estimate of people below BNI, was highly atypical. Furthermore, the drastic plunge in 1984 prices resulted in very low incomes for most rural households. Hence, the combined effect of these two events accounts for the large observed numbers of people below BNI. By 1986, as the economy adjusted to the double shock, many of these rather temporary rural residents quit farming, and the cropping pattern, as well as prices, returned to normal. The ERP probably had little to do with these developments.

In 1986, it was estimated that 66.8 percent of all smallholders, or 50.6 percent of all farm holders, had household incomes below the poverty line. In terms of numbers, 3.8 million rural people, or 54 percent of the total farm population, were estimated to be below the poverty line. This represents almost a doubling from 1970 while the total rural population over the same period increased by only about 43 percent. Considering that the income figures which formed the basis of the calculations were most likely underestimates of true incomes, the results present a rather bleak picture.

In terms of regional patterns, the increase in poverty between 1970 and 1986 was highest in the Northern Region where the number of farmers below the poverty line increased 4.5 times. This is directly followed by the Western, Ashanti and Brong-Ahafo Regions, where the number of those below the poverty line increased by 2.2, 2.3 and 2.1 times respectively. These latter regions absorbed most of the migrant labour force from the north. In some regions, notably the Central Region, the number of rural people below the poverty line seems to have stayed roughly unchanged.

In terms of numbers of the poor, there are more than 200 000 rural people below the poverty line in each of the regions except the Greater Accra and Upper West Regions. The largest number of rural poor appear to live in the Ashanti Region. This contrasts sharply with the fact that Ashanti is a relatively rich region. The large numbers of poor there, as well as in some other regions considered to be rich (such as Western, Eastern and Brong-Ahafo), should dispel the notion that interventions should be concentrated only in those regions considered to be underprivileged.

In summary, large pockets of rural poverty are to be found in all regions of Ghana. The concentration of rural poverty is not necessarily confined to resource-poor regions, but is also prevalent in rich regions. The implication for development strategy is that, while in resource-poor areas (for instance, the Upper East) targetting the smallholder will not be a problem as almost all rural people there are poor, interventions in richer areas (such as Ashanti) will have to be innovative in the way they specify smallholders who are most in need.

Other Rural Poor Groups

Artisanal Fishermen

A brief overview of fisheries with respect to government policy, distribution, and marketing was given in Chapter 2. This section considers some socio-economic aspects of artisanal fishing. Artisanal fishing is located along Ghana's coast and on its inland water, especially Lake Volta, and is canoe-based. Very many of the canoes are motorized as a result of state intervention, mainly through the Agricultural Development Bank (ADB). A limited amount of pond-based fishing has been developed in the Upper and Northern Regions and more recently in Ashanti.

The fishing industry is family-based and, although the crew are generally kin, contracted labour does occur. Payment is usually in kind; a share of the catch is calculated according to complex criteria which vary from region to region. As a result of the seasonal nature of much fishing and the variability of the catches, many fishermen are obliged to do other work, usually agricultural wage labour. In some instances this can lead to formal patterns of migration, such as the seasonal movements of men between the Dangbe District of Greater Accra and the Central and Western Regions. The dependence on family labour, the riskiness of the enterprise and the frequently marginal returns mean that unmotorized fishermen in particular are among the poorest of the community. These factors have also contributed to a relatively low level of socio-economic differentiation among fishermen, since the enterprise does not encourage high levels of investment. Safer profits are to be made from investment in marketing rather than production. Despite the individualistic character of the business, groups of fishermen have formed in some districts with the encouragement of Fishery Department extension personnel. The four main fishermen's groups in Brong-Ahafo are the National Inland Canoe Fishermen's Council, the Lake Canoe Fishermen's Association, the Ada-Okor Cooperative Fishing Society, and the Volta Lake Transport and Fishermen's Association. In Ashanti the principal organizations are the Ashanti Fish Pond Farmers' Association, the Lake Bosomtwe Fishermen's Association, and the Agogo-Afram Plains Fishermen's Cooperative. It would seem that the main function of these groups is to facilitate the acquisition of inputs, while production and marketing remain individualized.

Artisanal fishing suffers from a number of problems. The principal one is the difficulty of obtaining credit. Formal institutions are discouraged by the small size of individual fishing operations, the riskiness of returns, and the ratio of administrative costs to loan size. There is, therefore, considerable dependence upon informal sources of credit, usually a local fishmonger/trader who charges high interest and gives loans against the prospective catch. The fishermen are consequently tied to the creditor, and the creditor's valuation of the catch. The Brong-Ahafo associations have achieved a limited solution to the problem. They apply as a group for a loan for bulk purchasing of inputs from the Ghana National Trading Corporation or other commercial sources, although credit is not always available. Even when the banks take delivery of inputs from the commercial firms on behalf of the fishermen's groups, there is insistence on full payment by the individual beneficiaries before items are released. Inability of the individual beneficiary to pay outright will result in the inputs being locked up by the bank, or the consignment going to a wealthier fishermen or agent who can afford to pay. Part of the poverty trap for poorer fishermen is that the far greater returns from motorized canoes are unavailable to them since the credit requirement for the change is high. Changing to a motorized canoe involves a complete reassembly of inputs; i.e., a larger boat, different nets and other tackle, and larger crews.

Finally, there are problems with the maintenance of engines, the procurement of spare parts and fuel, and the inadequate provision of extension support, due to lack of personnel and transport.

Landless and Near-landless

With only an estimated 12 percent of Ghana's total land currently under cultivation, the notion that there is a class of Ghanaian landless or near-landless is, at first sight, odd. The common response to land availability questions is that no such problem exists in Ghana, with the possible exception of the Upper East Region and the far southeast of the Volta Region. The argument is that those who are landless are so by choice. While it is true at the macro-level that there is no overall land constraint, some considerable localized land pressures have developed in the vicinity of export cash cropping and commercial food crop production. The major reasons are that:

- in recent years, large-scale land acquisitions for agricultural projects involving the State, some multinational agribusiness companies, or some bilateral and multilateral funding agencies, have aggravated the difficulties relating to land accessibility (Arthur 1985), such as in the Osudeku Traditional Area, where more than 70 percent of available productive land is reported to have been compulsorily acquired for sugar plantations;
- because of demand, the cost of acquiring land in some areas has become prohibitive for poorer people;
- demand for land appears to have increased during the food shortages of the early nineteen-eighties as urban people applied for land for subsistence production, and in some areas this seems to have led to shrinkage of holdings;
- ecological degradation has created land pressures, particularly in the Upper East and down-stream of the Akasombo Dam; and
- it has been a feature of resettlement and irrigation schemes that the conditions of access to land in such projects have removed operators' tenurial rights, making them, at least technically, "landless".

In conclusion, it can be argued that, while at present there is no overall land constraint in Ghana, there are nevertheless increasing signs of economic, legal and social stress as the existing land tenure system adapts to current agricultural development and the general economic condition of the country. One expression of this tension is land pressure which, although hitherto localized, has given rise to occasional outbreaks of violence between groups competing for land. Although the possibility of internal rural migration still exists, this option raises a complex set of policy issues with respect to what action should be taken in the modernization of tenure and the direction of agricultural production in order to make such migration economically attractive and viable.

Chapter 4

Social Dimensions of Rural Poverty

Apart from income-generating activities considered in the previous chapter, there are several other dimensions to the rural economy. Land tenure, health and nutrition, water and sanitation, and education in the rural areas are quite important for the well-being and security of smallholders. This chapter is devoted to these aspects. At the end of the chapter, an attempt is made to shed light on the process of economic and social differentiation in rural Ghana. The object is to discover whether historical as well as economic factors have conditioned the social and regional dimensions of rural poverty in Ghana and whether these processes constitute a further constraint to smallholder development.

Land Tenure

Types of Tenure. The 1962 Lands Act empowers the Central Government to acquire any lands in Ghana "in the public interest". In principle, therefore, land is accessible to the State for the promotion of state agricultural enterprises such as block farming or plantations. In practice, however, the vast majority of land is vested in traditional landowning groups, essentially lineages. This land is "stool land". The heads and office bearers of these lineages are customarily regarded as the custodians of group lands and traditionally are not allowed to alienate any of that land without group consent. Any adult member of the group, male or female, is in principle (discussed further in Chapter 5) allowed to farm any portion of group land not already claimed by other members of the group, and to establish his or her right to that land by being the first to clear it. The established right, however, is usufructuary. Although the land may be heritable and can be pledged against debts, it cannot in principle be sold. The basic customary tenure, therefore, may be described as communal tenure or corporate ownership. It is important to recognize, however, that fundamental to such a system is an intransigent ambiguity with respect to group and individual rights. This ambiguity is the source of many problems in land tenure relations in Ghana. The two main categories of problems associated with this ambiguity are, first, the interpretation of land allocation and tenurial arrangements by the hierarchies of chiefs and other office bearers with respect to the boundary between their custodial responsibilities and their private interests and, second, tenurial agreements with "stranger" farmers. Stranger farmers are those seeking land in an area but who have no rights to that land by virtue of lineage, i.e., membership of the landowning group.

Five basic categories of tenure have been identified in Ghana (Benneh 1985; Ewusi 1983). These are:

(a) the allodial title (an absolute ownership right), which is supposed to be the highest grant or right in land;
(b) the customary freehold;
(c) the leasehold (usufructuary right for an agreed period in exchange for an initial agreed payment);
(d) the *abusa, abunu* and *abehyem* sharecropping tenures; and
(e) *nto*, a cash rental tenure.

Categories (a) and (b) primarily concern members of owner groups while (c), (d) and (e) affect stranger farmers. Under the terms of *abusa* and *abunu* share-tenancy, the rent is a stated proportion of the tenant farmer's yield either in kind or in cash. Traditionally, the ratios for *abusa* are one-third to the tenant, one-third to cover the costs of production and one-third to the landlord. In *abunu* the tenant and the landlord share either the farm or the yield equally. There can be considerable deviation from these traditional terms. Under both systems the landlord's contribution may only be the land, though formerly the general custom with *abunu* was that the landlord also made some contribution in terms of labour, capital and seedlings. *Abehyem* tenure occurs where the tenant occupies "palm land". He is expected to deliver an agreed quantity of palm oil to the landlord each year. With *nto*, the original principle was that the tenant paid a cash rent equivalent to 10 percent of the yield value each year. In fact an *nto* tenant may well find that the annual reassessment of his rent may be quite arbitrary, since what was originally regarded as "tribute" is now perceived as "ground rent" and hence assessable on the basis of commercial rather than social criteria. In addition to the rents entailed by their sharecropping agreements, tenants are liable for a variety of supplementary charges. These can include contributions to their chief's funeral costs, enstoolment payments, land litigation costs and festival costs. There is a great deal of variability in the operation of the *nto* tenure arrangement. Generally, however, the tenant pays the *nto* to the local District Council (now District Assembly) and only one-third to two-thirds goes to the local chief depending upon whether he is a sub-chief or a paramount chief. Sometimes, payment of *nto* is accompanied by a sheep or the equivalent. This amounts to an annual tribute and is a constant reminder that the tenant is a stranger farmer.

Land Tenure Problems. There are a number of important land tenure problems, principally:

- The difficulty of defining ownership and tenancy boundaries, coupled with the running down of the government survey capacity, has given rise to many disputes, putting operators at risk.
- The custodial hierarchy is so complicated that stranger farmers can find that the sub-chiefs with whom they have negotiated are overruled at some later stage by superior office holders.
- Changes of custodians through death or replacement can lead to a reassessment of tenancy agreements.
- Land administration and land use planning is often made time-consuming and haphazard by the traditional system of allocation.
- The heritability of land, usually by nephews, can lead to fragmentation and the acquisition of the land by persons who either do not use it or are unfamiliar with farming.
- Tenants can be exposed to the unscrupulous practice of open-ended agreements in which the landlord's assessment of rent is postponed until the yield is seen. The tenant has difficulty rejecting the terms since he cannot leave the farm he has developed.
- Tenants are subject to arbitrary increases of rent, with costs of litigation being usually prohibitive for the tenant.
- It has been known for chiefs to sell the same piece of land to more than one migrant farmer or give to farmers lands which are in fact in government-declared reserves, and this enables officials to issue threats or extort money from farmers (Arhin 1985b).

The Impact on Terms of Cash Cropping. In the past, the availability of land and the predominance of a subsistence-oriented rural economy meant that the various tenurial arrangements could operate on the basis of goodwill between the contracting parties with the payment of essentially minimal or token rents. With the introduction of cash cropping, specifically cocoa and to a lesser extent rubber, the land suited to these crops acquired an unprecedented value. Pressure on such land increased and the rural economy was rapidly monetized. Tenurial relations came to be perceived in a much more commercial perspective. Above all, the issue of security of tenure became important, given the investment in labour and capital and the lengthy maturation periods of such crops. "Strangers" sought increasingly to enter into binding contractual agreements with landowning groups, while custodians were reluctant, in their own interests, to alienate land which could prove extremely profitable.

Landowners, in many instances, were keener to develop sharecropping arrangements and, if possible, to extend their own enterprises on the basis of wage labour. However, the availability, and hence cost, of labour was a key factor. In this context, the *abusa* system provided to some extent a viable compromise, as it gave both tenant and landlord the opportunity to increase their access to the cash required by the monetization of the economy. It is still the case, therefore, that some 75 percent of all cocoa farms are operated under sharecropping arrangements. The customary arrangement has been that tenants take responsibility for their own subsistence, usually by intercropping cocoa with food crops in the first years and then transferring food production to a small secondary plot allocated by the landlord and, as a rule, free of any charge.

In the nineteen-seventies, the decline in the cocoa price and the rise in food prices had some impact on tenurial arrangements. Tenants in some instances attempted to switch to food crops. Landlords reacted either by evicting tenants for breach of the terms of their tenurial agreement, or else by extending *abusa* conditions to cover food crops, where customarily this was never the practice. Alternatively, landlords sought to recoup some of their loss of income from cocoa by converting from *abusa* to *abunu* tenancies, thus recovering half rather than a third of the value of the yield.

With some provisos, land tenure problems have more often arisen in areas given over to export, cash crop production than on food production land. This is quite simply because landlords require tenants to generate income for them and the balance of economic opportunity in this regard has generally not favoured subsistence or food crops. When the commercial development of maize or rice occurs, similar tenurial revisions arise. The potential for mechanization in these instances seriously weakens the countervailing force, from the smallholder's point of view, of the need for labour and hence the prospect of more equitable terms of tenure.

Dynamics of Land Tenure and Poverty. Land tenure issues lie at the heart of Ghana's rural political economy. The "traditional" system of land allocation has proved itself to be very far from a static set of customary rules. On the contrary, the system is essentially dynamic and reflective of historical and economic changes. Any land allocation and tenurial arrangement, be it to a member of the landowning group or to a stranger farmer, is a direct function of the relative socio-economic status of the custodian-landlord on the one hand and the allocatee on the other.

The consideration of size of landholding and/or tenurial status provides a direct indicator of the pattern of poverty. *Abunu, abusa* and *nto* tenants form the lower levels of the rural social strata in the context of stranger farming. Among stranger farmers, the comparatively influential ones (in socio-economic terms) have been able to secure their lands through outright purchase or leasehold, despite tradition. Indeed some of them have become landlords despite their own stranger status. Similarly the size of landholding of the lineage member reflects his position in the hierarchy of the landowning group. Obviously judgements based solely on landholding size must be considered in relation to the overall holding of the landholding group and also in relation to the actual or perceived potential productivity of the land.

Table 4.1 shows the numbers and proportions of "owned" (including tenure systems under categories (a) and (b), described earlier in this section) and rented farms (including the remaining three land tenure systems) in 1970, 1974 and 1986. The percentage of total farms owned by farmers was as high as 94 percent in 1970. However, renting of farms was more common in Central and Eastern Regions (14 percent and 13 percent respectively), whereas all farmers in the Northern Region owned their farming land in 1970. This regional picture remained unchanged in 1974 despite an increase of 17 percent in total number of farms from around 2.2 million to 2.5 million. A decline of 6 percent in total number of farms was observed in 1986 (compared to 1974). This decline was accompanied by a decline in the number of farms owned in the Western, Central, Eastern, Volta and Ashanti Regions, whereas in the Northern and Upper Regions the number of farms owned increased. In terms of proportions, the share of rented farms in total figures increased in all of the south, with the largest increases noted in the Ashanti and Brong-Ahafo Regions. The shares of rented farms remained unchanged in the Northern and Upper

Table 4.1: Land Tenure by Regions, 1970, 1974, 1986 (thousand farms)

Region	1970				1974				1986			
	Owned	(%)	Rented	(%)	Owned	(%)	Rented	(%)	Owned	(%)	Rented	(%)
Western	165	(94)	10	(6)	306	(97)	10	(3)	192	(82)	41	(18)
Central	181	(86)	30	(14)	212	(86)	34	(14)	147	(70)	63	(30)
Greater Accra	-	-	-	-	-	-	-	-	27	(72)	10	(28)
Eastern	375	(87)	54	(13)	370	(87)	55	(13)	199	(72)	76	(28)
Volta	292	(92)	25	(8)	309	(92)	26	(8)	195	(86)	31	(14)
Ashanti	450	(97)	12	(3)	570	(95)	33	(5)	380	(87)	55	(13)
Brong-Ahafo	183	(99)	2	(1)	213	(99)	2	(1)	230	(85)	41	(15)
Northern	113	(99.5)	1	(0.5)	130	(100)	-	(0)	220	(99.7)	0.7	(0.3)
Upper	257	(98)	4	(2)	256	(99)	3	(1)	454[1]	(98)	10	(2)
Ghana	2 016	(94)	138	(6)	2 366	(94)	163	(6)	2 044	(86)	328	(14)

[1] In the Upper West Region 118.7 thousand farms were owned (98.5% of total) and 1.9 thousand rented (1.5% of total), while in the Upper East Region 335.7 thousand farms were owned (97.6% of the total) and 8.4 thousand were rented (2.4% of total).

Source: Derived on the basis of Republic of Ghana 1972: 48-49; Republic of Ghana 1975; Giri, Oku and Fukai 1987; and Republic of Ghana 1987h.

Regions. These observations may be taken as an indication of rural-rural migration of farmers from the northern regions to the southern regions of the country over the last 15 years.

For 1987, Table 4.2 gives a breakdown of the ownership and rental systems by number of farms and percentage, and a further breakdown of the rental system into cash, fixed amount of produce, *abunu*, *abusa* and others. The cash rental type (40 percent) ranks high followed by *abusa* (30 percent), *abunu* (25 percent), and fixed amount of produce (5.3 percent). In 1987, with increased farming activities in Brong-Ahafo and Northern Ghana, reflecting the renewed interest in maize, tomatoes, and the industrial crops (tobacco and cotton), the percentage of rented land went up.

Land Tenure and Agricultural Development Projects. Formal development interventions in agriculture invariably affect tenurial relations directly or indirectly. In Ghana, the interaction between the tenure systems and projects has expressed itself in a number of different ways. In the first place, the development of commercial farming and plantations has, on occasion, been impeded by difficulties of resolving ownership or security of tenure issues firmly enough to justify proceeding with the high levels of investment required. Second, resettlement and irrigation schemes have been hampered by the complexity of reallocating land. Third, there has been a general tendency in Ghanaian agricultural projects for the land interests of smallholders to be subordinated to the "public interest" of the State or to the private interests of those with close contacts with the relevant banks and state institutions. Projects designed to strengthen the economic base of the smallholder are bound to have an impact upon issues of land ownership or tenure either by facilitating the smallholders' capacity to farm more land or by increasing the productivity of the existing holdings and hence their market value. Smallholder development, therefore, requires clear and effective policy commitments from the Government with respect to accessibility of land, rent regulation and security of tenure.

The Land Allocation Committee. The principal body, and the first court of appeal with respect to land allocation and tenurial issues, is the District Land Allocation Committee. The Committee consists of district chiefs representing custodial interests and the District Provisional National Defence Council (PNDC) Secretary representing the Government and government policy. The Committee deals with issues of demarcation disputes, land use and planning. For example, in the case of irrigation projects, the Committee is responsible for sorting out the reallocation of irrigated land. Disputants can, if necessary,

Table 4.2: Farms Under Different Tenancies, 1987

Region	Total No. of sample farms	Ownership				Types of rental arrangements								
		Owner		Rent		Fixed amount				Abunu		Abusa		Others	
						Cash		Produce							
		Number	%	Number	%	Number	%	Number	%	Number	%	Number	%	Number	%
Western	182 612	159 474	87.3	23 138	12.7	9 393	40.6	143	0.6	6 504	28.1	6 989	30.2	109	0.5
Central	172 308	129 086	74.9	43 222	25.1	25 489	59.0	1 652	3.8	5 405	12.5	10 676	24.7	-	-
Greater Accra	72 071	53 765	74.6	18 306	25.4	11 935	65.2	824	4.5	1 648	9.0	3 899	21.3	-	-
Eastern	298 549	220 932	74.0	77 617	26.0	19 820	25.5	4 029	5.2	24 074	31.0	28 595	36.9	1 099	1.4
Volta	178 408	56 483	87.7	21 925	12.3	6 59	30.8	2 657	12.1	1 922	8.8	9 042	41.2	1 545	7.1
Ashanti	459 100	400 537	87.2	58 563	12.8	15 308	26.2	665	1.1	28 229	48.2	13 593	23.2	768	1.3
Brong-Ahafo	223 221	182 355	81.7	40 866	18.3	21 514	52.6	2 488	6.1	4 060	9.9	12 444	30.5	360	0.9
Northern	167 467	161 607	96.5	5 860	3.5	2 877	49.1	2 432	41.5	551	9.4	-	-	-	-
Upper West	123 412	123 331	99.9	81	0.1	-	-	-	-	-	-	-	-	81	100.0
Upper East	297 048	284 779	95.9	12 269	4.1	3 111	25.3	1 188	9.7	2 965	24.2	4 806	39.2	199	1.6
Total	2 174 196	1 872 349	86.1	301 847	13.9	116 206	38.5	16 078	5.3	75 358	25.0	90 044	29.8	4 161	1.4

Source: PPMED, Ministry of Agriculture, 1988.

appeal to a higher authority at the regional level in the event of being unable to settle their quarrels at the level of this Committee. In most cases, however, committee decisions are accepted.

Health and Nutrition

Background. The health status of the majority of Ghanaians, particularly those living in the rural areas, is poor. Diseases related to poverty and underdevelopment, such as intestinal parasites, scabies, diarrhoea, bronchopneumonia, malnutrition and malaria, are common. Moreover, there is evidence that during the period 1970-83 the economic decline of Ghana was reflected in a sharp deterioration in the health of its population. Diseases virtually eradicated by campaigns in the nineteen-fifties and nineteen-sixties, notably yaws and yellow fever, reappeared in the late nineteen-seventies with major epidemics in the Northern and Upper Regions in 1977, 1981 and 1983. Infant and child mortality rates rose; visits to health facilities dropped; the per capita calorie supply as a percentage of daily requirements declined; and the ratio of physicians to population worsened sharply. While government expenditure on health as a proportion of total government expenditure increased in 1984, following a decline experienced during the mid-seventies, this is only in apparent terms since real per capita expenditure on health in 1982/1983 was only 23 percent of its value in 1974. Expenditure on health care for the rural poor has consistently suffered from a strong urban bias in the health budget allocations. No specific allocation is made to primary health care, the main rural requirement, since allocations are made to the Ministry of Health (MOH) divisions for medical care, maternal and child health and nutrition, and control of communicable diseases.

In 1975-76, medical care received 79 percent of the total resources allocated to health, of which 22 percent was allotted to the main teaching hospital in Korle Bu; public health services received 12 percent; and training 6 percent. These proportions have remained the same. Eighty percent of the allocation is spent on recurrent expenditure, and 20 percent on capital expenditure. For the past five to seven years, however, hardly any capital expenditure has been made.

Regional Variations. Considerable regional variations exist in the provision of health services. It is clear from all the data (a sample is exhibited in Annex A, Table A.13) that health facilities and staffing are weaker in the north of Ghana than in the south. The northern regions are particularly dependent on non-governmental organization

(NGO) health assistance to make up for the relative lack of government services. The major NGO contribution comes from the Roman Catholic Church. While the Government has drawn up a primary health care strategy for the country, provision of health services to the rural poor is still very inadequate.

The nutritional state of Ghanaians is generally low and was considerably aggravated by the 1982-83 drought. The most vulnerable groups are pre-school children, school-age children, and pregnant and lactating women. In 1986, 36.1 percent of all children fell below 80 percent of the Harvard Weight-for-Age Standard, with the incidence of malnutrition higher in the Northern and Upper Regions. In the drought year of 1983 this proportion was as high as 47 percent. From survey work, it appears that adult males and females other than those considered above are able to achieve acceptable nutritional levels except during the rainy seasons and the run-up to harvest. Seasonal malnutrition has been severe in all years (see Figure 4.1) and particularly so in the Northern, Upper East and Upper West Regions, where during the hungry season food intake is reported to drop to 60-70 percent below average requirements. There is broad cause for concern with regard to both calorie and protein intake deficiencies.

Nutritional problems reflect ecological variations from region to region. For example, the heavy dependence on starchy roots contributes to a high incidence of kwashiorkor in the forest zones of southern Ghana. In the Northern Region, where marasmus is more common, calorie intake is low, but the consumption of cereals permits an adequate intake of protein. Although the Northern and Upper Regions are large net exporters of groundnuts, yams, cattle and rice, they are nevertheless nutritionally deficient as a result of having to sell food items to raise cash for non-food needs. Other nutritional problems are goitre from iodine deficiency in the Upper, Northern and Mampong Ashanti areas, and vitamin A deficiency in these areas and in Axim and the Western Region.

Nutritional Programmes. Nutrition rehabilitation is an important element in the work of the Nutrition, Maternal and Child Health, and Health Education Division of MOH. There are 11 nutrition rehabilitation centres in the country: four in the Greater Accra Region; three in the Upper Regions; and one each in the Eastern, Volta, Ashanti and Northern Regions. Two of the three Upper regional centres are run by NGOs: the Presbyterian Church and the Christian Council of Ghana. Other government organizations involved in nutrition and nutrition education programmes are the MOA Home Extension Unit, the Community Development Department of the

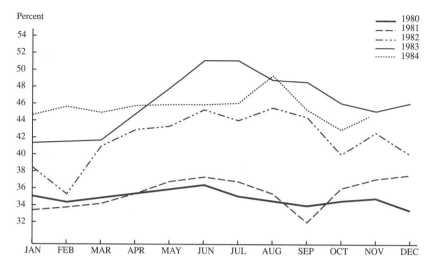

Figure 4.1: Malnutrition Among Children Under Five Years Old: 1980-84

Source: Catholic Relief Services.

Ministry of Local Government and Rural Development, the Social Welfare Department and the Food Research Institute. In addition, a large number of NGOs are concerned with nutrition, notably Catholic Relief Services, who have been supporting supplementary feeding programmes through over 300 government and private health centres for more than 20 years. Finally, the international agencies FAO, WHO and UNICEF have nutritional programmes focussing, *inter alia*, on nutrition education at the primary school level, on the production of weaning food (mainly by women's groups) through a group development approach in which grinding mills are provided on credit, and on food preservation and storage, especially fish-smoking promotion and dry-season gardening.

Outstanding Nutritional Issues. Despite the large number of agencies concerned with nutrition improvement, the problem of deficiency has remained difficult to resolve. This is due in part to pricing policies which lead to low food production because producers have gone into trading or wage labour; poor infrastructure which constrains distribution of inputs and produce, especially meat and fish; land pressure which leads to short fallow periods and poor yields; the high price of inputs (when obtainable); the lack of storage facilities; and the increasingly aged producer population as the young leave the rural areas.

Maternal and Child Health and Family Planning. The regional distribution and source of operation of maternal and child health clinics conforms to the usual pattern for regional variations in health facilities. The outreach of these clinics can be severely limited, as demonstrated by the large urban concentration of maternal and child health staff. Maternal and child health clinics provide antenatal and postnatal care, but, in general, are inaccessible to rural women, who are dependent upon traditional birth attendants. The Ghana National Family Planning Programme under the Ministry of Finance and Economic Planning started operations in 1970. By 1979, 221 family planning clinics were registered with the Programme. Family planning appears to be practised most in Accra and least in the Upper and Brong-Ahafo Regions, but family planning would seem to be marginal in a society where the average expectation is six children.

In conclusion, the existing infrastructure for delivering basic health services faces three major problems: low population coverage, shortage of supplies and insufficient manpower. The urban bias means that at most only 30 percent of the rural population is estimated to have access to any health care. The network of primary health care centres has not expanded to keep pace with population growth. Foreign exchange constraints and the devaluation of the cedi contribute to the high cost and short supply of basic drugs such as nivaquine and aspirin and consumables such as cotton wool, gauze, bandages, needles and syringes. Poor infrastructure has hampered supply distribution. The Government is evidently well aware of the problems, as the PIP provides for primary health care strengthening in which 15 districts will initially receive staff training support. All other elements of the health programme are rehabilitative. Nutrition is not mentioned. While it is the Government's intention to provide modest increases in the health budget, it is nevertheless clear that it is likely to be some time before significant improvements in access to rural health care are achieved. Meanwhile, a heavy and increasing reliance upon a combination of NGO support and community involvement to alleviate the burden upon government in this sector can be expected.

Education

Background. Since at least the early nineteen-seventies, the range and quality of state education in Ghana has been in serious decline. In 1970, the education budget comprised 3.9 percent of GDP. This fell to 0.85 percent by the early nineteen-eighties. Despite a rapidly growing population, state expenditure in 1984 was about one-third in absolute terms of that of 1976. The effect on the schooling system was virtually catastrophic. Buildings fell into disrepair; textbooks and stationery became largely unobtainable; equipment was neither repaired nor replaced; over 50 percent of the teaching staff were untrained, a state of affairs aggravated by the emigration of many trained teachers, along with other middle-class Ghanaians, either to neighbouring countries or the US and Europe; drop-out rates rose and enrolment ratios fell so that it is now estimated that 60 percent of the adult population are illiterate (though enrolment ratios are now estimated to be rising again). Rural schools were harder hit than urban institutions and girls more affected than boys.

Regional Variations. Long-standing regional variations in the accessibility and quality of education were also exacerbated to the extent that reliable data collection makes such judgements possible. While the capacity for official data collection was already shaky before 1980, it collapsed entirely shortly thereafter. The quality of the data must, therefore, be taken with caution. Nevertheless, a clear regional pattern emerges, as shown for instance in Table 4.3. The strongest educational base is found in the metropolitan areas of the Greater Accra Region and in the cocoa belt regions of Eastern and Ashanti. At the other end of the spectrum, educational provision and attainment is exceptionally weak in the Upper East, Upper West and Northern Regions. Brong-Ahafo is also a relatively weak region in educational terms. These problems are long-standing. They originated in colonial policies which, quite deliberately, discriminated against the northern half of Ghana with respect to the provision of social services. Thus, secondary schools are rather inaccessible since they are located exclusively in the few urban centres of these regions and the nation's three universities are located in the south of the country. To some extent the pattern has been self-perpetuating, since graduates from the teacher training colleges are reluctant to take up posts in the comparatively remote and poorly serviced northern areas.

Rural Water

Background. The relationship between rural poverty and lack of access to potable water and adequate sanitation is clear in Ghana. About 4.4 million people, approximately 37 percent of the national population, do not have access to clean water or effective sanitary facilities. The majority of these people live in small rural communities.

Table 4.3: Selected Educational Statistics in 1980

Region	Percentage of adults who have attended school	Primary enrolment ratios	Primary Schools			Middle Schools		
			Number of schools	Number of teachers	Pupils per teacher	Number of schools	Number of teachers	Pupils per teacher
	(1)	(2)	(3)	(4)	(5)	(6)	(7)	(8)
Western	37.9	65.4	857	4 039	35	413	1 797	26
Central	33.3	60.1	751	4 350	35	481	2 531	23
Greater Accra	50.9	74.0	571	3 816	35	414	2 128	28
Eastern	42.8	70.1	1 540	8 330	35	923	4 428	23
Volta	37.5	60.3	1 052	6 149	24	640	2 949	24
Ashanti	27.9	71.6	1 383	1 160	27	865	4 765	24
Brong-Ahafo	38.0	55.9	870	5 669	25	460	2 319	21
Northern	7.7	17.3	477	3 117	19	106	760	18
Upper	7.4	19.3	347	2 291	25	147	822	14

Sources: Ewusi 1984; Education Statistics, 1981–82, Ministry of Education.

Regional Status of Water Supply. In Ghana as a whole, 43 600 or 91.3 percent of all communities, comprising 34.7 percent of the total population, are not served by any water supply. Of these communities, 43 000 have populations of less than 500 people and they comprise 26.4 percent of the total population.

Since all the small communities are rural, it is evident that people in small villages almost totally lack adequate water supplies. Of the rural pipe-borne water supplies, 43 percent of the surface sources and 39 percent of the groundwater sources need rehabilitation. All the rural water sources needing rehabilitation are in the Ashanti, Brong-Ahafo, Western and Volta Regions. The region with the greatest population without potable water supply is the Northern Region, followed in descending order by the Eastern, Ashanti, Volta and Brong-Ahafo Regions. By comparing the distribution of population between community size categories, it is clear that the reasons for an existing unserved population are different for the Northern, Brong-Ahafo and Volta Regions as compared to Eastern and Ashanti. Basically, in the Northern Region the lack of services is attributable to the relative remoteness and physical dispersion of settlements. This pattern has limited the cost-effectiveness of water supply provision and thus discouraged investment. The same is true to a lesser extent for the Brong-Ahafo and Volta Regions, especially the northern half of Volta. In the Eastern and Ashanti Regions it is clear that some effort has gone into supplying the larger settlements, but that investment has not kept pace with the high levels of population. The Upper East and Upper West Regions appear atypically well serviced because of a massive well-drilling campaign by the German and Canadian Governments. As a result, the Upper East in particular is now arguably the region with the best water supply.

Rural Sanitation

Background. There are no reliable data for rural sanitation coverage despite the 15 percent figure assumed in official documents. It is probably more realistic to accept the 4 percent coverage which appears at the bottom end of the range estimated in recent sanitation reviews. Basically, five types of latrine appear to be in limited use: pit latrines, bucket (or removable pan) latrines, the aqua-privy, KVIP and the water-closet (the KVIP is an improved pit latrine that produces no nauseating odours. It is built in such a way that the use of a pair is alternated so that when one pit fills up users switch to the other. The filled up pit is left to atrophy, and later dug up to become usable again). Where facilities are available to rural communities they consist mostly of the pit or bucket type usually located 50-100 metres from the nearest houses. In practice, all rural people simply resort to bush or beach defecation.

Rural Sanitation Problems. The two main problems of rural sanitation may be summarized as follows: on the one hand, government services are severely constrained technically and financially; on the other, progress has been impeded by the lack of public knowledge and understanding of the causes of diseases, an antipathy to the functioning of various latrine systems, and practical objections to the high costs of installing private facilities. The principal water-related diseases in rural Ghana are diarrhoea, dysentery, schistosomiasis, onchocerciasis, typhoid, cholera, guinea-worm, malaria and bilharzia.

Mechanisms and Process of Socio-economic Differentiation

The mainspring of socio-economic differentiation in rural Ghana has historically been the cocoa industry. It put a premium on access to capital; intensified internal migration; increased agricultural wage and sharecropping labour; fuelled the demand for goods and services; accelerated the monetization of rural relations of production; enhanced the spread and power of informal credit systems; and became the major internal source of revenue for financing the public sector and industrial development. The importance of this single export cash crop to the Ghanaian political economy dictated, to an unusual degree, the pattern of national socio-economic differentiation. Policies with respect to cocoa production and state control over pricing, taxation, and marketing of the crop have had a major bearing on the process of social differentiation.

Prior to the development of cocoa in the south there was, of course, some socio-economic differentiation based on the traditional chieftaincy hierarchies and, to a limited extent, upon trade in commodities such as food crops, palm oil and rubber. Nevertheless, the range of differentiation was quite narrow. For example, a typical Akan household comprised the household head and often his younger brothers and sisters belonging to the same clan; wives of the father belonging to different clans; his children belonging to their mother's clan; and house "pawns and slaves" belonging to or having close ties with the household head. The head of the household had a religious function, acting as an intermediary between the living and the dead members of the family. He also exercised considerable control over the labour power of the household members, even those belonging to a different clan. Because of the low level of technology and the nature of the terrain, it was, above all, the number of household members that determined the acreage under cultivation; the more members, the more land. A system of shifting cultivation was made possible by the abundance of forest land and every two or three years a patch would be abandoned and a new one developed.

While lineage combinations may have been different, the majority of northern households were very similar to this typical model, particularly with respect to the household head's religious as well as secular power and his command over household labour. An important element of this authority in most, but not all, northern societies was the requirement for young men to pay bride price. The elders controlled access to wives, land and cattle and their acquisition depended on young men giving their labour power. Compared to the south, traditional socio-economic differentiation was even narrower, since northern patterns of kinship obligations were expressed through distributive mechanisms which reduced the individual's opportunity for personal accumulation.

These traditional, subsistence-oriented, food-producing households were transformed by cocoa development in the south. The processes of cocoa-related differentiation took different but interrelated forms in the north and south of Ghana. Northern Ghana was, and still is, relied upon as a labour reserve for the development of cocoa in the south. Initially coercion was used, sometimes with the cooperation of some northern chiefs. A number of policies were subsequently developed to maintain the migratory form of labour. Measures were taken to prevent the north from acquiring funds to build up physical and social infrastructure. All lands were vested in the State, thereby preventing the development of a land market.

In the south, new socio-economic categories were created as cocoa production spread. At the top end of the new income range were the capitalist farmer-traders. These individuals had acquired capital in other businesses, enabling them to establish themselves as stranger farmers on a large scale and take advantage of the economic opportunities of cocoa. Included in this category of the richest were also a number of chiefs who were able to exploit their traditional custodial authority over the land for personal gain. Below this level, three distinct categories of "peasant" producers emerged: rich, middle and poor (Konings and Rowell 1986).

The criteria for categorization was the number of 60 lb (27.25 kg) "loads" produced by the peasant cocoa farmer rather than the size of holding. The data was based on research done in 1979/80. Rich peasants were defined as those producing more than 200 loads in the 1979/80 season. Twenty-four percent of the cocoa-growing peasantry in Brong-Ahafo was estimated to be rich that season. Middle peasants were classified as producing between 50 and 200 loads and were estimated as 46.5 percent of the population. Poor peasants were the remaining 29.5 percent, and produced less than 50 loads. Although the data comes from only one survey, it provides an indicator of different levels of production and distribution. The farmers in the middle and poor categories do not produce enough to meet their subsistence requirements. They are obliged not only to ensure their own production, but to hire themselves out as labour, and to borrow from rich peasants or even richer farmer-traders. In the case of such loans, crops are pledged as collateral. If middle-level peasants cannot pay, they slide into the poor category; and if the poor peasants cannot pay, they can enter into a form of debt bondage where they have to work off all their debts. Some never do. In the case of middle-range producers, supplementary sources of income, besides rural wage labour, include labour in the industrial sector and trade or small-scale commercial food production. Poor peasants can sell their labour to middle or rich peasants or, particularly in the case of poor peasant women, they will go into food production and processing and petty trade. At the same time, some poor cocoa producers buy labour, either by leaving their newly established or otherwise low-producing cocoa farms to an even poorer sharecropper while they go off and sharecrop on a richer farm, or by hiring casual labour (though not annual labour). In the middle and lower strata, therefore, the same individual may be a producer-owner, a labourer, and a hirer of labour.

The four forms of labour underpinning cocoa production are family, sharecropping (usually *abusa*), annual, and casual labour. *Abusa* labourers are recruited mostly from the ranks of illiterate males who are generally younger and of a different ethnic origin than their employer. The majority, 60-70 percent, are from northern Ghana. In general, *abusa* labourers do not send their children to school, either because they cannot afford the fees or because they need their labour. *Abusa* labour is apparently preferred by both employers and employees. From the labourer's point of view, income is potentially higher since wages depend on the level of production rather than on a fixed annual sum determined irrespectively of returns. Moreover, after the main cocoa season, the *abusa* worker can concentrate on food production or other wage employment. From the employer's point of view, sharecropping shifts some of the production risk onto the *abusa* labourer and enables postponement of payment until after the harvest when cash is more readily available. By comparison, annual labourers have no access to land, cannot generate income from other sources and essentially are only hired by rich producers. Middle and poor producers must settle for casual wage labour, if any, which is paid by the day.

It can be seen that cocoa development changed a relatively undifferentiated rural economy into a socio-economic hierarchy where access to cocoa land, capital and labour became crucial. Land ceased to be freely available. The costs of acquisition rose steeply. Land extent was no longer governed by the size of family labour but by the hiring capacity of the operator who became, in many cases, an absentee landlord with none of the traditional obligations binding the household head. Access to the potential profits of cocoa, for many, depended upon their entering the credit system as debtors in cash or in kind (including labour). The attendant monetization increased the demand for cash to pay rents, obtain inputs, pay labour, or pay for education. Labour was in high demand and cocoa had to compete with other sources of employment, such as the mines or timber industry. As cocoa allowed the development of the public and industrial sector, labour was also diverted to the urban areas.

In this context, food production was seen to decline from as early as the nineteen-thirties. The family labour which was needed in the past was often no longer available in the north or in the south. Traditional patterns of authority began to break down. Bride price, for example, was no longer a source of leverage for elders over the labour power of the young. In the south, food production was not only displaced economically, but physically, as it was moved to plots distant from the communities in order to make room for cocoa farms.

Other mechanisms and processes of socio-economic differentiation were dwarfed by comparison with the impact of cocoa. The migration precipitated by its development greatly contributed to the creation of an essentially "national" population where religious and ethnic considerations of identity were retained but became of secondary importance. Family ties were effectively broken and the traditional kinship systems of social and economic security weakened in favour of the informal credit system.

Since the end of the Second World War, both colonial and independent governments have recognized the developing crisis in food production. In particular, the north has come to be redefined in terms of policy not so much as a labour reserve for the south, but as a potential area for the development of large-scale food production which would feed the southern economy. In the period up to the late nineteen-seventies, the State's attempts to solve the food problem oscillated between the promotion of state-based agricultural enterprises and the encouragement of large private farmers. Neither approach was conducive to the development of smallholders. Although the socio-economic impact of these policies upon the smallholder sector was usually adverse, it also appears to have been rather limited, simply because both private and public sector schemes were capital-intensive, and placed heavy emphasis on mechanization. As such, they tended simply to bypass local communities in the development of the production process. For example, the Fumbisi Valley rice farmers on the borders of the Northern and Upper Regions, were a group of entrepreneurs largely drawn from business, the military and the bureaucracy, groups which, unlike the local people, had the contacts necessary to take advantage of government subsidies and bank credit. Permanent skilled labour was brought in by these mainly absentee farmers often on the basis of kinship, and was drawn principally from literate, urban young men who had formerly been involved in petty trade, lorry driving and so on.

A rather similar pattern developed in the cases of the Vea and Tono irrigation schemes, state-based enterprises, where, in the early days, land was taken away from local smallholders and reallocated, post-irrigation, to influential outsiders. The impact of these various schemes on the local socio-economic structure was that the local communities became suppliers of cheap, casual, unskilled labour. The schemes did not, as a result of mechanization, provide as many unskilled labour opportunities as they could have. They did to some degree, however, contribute further to weakening local food production and household organization by enabling young men and, in particular, young women to leave household control and family labour for alternative sources of independent income. In the cases of Vea and Tono, land was ultimately reallocated back to the local people after considerable political upheaval. Their incomes have gradually improved as they have adapted to producing a mix of upland subsistence and irrigated commercial crops. By the time of the restitution (13 years after project commencement in the case of Vea and five years in the case of Tono), however, a large number of the displaced peasantry had already migrated. Finally, even with the change in public emphasis toward smallholder-oriented projects, which happened in the late nineteen-seventies, there seems to have been a lack of attention to labour-intensive techniques of production which perhaps could have led to a more beneficial socio-economic impact.

From the mid-nineteen-sixties onwards, cocoa farmers' income began to drop rapidly. This decrease was mostly due to enormous government levies. At the same time, food prices began to rise steeply as disincentives affected smallholders. The result was that many "poor" and "middle" peasant cocoa farmers became impoverished and even the capital resources of the "rich" peasants and large producers became severely depleted. New investment in labour and expanded cocoa production ceased and much of the cocoa acreage was allowed to deteriorate. An increasingly high proportion of the cocoa that was produced was smuggled into the Côte d'Ivoire and Togo. These changes brought with them a new pattern of socio-economic differentiation in the south. There appears to have been little thorough analysis of these changes. What seems to have happened is that poor people turned to food production in greater numbers, though not on cocoa land because of tenurial problems. The result was an increase of small subsistence holdings. At the same time, male labour migrated out to Nigeria or other nearby countries. This must have constrained the size of food plots further since it left a growing number of female-headed households without adequate labour power. In 1984, following the expulsion of Ghanaian migrants from Nigeria, there appears to have been a further increase in the proliferation of southern food-producing smallholdings. At the same time, women who had been without male labour support learned a new role for themselves in smallholder food production.

Chapter 5

Women and Rural Development

Women play a very important role in rural Ghana. They constitute 51 percent of Ghana's total population and 51 percent of the country's workforce. Ghanaian women are a major force in agriculture, and farming is their main occupation in the rural areas. Hence, a discussion of rural development would be incomplete without an examination of their potential. This chapter is fully devoted to this task. Nevertheless, while women are an important force in Ghana, they do not share equally the benefits accrued from overall national efforts, and remain disadvantaged in certain respects. Women receive fewer of the services the nation has to offer, such as education, agricultural extension and access to capital. These and other aspects of the situation of women are highlighted below.

General Aspects

According to the preliminary results of the 1984 Population Census (Republic of Ghana 1984c), there are 2.5 million households in Ghana, of which 64 percent are located in rural areas or communities with a population of less than 5 000. Thirty-two percent of all the households in Ghana are female-headed, a 3 percent increase from 1970. In urban centres, 36 percent of all households are female-headed, while the proportion in rural areas is 30 percent. The average household size for the entire country is five persons. In urban areas the average family size tends to be slightly smaller (4.4 persons), than in rural areas (5.3). The definition of the household is expressed in economic terms: the household unit is the unit around a common "cooking pot" and its members are those who eat from it. All members contribute to the pot in different ways, but that does not mean that the resources of individual members are pooled. In fact, husband and wife usually keep separate economies. The demographic definition of the conventional household structure traditionally recognizes the man as head of the family and head of the household, which consists of an

92

extended family unit with one or more wives, their children and often elderly or unmarried relatives.

Women in Ghana must care for their families and at the same time be economically active. They are expected to have their own sources of income and to assume part of the economic burden for the support of their households by providing for their own material needs as well as those of their children. Quite often, however, despite the significant economic contribution women make to the household budget, the males dominate in deciding how to spend the earned income. Areas in which women have greater control in deciding how to allocate resources are clothing, household goods, food and cooking utensils. Nonetheless, in a large number of households the wife alone must pay for these basic expenses.

Women-headed Households

With the introduction of cocoa farming and the cash economy, when cash cropping replaced food production as the main activity, men began to migrate to other areas to set up their own cocoa farms or to work as labourers. At the same time, others began to migrate to urban centres in search of cash and job opportunities. Women took over many of the roles and responsibilities that previously had been male-dominated. They found, however, that their work burden increased while their access to resources did not. As mentioned in the previous section, 32 percent of all households in Ghana are headed by females; the proportion is higher in urban areas. This is probably due to the migration of women to urban centres to set up activities of their own, and to the more relaxed social structures there (Table 5.1). Differences also exist among regions. The urban areas in the Central, Eastern and Volta Regions have the highest proportions of female-headed households in Ghana with 47 percent, 40 percent, and 40 percent respectively. Conversely, although the Northern and Upper Regions have had the greatest net outflow of migrants together with the Eastern and Volta Regions, they also have the lowest proportion, 8 percent and 11 percent respectively, of female-headed households in rural areas. This may be explained by the traditional extended family structure of northern Ghana where, when males migrated, another male family member remained to head the household. Another factor may be that a substantial percentage of migration is seasonal. Northern farm labourers would move to cocoa-growing areas in Ashanti and Brong-Ahafo during the long dry season, and return home later in the year.

Table 5.1: Heads of Household by Gender, 1970 and 1984

	1970	%	1984	%
Urban	587 302		888 595	
Male	405 819	69.1	570 429	64.2
Female	181 483	30.9	318 166	35.8
Rural	1 206 278		1 590 315	
Male	873 722	72.4	1 118 556	70.3
Female	332 556	27.6	471 759	29.7

Source: Republic of Ghana 1970 and Republic of Ghana 1984c.

Women's Workload Responsibilities

Ghanaian women have always worked both inside and outside the home. Indeed, it is often stated that the idea of a full-time housewife is unknown in traditional Ghanaian society. The percentage of women aged 15 and over who are classified as employed is almost 80 percent for the whole country, while the urban and rural figures are 71 percent and 84 percent respectively (Table 5.2). Rural women's tasks include farming, processing and marketing of food, child care and household duties.

Traditionally, men and women farmed together on the same plot of land, producing solely for the household's consumption. The division of labour was clearly defined in a system based on age and sex. The development of the market economy and the introduction of cocoa cultivation brought about a new sexual division of labour: men were primarily cash crop producers and eventually migrant workers, while the burden of growing food crops to feed the family fell heavily on the women. This new sexual division of labour also resulted in yam (previously the most important crop) being replaced by other crops, such as maize and cassava, which are less labour-intensive. Before cocoa was introduced, men were the food producers, while the women helped on the family farm during weeding and harvesting. Because earnings from cocoa went into new crop investment or general household needs, women were left with little or no money at all. Consequently, they began to establish separate farms, in addition to the family farm, to raise crops for sale. Women became almost exclusively responsible for the daily subsistence needs of most households. In addition, with the rural-urban migration of males in search of jobs, many women were left to run the household on their

Table 5.2: Female Working Population, 1984 (thousands)

	Total	Urban	Rural
Female population Aged 15 and over	3 500	1 170	2 330
Employed women Aged 15 and over	2 786	834	1 952[1]
Percent employed	79.6%	71.3%	83.8%

[1] Obtained by summing up regional figures.
Source: Republic of Ghana 1984c.

own. This greatly affected their workload since they became the head of the household, and assumed all the responsibility.

Cultural diversity makes it difficult to generalize the status and situation of women in Ghana. For example, traditional northern Ghanaian societies differentiate sharply between men's and women's work responsibilities (e.g. what they are supposed to "pay" for), and their territory. Women in traditional societies occupy themselves with household duties and the lighter tasks of farming. In the Northern Region, farming activities such as land cleaning, tilling, and the raising of mounds and ridges are done by men, while women do the planting and weeding and help in harvesting. In fact, in areas such as Mamprusi, Dagomba, Gonja, Sessala, Wala, and Nanumba in the Northern Region it is absolutely forbidden for women to participate in the actual tilling of the land. By contrast, in the southern regions of Ghana women often keep their own farms and either carry out tilling of land themselves or hire labour to do it.

Food Processing. Processing of food crops is mostly done by women. They process food crops into various forms, mainly to prolong their availability during the lean seasons, and not only for family consumption but also for sale. Foods which undergo such processing are the starchy staples; e.g., cassava into gari (grated, fermented and roasted) and tapioca, and maize into fine meal (polished and unpolished). Rural women also process cooking oil from coconut, groundnut, palm nut and palm kernels. Fish smoking and salting is another common food preservation technique and a major activity of rural women along the coast. Other food processing activities include drying of tomatoes and peppers.

Domestic Chores. Traditional sex roles delegated certain domestic tasks to women. The handling of what the family ate, gathering firewood for fuel, fetching water, and looking after large numbers of children traditionally were, and still are, within the women's domain. Today the lives of Ghanaian women are still characterized by hard manual work, using traditional implements and methods. The rural woman's workday often starts at 5:00 or 6:00 a.m. and continues until 7:00 or 8:00 p.m. A study done in the Greater Accra Region shows that during a woman's 14-hour workday, more time is spent on domestic activities than on income-generating activities (Ardayfio-Schandorf, 1986). For example, an average of 1.3 hours a day is spent on water collection, 2.1 hours on cooking and food processing, and 0.8 hours on firewood collection. These averages change according to the season as, for instance, during the dry season much more time is needed to collect water.

After cooking, fuelwood collection, along with water fetching, remain the most time-consuming domestic tasks for women. According to a household survey (Republic of Ghana 1979), 75 percent of all households relied on wood and charcoal for cooking. In rural areas, however, all households rely primarily on wood. Women bear the burden of collecting wood as it is regarded as compatible with women's domestic activities but not with men's work. Usually fuelwood collection involves walking long distances.

Since domestic activities take up most of women's time, the introduction of technological devices, or of more efficient methods, would lighten their workload. First and foremost should be the provision of a good and reliable water supply. Also, technologies for milling or processing food would free women from many burdensome tasks. Appropriate technologies for income-generating activities, such as fish-smoking ovens, could also be introduced.

Women's Role in Agriculture

In 1984, 61 percent of all those employed were working in the agricultural sector and of this number 47 percent were women. The number of women farmers has been increasing faster than that of males. From 1970 to 1984 the number of women farmers increased 102 percent from 771 100 to 1 561 200, while the number of male farmers increased by 72 percent from 1 015 100 to 1 750 300. The slower increase in the number of male farmers is due to the large migration of males to urban areas and out-migration to neighbouring countries. While final results from the 1984 census are not available, 1970 data show that 70 percent of women farmers were in food cropping, where they outnumbered men. This was a significant change from 1960, when male farmers of food crops significantly outnumbered women. The second most important agricultural occupation for women in 1970 was cocoa farming; it employed 27 percent of the women.

In addition to farming their own piece of land, women farmers usually assist their husbands on the family farm. On their own farms, they may cultivate crops such as maize, cassava, cocoyam, peppers, tomatoes, garden eggs and okra. While the Agricultural Census does not distinguish between men and women farmers with respect to total area planted, it is commonly thought that women, on the average, have smaller farms than men. Additionally, women's farms are usually farther from the village than the family plot and have less fertile soil, since the most fertile lands are used for cash crops. While the initial task of clearing the land and felling trees is done by men (husbands or hired labour), women carry out the remaining tasks of planting, subsequent weeding, harvesting and carrying home produce from the farm.

The breakdown of persons aged 15 and over, employed solely in agriculture and hunting in 1984, is shown by sex and by region in Table 5.3. It is interesting to note that women farmers outnumber men in half of the regions, namely in the Western, Central, Eastern, Volta and Ashanti Regions. The Northern Region is the only region in which women farmers are significantly fewer than male farmers. This is mainly due to the more traditional nature of the Northern Region's family structure and the division of labour, as previously mentioned. The limited participation of women in agriculture in the north may also be due to the environment. Because of its arid savannah conditions, women must spend much more time fetching water and firewood than their southern counterparts. In addition, vegetable or backyard gardening is widely practised by women in the Northern and Upper Regions, and so it is possible that the actual number of women farmers in the Northern Region may be underestimated.

The participation of women in agricultural production involves certain special aspects. Marketing of produce begins with its transportation. For the small farmer, transporting produce from the farm to the village or market usually means headloading it many miles to the village so that traders and vehicles can transport it to markets. The average weight of headloads of cassava, maize and plantain is about 30 kg each. Table 5.4 gives an estimate of the person-days required to headload produce from one hectare of various crops from farm to village. These estimates are based on carrying two loads of approximately 30 kg each, over an average distance of 5 km a day. On this basis, it takes about 50 person-days for one ha of cassava; 12

Table 5.3: Persons Aged 15 Years and Over Employed in Agriculture, by Region and by Sex, 1984 (thousands)

	Male		Female	
	Number	as a %	Number	as a %
Western	160.15	48.22	171.94	51.78
Central	140.88	46.57	161.65	53.43
Greater Accra	36.36	58.24	26.07	41.76
Eastern	250.44	49.35	257.02	50.65
Volta	159.99	46.60	183.33	53.40
Ashanti	259.82	45.71	308.55	54.29
Brong-Ahafo	216.37	51.28	205.53	48.72
Northern	208.25	73.91	73.50	26.09
Upper West	78.01	51.94	72.17	48.06
Upper East	134.27	59.94	89.67	40.04
All regions	1 644.32	51.49	1 349.42	48.51

Source: Republic of Ghana 1984c.

Table 5.4: Estimated Person-days Required to Headload Various Crops from Farm to Village

Crop	Yield with traditional technology (kg/ha)	Person-days required to headload produce from 1 ha
Cassava	3 000	50
Maize	700	12
Palm fruits	5 000	83
Plantain	1 725	29
Cocoyams	900	15
Yams	3 250	54

Source: Computed from Dapaah 1984.

person-days for one ha of maize; and 29 person-days for one ha of plantain. Headloading of food crops is almost always done by women and children. In fact, it is regarded as demeaning for a man to be seen carrying headloads of foodstuffs, water or firewood in traditional Ghanaian societies. The large amount of female and child labour required to headload food crops from the farm to the village implies that the farmer is often forced to sell to the trader on the farm at a lower price.

The traders responsible for buying produce at farmgate, transporting it to markets and selling it are also women. Their activities involve all stages of distribution: assembling, storage, and even providing wholesaling and warehousing services. Women traders usually establish personal contacts with farmers and arrange to buy their produce during the harvest period. Each trader has her own personal customers and villages, and exercises tight control on the market by maintaining specific producing areas as her own personal domain. Therefore, women traders who deal with one commodity in one village usually do not infringe on another trader's commodity or village. In this manner, traders deliberately limit the number of prospective buyers, thus restricting access to the marketing of these commodities. The result is that small farmers are often pushed into exploitative patron-client relationships. Such relationships are further reinforced when traders are the only source of credit. Traders advance credit to small farmers mainly to secure their contacts and produce supply and to keep their suppliers in business. Loans are given for both social as well as economic reasons. It is not uncommon for women farmers to need emergency cash for the medical needs of a small child, and often their natural choice is the trader with whom they have an immediate business contact. In return, the farmer is obliged to sell all her produce to the trader.

Hired labour is used by women farmers mainly for land clearing and weeding. It appears that a shortage has been developing of available labourers, resulting in high prices. The daily wage ranged, at the time of writing, from ₵ 200 to ₵ 300 in addition to lunch and some crops at harvest time. Many farmers estimated that by 1988 wages for daily labourers would be as high as ₵ 500 a day.

Other constraints to women's productivity may be summed up as follows:

- the small sizes of their farms, since they cannot afford to cultivate larger plots, especially when children are attending school;
- the rudimentary nature of their tools, whereas some of the men have access to tractors;
- the land-tenure system, which sometimes discriminates against women in the allocation of land for farming;
- the fact that women are often not reached by male extension workers and lack inputs such as fertilizers, since agricultural extension is still mainly directed towards male farmers;
- the considerable distance of farms - often 5-7 km - from the village, which means that women spend much time and energy simply walking to and from the village, often carrying their babies on their backs; and

- lack of access to credit. It has been observed that the Agricultural Development Bank, the main bank in Ghana lending to small-scale farmers, has not done much business with women farmers because they tend to lack collateral, such as their own houses. Women therefore have to rely upon their own, often inadequate, savings to cultivate their farms or borrow from moneylenders or traders at high interest rates.

Marketing is another major problem for women producers. Even though most of them sell much of their produce on the market, they lack marketing expertise and have neither access to storage facilities nor to transportation to those markets which are located farther away. They cannot afford to delay selling their produce, as it would spoil, and this makes many women dependent on intermediaries and leaves them at a relative economic disadvantage.

Women in Off-farm Activities

Trading is the main activity of women after agriculture. In fact, this sector is dominated by women, who make up 86 percent of the persons employed in it (Table 5.5). On a regional basis, the percentage of women traders (known as "market mammies") ranges from 83 percent in the Greater Accra Region to 93 percent in the Volta Region. Within the commercial sector, which is defined as wholesale and retail trade plus restaurants and hotels, most of the women are engaged in the retail trade. In 1984, 97.9 percent of the women employed in the commercial sector were retail traders. Within retail trading, petty trading, hawking and peddling were the main areas. Of all people employed in the retail trade, 88.5 percent were female. There are, however, a few women in wholesale trading who operate on a large scale and are very powerful. Among the different types of women intermediaries in the distribution system, the wholesalers are the most resourceful and successful. They are also the most powerful and exert a tremendous influence on food supply as well as prices in the urban centres. Still, of the 680 650 women in the commercial sector, less than 1 percent are classified as wholesalers.

Retailers are less influential than wholesalers, but they are supported by a strong organization. According to the commodities they sell, women form groups headed by "market or commodity queens" who are recognized leaders of all sellers of their particular commodity.

Table 5.5: Persons Aged 15 Years and Over Employed in Commerce, by Region and by Sex, 1984 (thousands)

	Male		Female	
	Number	As a % of both	Number	As a % of both
Western	7.52	11.89	55.69	88.11
Central	7.16	9.27	70.10	90.73
Greater Accra	32.18	17.30	153.85	82.70
Eastern	10.14	11.64	76.98	88.36
Volta	4.84	7.08	63.50	92.92
Ashanti	26.78	20.80	101.97	79.20
Brong-Ahafo	7.14	19.90	28.73	80.10
Northern	5.62	7.55	68.89	92.45
Upper West	1.38	12.09	10.06	87.91
Upper East	8.79	14.73	50.89	85.27
All Regions	111.55	14.08	680.66	85.92

Commerce = Wholesale and retail trade, restaurants and hotels.
Source: Republic of Ghana 1984c.

These traders engage in either local or long-distance trade. Local trade is carried out within the region in which the commodity is produced. Women local traders are really retailers since they tend to travel a distance of 10-20 km to buy their produce and then sell it directly in the local market. Six or seven of them usually hire a truck together to go and buy their goods. Each will handle one or more specific commodity. Long-distance trade involves handling and transporting commodities outside the area in which they are produced. Women wholesalers operate in this type of trade and have large amounts of capital in comparison to local traders, in addition to a well organized transportation system.

It should be noted that women traders fill an important gap in the marketing system. Farmers located in remote villages with no means of transportation would be at a loss to sell their produce if it were not for the market mammies. Feeder roads are often in poor condition and during the rainy season many producing areas may be cut off. Despite these conditions, the women traders manage to reach the farms and transport the produce to markets. As a part of this trade, women traders have established wholesale markets and warehouses at strategic points to facilitate the storage of farm produce. These facilities range from open spaces at collection centres to various types of structures in the large markets.

Small-scale manufacturing of shea-butter, soap, charcoal and pomade is often undertaken by women, cooperatively organized into groups. It should be noted, however, that these groups are still few in number and their members appear to be women who have already been economically active as individuals and have resources and skills to contribute to group activity. The majority of these groups operate on a small scale, partly because they lack the necessary capital to expand, and partly because they lack knowledge about new and more efficient methods of operation. Another important factor is that many women are risk-adverse.

Fish Smoking. Fish smoking is a major activity with rural women along Ghana's coast and on Lake Volta. It is estimated that 60-70 percent of all fish landed in Ghana is smoked - about 200 000 tons of fish in 1986 alone. The fish smokers and the fishermen working together usually are a family unit; the wife buys the fish from her husband, then smokes and markets it. Even if they are not in a husband and wife team, the men usually do the fishing and the women the smoking. In some cases, the woman may even sponsor the fisherman, in the sense that she will commission his fishing trips and receive his entire catch. On the average, each fish smoker handles about 50 crates of fish per week of five working days; each crate weighs about 30 kg. The major problem for these women fish smokers is the lack of adequate funds to pay for bulk purchases from the fishermen. Even though most of these women are married to the fishermen, they must pay for the fish landed or the men will sell it elsewhere.

Traditional fish smoking is done in large, thatched cylindrical ovens built of mud and fuelled by firewood. During the fishing season, women work the ovens 12 to 14 hours a day, taking little time off to eat and ignoring all other domestic tasks. The main drawbacks of the traditional ovens are that they wear out after one or two seasons, are very time-consuming and smoky to operate, do not give uniform smoking and have a limited capacity. More important, it seems that the traditional method of smoking considerably reduces the protein value of the fish and lessens the storage time. Fish that is properly smoked can go six months without losing much of its nutritional value.

In 1969, the Food Research Institute in Ghana designed a new type of oven for improved fish smoking called the Chorker oven (sometimes called the Kagan oven). Since then, this technology has been disseminated in some villages along the coast but it is still not widely available. UNICEF sponsored the initial Chorker oven research and issued a manual. In addition, UNICEF, ILO and FAO have provided the initial credit for women to buy the ovens in some 20 villages. However, lack of funds has prevented many women from adopting this new technology. The advantages of the improved oven are that it has a larger capacity (270 kg of fish compared to 60 kg) and a longer life and smokes the fish more uniformly. More important, with the improved oven women can smoke up to 15 crates of fish a day compared with a maximum of six with the traditional ovens.

Although this improved technology has proven successful in reducing women's drudgery and although the women have accepted it, most women fish smokers have yet to be introduced to the ovens because of lack of credit. Similarly, those women already using the Chorker ovens have not been able to realize their potential fully because of lack of working capital and the non-availability of low-interest credit.

Palm-oil Processing. Oil processing is another major activity for rural women in Ghana. The major types of vegetable oil produced include palm oil, palm-kernel oil, coconut oil, groundnut oil and shea-butter. The Western Region in particular is rich in palm nuts, but lacks the machinery to utilize fully this resource. In the palm-oil processing industry, the sexual division of labour is very clearly defined. Men own the plantations and supply the palm fruit (usually on a credit basis) and women process them into oil. Oil processing is a job for women only, using traditional methods. Paid labourers may help with the pounding of fruit for a fee.

Palm-oil extraction, using the traditional method, is a very tedious and time-consuming activity, involving boiling and pounding. A cold method involves the mixing of pounded palm fruits with cold water. Palm oil can be stored up to one year without spoilage; if it does spoil, it can eventually be used to make soap. A very important by-product in palm-oil processing is the palm kernel which can be further processed to yield palm-kernel oil which is also used for cooking but on a smaller scale than palm oil. Palm-kernel oil processing, however, is more laborious than palm-oil processing. Women have to spend a day cracking palm nuts one by one with a stone. In some districts, a mechanized nutcracker has now been introduced. At present, no improved tools exist for many of the other processes, with the exception of nut grinding.

Through a joint effort by the Technology Consultancy Centre of the University of Science and Technology, Kumasi, and an equipment manufacturing company, Science Import Simulation Engineering, an improved palm-oil-processing machine which consists of a mechanical fruit pounder and oil presser has been designed. The oil-extracting machinery has ensured a high-quality product with a reduced working time, easy operational facilities, lower fuelwood consumption and a longer life span. The diesel-powered pounding machine, however is the most fully accepted part of the total equipment. It effectively accomplishes the task women consider the most arduous and time-consuming, pounding a batch in five minutes - at least three times as fast as the traditional method. To adopt this improved technology it should be operated reasonably near capacity so as to pay its costs from increased income. This means processing a larger quantity than required at the household level and having a ready market for the oil. While women need to form a group in order to take out a loan and, in general, be responsible for the machine, this does not necessarily mean that they must make palm oil always as a group. Each group member may have a certain day or hour in which she uses the machinery for her own individual purposes.

Gari Processing. Gari has become a very popular food item in recent years because of its relatively long storage life (up to six months when well prepared) and ease of preparation. For the latter reason, it is also a favourite food item among educational institutions and workers' canteens. With the growing urban metropolis, gari has a ready and expanding market and great export potential. With the introduction of mechanized cassava grating and gari roasting and melting machines women have increased production to meet demand and taken the drudgery out of traditional cassava-processing methods. These involved many manual operations, including peeling, washing, grating, pressing, sieving, roasting, and bagging. It is in grating cassava that most time is saved through mechanization. Manually, the task is very tedious and even dangerous.

Other Activities. Activities which, for a very long time, have earned women some income, especially in the north, include pito brewing, a local drink made from guinea corn (sorghum); the production of shea butter, dawa-dawa (seasoning for soup), and local soap; and handicrafts. In rural areas, women who specialize in pito brewing are often regarded as "rich". Pito is brewed for market days, festivals, funerals and special occasions. In recent years, shea butter has been in great demand, helping to increase the income-earning opportunities for women. So far, no technology has been designed for shea butter extraction, a very time-consuming manual task.

Projects aimed at providing women with income-generating activities usually meet with strong community support. Chiefs and local officials extend their support to the groups, and the men of the villages even encourage their wives and other women to participate if they prove hesitant or shy.

Group Formation. In order to take advantage of new technologies, women need to form groups. In groups women are in a better position to mobilize credit, to adopt new technology, and even to develop appropriate technology than when operating as individuals. While there are many women's groups in Ghana, it is not always easy to start one. In introducing some of the new technology discussed above, it is usually best to start in those villages where groups are already formed and working, using traditional methods of food processing. Working with and through local women's groups requires developing strong leaders as well as broad-based participation. One of the social benefits to women of improved access to technology is increased standing in the community. At the village level, compromises must be reached between traditional leadership forms and modern methods. The illiterate majority of women will feel excluded if undue emphasis is placed on literate leaders. A combination of both prevents tension. In any case, group leaders will usually need new skills in record keeping and in negotiating with outside contractors.

In supporting the use of improved processing technologies in villages, several factors should be kept in mind. First, if the women have no experience in any of these food-processing activities, women from other villages may be asked to visit and to train the women in the skill. Also, some experience or training is needed to market the new output and to collect and account for money earned or spent. Increased food production and processing facilities need to be looked at together with marketing opportunities or constraints. The processing machines should be located very near the sources of raw materials to save transport costs. Information on additional work done by women is also necessary to see how it can conflict, or fit in, with existing activities. Childcare arrangements and domestic responsibilities might require a short working day. Those with distant farms might want a full day off. Where women also work on a husband's farm, this needs to be taken into account as well. Where women have had negative experiences with machinery in other developing countries, this has most often been because they were not given proper training. Moreover, sometimes a technology which is aimed at alleviating the work burden of women has been found to displace them from what was previously a female preserve, as men step in and take over. Finally, women themselves have identified inadequate working capital as the most serious constraint.

Careful sequencing of assistance would greatly improve its effectiveness. Preparatory work with participating groups should begin well in advance and take up a substantial part of total training time. Basic group formation and skills acquisition should take place before new equipment is made available. This reduces the risks of failure since any mishaps take place at lower investment levels. Extensive consultations with women's groups should precede both their agreement to participate and the project's agreement to assist them, and more attention should be paid to increasing women's access to working capital. Technical problems identified by women should be followed up and resulting modifications should be made in subsequent equipment. The scale of technology should be commensurate with raw material availability and managerial skills. Under-utilization and excess capacity, arising from the seasonal nature of an activity and the current scale of operation, should be minimized by encouraging renting of equipment to non-members or individual members (raising additional revenue for the group).

The acceptance and success of a new technology depends not only on low cost and high return but on simplicity of design and conformity with traditional practices. As mentioned earlier, several varieties of fish-smoking ovens had been developed before the Chorker oven, but the Chorker was the most widely accepted because it was the simplest and least expensive and varied little from the traditional mud ovens. Technologies that will have the greatest success are those which are the most affordable and appropriate for women, and do not conflict with traditional beliefs, taboos or values. By involving women in the identification of a felt problem and in the design of a technology to counter that problem, there is a greater chance of introducing a new technology successfully. Finally, it should be kept in mind that the introduction of income-generating activities *per se* does not solve all the welfare problems of a rural community. Maternal and child health and sanitation facilities are still urgently needed. In addition, steps should be taken to ensure that new technologies or activities do not increase, rather than decrease, women's workload.

Women's Access to Resources

Although women contribute directly to almost all agricultural processes and play such a major role in the nation's food production, they are seldom the direct beneficiaries of resources such as land, credit, agricultural inputs, training or extension services. This limits their ability to increase their productivity and provide a better life for themselves and their children.

Land. Land is probably the most significant productive resource over which women still do not have much control in Ghana. Women's choice of land is influenced by the male control of land tenure systems and by the restrictions imposed on them by their limited labour resources. These in turn, restrict their access to other resources such as credit, inputs and extension services. The land tenure system in Ghana has been discussed in the previous chapter; the point made was that land, in general, belongs to a community or lineage or "stool" and, in principle, any member of the lineage - male or female - is entitled to occupy a portion of unused communal land. In practice, however, this is not always the case since women's access to land is clearly inferior to that of the men, although rules and practices vary among ethnic groups and around the country.

Within the matrilineal system of descent, both men and women in the matrilineage have equal rights and access to land belonging to the lineage. When a man marries, however, his wife and children are limited to usufructuary rights over land belonging to the husband. That is, a wife can only cultivate land belonging to her husband as long as the marriage lasts. She cannot claim any rights of ownership even if her husband "gives" her a tract of land to farm for herself. When a man dies, it is his sister's son who inherits the land. This nephew assumes responsibility for the dead man's wife and children, although this assistance is usually temporary and, more often than not, the wife and children are left without anything. While in theory a woman under the matrilineal system could inherit from her uncle, in practice her brothers or the male descendants are more often recognized as heirs.

With respect to the patrilineal system, succession moves from a man to his children. Female children have a right to inherit property just as male children do, although their share is usually smaller. Under this inheritance system it is important to note that women can own property in their own right. Sometimes women will transfer their property to daughters while sons inherit from their fathers. This results in a particular type of inheritance called *nonududu* - inheritance of female-owned property through females. If a woman marries outside her village and the marriage terminates in death or divorce, she and her children may return to her patrilineage. She will have access to the family land temporarily but her children cannot inherit it. This is done to prevent the children from diverting land to their own patrilineage, that is, their father's lineage.

Under both systems, widows are disadvantaged because they are regarded as outsiders by their husband's lineage. Sometimes, widows may agree to marry the dead husband's brother or successor to the land, so that their children may inherit the land; but they themselves will have no right to it except for what may be allotted to them by their children. Among the Moslems in northern Ghana, daughters have rights to inherit property, but only half of the amount allotted to sons. A widow receives one-eighth of her deceased husband's estate if she has children and one-quarter if she does not. A widower, on the other hand, receives one-quarter of his deceased wife's estate if he has children and one-half if he does not. In this respect, Islam is one of the few religions that recognizes women's rights of inheritance and land ownership.

The enactment of a new inheritance law in Ghana in July 1985 - the Interstate Law - makes further provision for wives and children to inherit shares of a deceased man's property. Women under both matrilineal and patrilineal systems now have legal rights of access to land. The new laws, however, apply only to property acquired by the deceased and not property held by him on behalf of his lineage. It should be noted that in practice two legal systems often exist. Although women have the same rights as men under constitutional law, in the villages customary law is applied to marriage and land tenure cases. In these cases, men decide and women have little to say in regard to their own fate.

Credit. A UNDP study has revealed that 70 percent of women have annual incomes under US$ 200. Although banks consider women to be generally credit-worthy, credit is most often cited by women as their biggest constraint. In theory, both urban and rural women can have access to credit with the ADB, Ghana Commercial Bank or the rural banks. The urban women engaged in the marketing and distribution of foodstuffs as well as processing can obtain "Agrobusiness Individual Loans" from the ADB. Rural women engaged in food production, processing and marketing can have access to the Bank's Commodity Credit Scheme or Group Lending Programme. In practice, lack of institutional credit and of the required collateral make it often very difficult for women farmers to receive loans.

Women received about 34 percent of the credit under the Commodity Credit Scheme of the ADB. Of this credit 80 percent was utilized for food production, 19 percent for food and fish marketing, and 1 percent in other areas. One of the reasons stated for the low number of rural women taking advantage of this scheme is that their participation is related to the number of female credit or project officers in the field. Since very few female credit staff are involved in the scheme, there seems to have been a tendency to organize more men than women. Some of the constraints women face are:

- The nature of the household as a production unit creates difficulties. For example, where husband and wife work on a farm together, the wife's work is often unpaid but returns from her labour accrue to her husband when crops are sold. If the woman farms her own piece of land, little of the produce is sold since it is mainly for household consumption. She thus has little income to pay back loans.
- Rural women are more often illiterate and need education as to what credit facilities exist or can be made available to them.
- More women than men are without legal title to the land they farm and thus lack an important form of collateral.
- Credit institutions favour larger farmers; this excludes most women farmers, who are usually small-scale operators.
- Traditional and cultural values (especially in the north) prohibit women from seeking credit on their own.

Women farmers in Ghana get most of their credit from the informal market which is made up of friends, relatives, traders, moneylenders, producers of various goods and services or distributors of farm inputs. Three main types of informal credit can be identified in Ghana:

- *Labour credit:* The labourer works for either a relative or moneylender and waits until the farmer sells the produce before receiving his wages.
- *Buyer's credit:* A trader will advance funds to a farmer, especially during the off season, to enable the farmer to maintain her farm or to pay for some emergency. The farmer will then sell her produce to the trader at harvest time.
- *Susu:* This type of cooperative is discussed in Chapter 9, and is frequently used by women traders.

Improving women's access to credit is an important way of helping to alleviate poverty, as the poorest families tend to rely heavily on women's income. Priority, of course, should be given to female-headed households.

Extension Services. The Department of Community Development, the Ministry of Agriculture and the Nutrition Division of the Ministry of Health all run extension services for women. Nevertheless, the services provided do not cover very many women, because the farmer-extension ratio is too high and problems with staff, funds and transportation are acute. The Women Farmers' Extension Division of the Ministry of Agriculture is responsible for ensuring that women farmers have full access to technology extension so as to improve their productivity. The main focus of this extension service is nutrition in relation to food production and diet improvement, food utilization, food processing, preservation and storage of produce and management of farm and home resources. The extension services are carried out on a group basis; follow-up is then attempted on a 1:1 basis according to the time constraints of the extension officer. Usually the local chief's permission is requested for the initial encounter with the village women and he or other men of the village may also sit in on meetings. The extension officer must have some background of the traditions and culture of the area she is working in but, more important, she must know the local language.

The Greater Accra and Volta Regions have received the best coverage thus far from these extension services with 17.9 percent and 14.5 percent of women farmers covered respectively (see Table 5.6). The Brong-Ahafo, Western and Ashanti Regions have the lowest coverage, with 0.4 percent, 0.8 percent and 1.1 percent respectively. But even the regions with the best coverage are virtually unserved. The reason for this is that there are only 145 women extension officers who are technical para-professionals working in all ten districts. Each extension officer is responsible for 20-25 villages and has two programme assistants who are trainers. The ratio of extension officers to women farmers covered thus far is 1:459; however, the ratio to total women farmers is over 1:11 000.

The Department of Community Development under the Ministry of Youth and Rural Development has a Home Science Extension Programme directly targetted at rural women. Its mandate is to assist them through the provision of extension services that focus on home management and income-generating activities. Staffing generally consists of one Regional Supervisor per region, one District Supervisor per district, and 6-10 field workers (community development officers, community development assistants and mass education assistants) per district. There were, at the time of writing, 400 women extension agents advising rural women on subjects like home-making and family life, health, sanitation, marriage and human relations, and the management of resources. Each extension agent is supposed to cover

Table 5.6: Regional Coverage of Women Farmers' Extension Services
(as of June 1987)

	No. of districts	No. of districts covered (1987)	No. of villages covered (1987)	No. of women farmers covered (1987)	Total no. of women farmers (1984)	Percent coverage
Greater Accra	3	3	134	4 654	26 074	17.9
Central	9	4	132	9 920	161 650	6.1
Western	5	2	42	1 371	171 937	0.8
Eastern	9	4	114	7 825	257 017	3.0
Volta	8	8	671	26 500	183 326	14.5
Ashanti	10	4	148	3 523	308 547	1.1
Brong-Ahafo	8	2	20	912	205 526	0.4
Northern	7	1	60	2 075	73 499	2.8
Upper East	4	4	60	6 212	89 666	8.6
Upper West	3	3	87	3 700	72 174	4.3
Total	66	35	1 468	66 692	1 549 416	4.3

Extension agent figures are for 1987, while the number of women farmers is from 1984 data.

Source: Data supplied by Ministry of Agriculture, Women Farmers' Extension Division; Republic of Ghana 1984c.

approximately three villages, and to form one or two groups per village with about 25-30 women in each group. In addition to general organizational training, basic instruction in some income-generating activities is provided. Skills taught include needlework, food preparation, backyard gardening, farming, animal husbandry, soap making, shea-butter extraction, groundnut oil processing, and various handicrafts.

The principal constraints faced by all the extension workers are: lack of transport for field workers, severely limiting the number of villages they can reach and the regularity of their visits; a scarcity of teaching aids and demonstration equipment; lack of financial incentives; low number of trained women extension officers; and the absence of any linkage between the dissemination of the extension message and the availability of financial resources or credit facilities to support the recommended investment activity.

Women farmers generally accept extension officers' advice but the rate of change is slow. Farmers are risk-adverse and when they are hard-pressed for survival they have little time for new technologies or methods. Female extension workers can play an important role in improving the productivity of women in food production and food security. As women, they are in a better position than men to get innovations accepted. It is, therefore, important that women's components in extension be strengthened.

Labour. Although a woman may be expected to be economically active and contribute to household expenses, the time she can devote to this activity is not all her own. She is also expected to take care of her children, which makes long, unbroken intervals of time hard to come by.

Education. The literacy rate in Ghana (percentage of population over 15 able to read and write to total adult population) is 59 percent for males and 37 percent for females. Over the last decade or so, Ghanaian women have increased their attendance in school. In 1970 women lagged behind men in all levels of education and constituted only 35.55 percent of total schoolgoers. By 1984, however, females made up 43.17 percent of all schoolgoers. Although there has been a significant increase in the number and proportion of females attending school, they still lag behind males, especially in the higher levels of education. While females make up 56 percent of those in primary school, only a very small minority (14 percent) of university graduates are women.

Patterns of school attendance vary considerably in different regions, especially for girls. This is particularly true in the Northern and Upper Regions, where attendance rates lag far behind the rest of the country. The training of girls in the Northern and Upper Regions is still traditional and generally geared to making them good mothers and wives. Formal education is even seen as dangerous for females. While the 1984 population census results for school attendance regionally are not yet available, the 1970 census gives an overall picture. Only 2.41 percent of females in the Northern and Upper Regions had ever attended school and only 4.35 percent were then presently attending. This is substantially lower than in the southern regions where between 11 and 28 percent of women attended school. Although parents now generally recognize the value of sending girls to school, there are still some factors which limit the chances girls have of completing their education. These include pregnancy, early marriage and the fact that mothers lose valuable domestic help. While the overall gap in literacy between men and women has been closing, it still remains wide.

Women's Development Organizations and Institutions

Many women-specific agencies and projects exist in Ghana, both at national and local levels, often focusing on rural women. What seems to be missing, however, is coordination. In addition, almost all institutions lack financial resources, which seriously hampers their ability to implement projects.

The National Council on Women and Development (NCWD) is the most important agency at the government level. It is a statutory body, set up by the Government of Ghana in 1975, to advise the Government on all matters relating to the full integration of women in national development at all levels. Other functions of the Council include:

- cooperating, co-ordinating and maintaining liaison with national and international organizations on matters relating to the status of women;
- examining and evaluating the contribution of women in the economic, social and cultural fields in order to advise the Government on specific areas where the participation of women may be strengthened or initiated;
- developing plans and proposals for the establishment of large-scale, informal education and training aimed at raising living standards and eradicating illiteracy; and
- devising a programme allowing the continuous review and evaluation of women's integration in the total development effort at local, regional and national levels.

The major task of the NCWD is co-ordination to ensure that the services of existing institutions in Ghana reach women. For example, the NCWD may act as the intermediary between farmers and the Ministry of Agriculture's district office for any assistance required.

The activities of the NCWD may be broadly summed up as follows:

- research, consultations and seminars on how Ghanaian women perceive their needs regarding education, skills training, income generation, employment, health and family welfare;
- income-generating projects aimed at improving the efficiency of traditional women's activities such as farming, food processing, food distribution, fish smoking, pottery and other handicrafts;

- informal educational programmes on sanitation, nutrition, child care and family welfare in general, as well as on civic and legal rights and responsibilities; and
- counselling services on the problems facing working women, as well as on personal, marital and family problems.

While the NCWD is funded by the Government (the budget for 1986 was about ₵ 6 000 000, approximately US$ 67 000 at the 1986 official exchange rate), it has also occasionally received financial and other assistance from multilateral and bilateral agencies, such as IFAD, ILO, UNICEF, CIDA, the Government of the Netherlands and USAID. Still, it does not have the funds or the staff to carry out effectively its prime responsibility, coordination. There is a NCWD office in each of Ghana's ten regions responsible for coordination at the operational level. To facilitate this, each regional office is supposed to have an Advisory Committee, with members drawn from government departments whose programmes most affect women. Each regional office of the NCWD is made up of a Regional Secretary, two to three project staff and three office support staff (typist, cleaner, messenger). Because of their very limited staff, most of the regional office's work consists of supporting initiatives by women's groups and other agencies. The offices are also constrained by a lack of funds and vehicles. For example, the Brong-Ahafo regional office had a budget in 1987 of approximately ₵ 200 000 (approximately US$ 1 200), and this was considered to be on the high side. As it had no vehicle, the office had to coordinate its work and field visits with the district office of the Department of Community Development. Although each regional office has a different budget and staff, the situation in the Brong-Ahafo Region is fairly typical.

The NCWD has devoted much attention to improving rural women's income-earning abilities by encouraging cooperatives and small-scale food-processing industries, and by obtaining credit facilities for women for business expansion. Its role is to act as a catalyst in organizing groups of women in income-generating activities. The NCWD, through its coordinating or liaison roles, has made it possible for these groups or communities to obtain grants of land from local chiefs for their farming activities as well as donations of equipment or technical expertise from international organizations. Each Regional Secretary has a small revolving fund of ₵ 2 000 (approximately US$ 12 at the 1987 exchange rate), from which she can make occasional small loans for the purchase of raw materials.

Generally the loans are to be repaid within six months at 5 percent interest. These are clearly insufficient to meet the existing credit needs of rural women.

The relationships between women's groups and NCWD varies, but is generally one of loose association. In some cases, NCWD was actively involved in the formation of the group and still provides regular contact and supervision. In other cases, existing groups have become more structured as the result of NCWD assistance. All groups see NCWD as their liaison with the Government and other institutions; however weak that liaison may be, it is better than none. The NCWD clearly has an important role to play in fostering women's development in Ghana. Its capacity, however, is constrained by lack of staff, funds and transportation, resulting in a small outreach.

The Ghana Enterprise Development Commission of the Ministry of Finance and Economic Planning is another government agency which aims at identifying indigenous, small-scale manufacturing units and providing financial, technical and managerial assistance. Priority areas for support, using locally available materials and resources, include indigenous industrial activities common to a particular area. These include smithery, handicraft production (basket weaving, leather work, spinning, weaving and ceramics), soap making, shea-butter and groundnut oil processing, and tailoring. Producers in need of assistance approach the Commission directly or are searched out by staff. Some women producers are directed to the Commission by NCWD. Producers are financed through the Small Scale Loan Scheme, which is administered by the Small Scale Enterprises Development Committee. The loan fund (for example, ₡ 500 000, approximately US$ 3 000 at the 1987 exchange rate, for the Northern Region) is meant to be a revolving fund. Loan terms stipulate a repayment period of 12-18 months at a 12 percent rate of interest with a two-month grace period before payments begin. The maximum loan per person was ₡ 5 000 (US$ 30) in 1987. Experience indicates that 60 percent of the loans have been received by women and that 65 percent of the loans have been recovered within the repayment period. Loans are often provided to groups, to be divided among individual members. The Commission faces a constraint in the scarcity of its resources for lending (at any given time the Small Scale Loan Scheme has about 20 outstanding applications that they are unable to satisfy), and a lack of staff and mobility to cover the outlying areas adequately .

The 31st December Women's Movement is the women's arm of the ruling party, the PNDC. The following are its objectives and aims:

- to mobilize and organize the women of Ghana into a concrete force to advance, defend and consolidate the cause of the 31st December Revolution;
- to defend the interests of women in all spheres of political, economic and social life;
- to help women understand the aims of the PNDC and take an active part in its deliberations;
- to engage women in productive activities, to raise their standard of life and eliminate their reliance on men;
- to eliminate all forms of oppression; and
- to maintain liaison with progressive sister organizations in other countries in order to share experiences.

Although many of the objectives are political in nature, the 31st December Women's Movement has become increasingly involved in lending assistance to rural women's groups, in setting up day-care centres, and sponsoring income-generating activities such as baking, tye and dye, soap making, etc. Offices are located regionally and all staff are voluntary.

Other major government agencies which directly target services at women include the Women Farmers' Extension Division of MOA, and the Home Science Extension Services of the Department of Community Development, Ministry of Youth and Rural Development, discussed earlier. MOH, under its Mother and Child Health Programme, and the Department of Nutrition also try to provide rural women with health and nutrition services.

Multilateral and Bilateral International Institutions which have given priority to assisting rural women in Ghana include IFAD, ILO, UNICEF, UNDP, the Government of The Netherlands, and CIDA. All these agencies focus on improving women's income-earning capabilities by introducing them to, or providing them with, the capital and equipment for starting up income-generating activities such as fish smoking, gari processing, or palm-oil processing. IFAD's project in the Northern Region has a component specifically designed to support the activities of women's groups by providing credit for vegetable growing and food processing. The ILO and the Government of The Netherlands have collaborated on a project on Technologies for Rural Women and, together with the NCWD, have produced technical manuals for income-generating activities such as soap making, palm oil processing, gari processing, fish smoking and coconut oil processing. UNDP's project on Integrated Community Actions for

Women in Development has been followed up by studies on the integration of women in development projects.

UNICEF has sponsored many small-scale food-processing industries. For example, it sponsored and produced a manual on the initial Chorker fish-smoking ovens for women's groups, and it has lent funds to women's groups to purchase gari processors. At the same time, it has also sponsored the Food Storage and Processing Project, which included the production of weaning foods for children by women's groups. UNICEF is especially involved with women's groups in the Northern Region. CIDA is implementing a new project in the Northern Region for women in development on a regional level. The project includes credit to finance income-generating activities. CIDA was previously, and still is, involved in smaller-scale women's projects in other regions. All agencies have worked together with the NCWD to implement their projects.

Non-Governmental Organizations. Many international, national, and local NGOs in Ghana have programmes or projects directly targetted at women. Most of the NGOs are concerned with increasing women's income-generating activities, although many also foster cooperative and self-help village activities and primary health care, including nutrition and immunization. All work at the village or district level and, though they are all very effective, most would benefit from an increased level of coordination.

Chapter 6

Government Support Services

As should be clear from the previous chapters, which emphasized the economic and social profile of rural Ghana, there are substantial possibilities for smallholder development. Furthermore, the large number of rural poor suggests that their development will have significant sectoral and macro-economic impact. Development interventions have traditionally been implemented through existing or new institutions, and their success crucially depends on the efficiency of these institutions in reaching the target groups. The attention in this and the following three chapters will, therefore, shift to a description and analysis of the institutions that serve the agricultural sector. This chapter is devoted solely to the support services provided directly by the public sector.

The Ministry of Agriculture

The primary responsibility for establishing agricultural policy and programmes rests with MOA, which, either directly or through various parastatals, performs a wide range of functions. As a Ministry, MOA undertakes planning, budgeting, and operational activities such as extension and agricultural engineering. Under the ASRP, MOA has been shorn of its input-dispensing function almost completely. It now handles only fertilizer, and importation/local production and distribution of that by MOA was to be phased out *in toto* by the end of 1991. MOA's overseeing and evaluative role includes programme monitoring and evaluation, economic analysis and market research. In addition, there are 18 autonomous or semi-autonomous parastatals attached to MOA. In spite of this vast institutional framework, two functions related to agriculture do not fall under the direct purview and control of MOA. These include cocoa production and general agricultural research. Research is conducted through various specialized institutions that fall under the umbrella of the Council of

Scientific and Industrial Research, which is attached to the Ministry of Industries, Science and Technology.

MOA has undergone reorganization. It is now headed by a PNDC Secretary (a political appointee), and is supported at headquarters by two politically appointed Deputy Secretaries. They are both technical; one is in charge of crops and the other of livestock. The Deputy for Livestock has also temporarily assumed responsibility for fisheries.

Each of the Regional Directors of Agriculture are supported by regional technical staffs (livestock, crops, fisheries, extension and PPMED). When the operations of MOA are decentralized, these Regional Directors will coordinate the activities of the technical departments. At present, however, the Central Ministry Department Directors control the budget of the Regional Technical Officers and because of this, the Regional Director's coordination role remains essentially ineffective.

Staffing. The exact MOA staff strength is not known, but is generally believed to be over 9 000. As with other ministries, there is significant overstaffing in the lower, non-professional grades and considerable understaffing in the technical and managerial grades. In the professional, technical and sub-professional grades, over half of the positions are vacant, largely owing to the unattractive wages offered by the civil service. Consequently, a number of staff have either left the country or joined the private sector. The shortages experienced in the professional cadres affect the implementation capacity of MOA and its ability to analyse and synthesize data and to formulate plans. For instance, in the professional cadres of the Crop Services Department 406 of the established positions are vacant. Similarly, the PPMED has 103 out of 127 established positions vacant. Thus, MOA's principal function of policy formulation, planning and evaluation remains severely handicapped.

Role of State-owned Enterprise. As mentioned earlier, there are a number of organizations affiliated to MOA. Most of these make losses and have become a drain on MOA's resources; total subventions account for over 35 percent of MOA's budget. A number of these operations and the roles of various parastatals are being questioned. Under the World Bank-financed ASRP, a review of all the parastatals is being conducted. It has been agreed that of the 18 organizations, four are significant, namely, Ghana Food Distribution Corporation, Ghana Seed Company, GIDA and the Ghana Cotton Company. Of the 18, one is to be liquidated, one sold, seven converted into joint ventures, five divested, and four retained as parastatals.

A number of institutional reforms are under way within MOA. Priority has been given to staff reductions, budgetary reallocations and parastatal reform. All these measures will pave the way for reorientation of the budget towards other recurrent expenditure. They will release funds for important routine supervision and administration, both of which are critical to supporting MOA's operations. Prior to decentralization of MOA, PPMED is expected to be strengthened in order to be able to undertake planning, monitoring and evaluation functions.

Implementation of all these actions is planned in the next three to four years. To judge from past experience, however, it could take longer. In the interim, MOA faces institutional problems and its capacity to implement projects at national level will remain constrained. Over the medium term, as an interim strategy, implementation of projects at regional level, managed by regional administrators with proper incentive structure and budgetary support, could prove more effective. Regional projects would also have better chances of success because of closer contact of MOA regional staff with projects and better project supervision. Moreover, the Government's plans for decentralization would be furthered, as it lacks the necessary cadres to strengthen district-level staff.

Agricultural Research

Some of Ghana's research institutions once had an excellent international reputation, but in recent years most have steadily deteriorated and are now unable to give the desired support to agriculture. Trained staff have left, equipment has not been properly maintained and much of it needs replacing, and research programmes have contracted.

There has been little national coordination of research priorities and programmes and links with extension services are practically non-existent at most levels. As a result, the impact of research on agricultural production is slight. MOA, until recently, had little influence on the programmes of the various research organizations. Since several research institutions are autonomous, there is a risk of unnecessary duplication in effort and even conflicting extension messages. Efforts are now being made to achieve some measure of coordination between the Council for Scientific and Industrial Research and other organizations and MOA. A senior staff member has been appointed in both the Council and MOA with specific responsibility for coordination. Some cooperation exists between the universities and other institutions in the conduct of specific research projects but it rests mainly on the personal initiatives of the research staff.

Agricultural research does not receive the priority it deserves in a country whose mainstay is agriculture. Progress in crop research during the last 25 years, with the possible exception of research on cocoa, has been very limited. But even cocoa research has not kept up with the previous traditions for high quality. During the decade 1958-68, research came to a virtual standstill because of insufficient financial support. From 1968 until now circumstances have not improved. Research on industrial crops has not been significant in the last three decades, while in food crops efforts have not been sufficient to make a positive impact on food production. The research institutions and organizations are all short of funds. The number of experiments they can conduct is therefore limited, and in some cases no work is carried out at all. Many of the more capable research scientists have emigrated.

The Crops Research Institute (CRI) is responsible for conducting research on all food, industrial and horticultural crops in Ghana except cocoa, cola, coffee and oil palm (which are handled by their own special boards or agencies). To implement the CIDA-funded Grains Development Project, CRI, based at Kwadaso, was named the executing agent for the Government of Ghana, with the Grains and Legumes Development Board of MOA as cooperating institution. CIDA named the International Centre for Maize and Wheat Improvement (CIMMYT) as its executing agent. IITA, with a seat on the Project Management Committee, has a subcontract to take responsibility for the cowpea component.

The general objectives of the project have been to increase the production of maize and cowpeas to make Ghana self-sufficient. The agronomic research and demonstration component of the project seeks to develop suitable agronomic practices for the various ecological zones of Ghana, appropriate technology to aid small-scale farmers and extension information for use by the Grains and Legumes Development Board and MOA. These objectives apply for both target crops. In order to meet these objectives, provision has been made for the training of manpower, both within and outside Ghana, and for the importation of equipment, supplies and transport. From the outset, the primary site of agronomic research, using an extensive network of trained staff scattered throughout the major maize and cowpea areas of Ghana, has been farmers' fields.

This bilateral programme has entered Phase II with a five-year planned expenditure of Canadian $ 6.3 million. Staff services and offices are provided mainly by CRI which also covers transport, maintenance and running costs, field trial inputs, clearing of imported goods and in-service training programmes plus a national maize workshop. The project has 15 research officers, 11 technical officers and a backup staff whose salaries represent a major share of the Government's financial commitment. The success of the maize-cowpea project at CRI indicates that the deterioration of working conditions can be halted with the provision of adequate funds.

The Northern Region is well served by the Nyankpala Research Station, a substation of the CRI, which concentrates on semi-arid lands research. The station has 400 ha of land and good laboratory facilities. Funds are received from two sources: the Ghana Grains Development Project, concerned with maize and cowpea variety testing, foundation seed production and adaptive research both on-farm and on-station; and German aid for adaptive research on maize, cowpea, sorghum and rice, low-cost soil fertility maintenance trials and appropriate technology research related to bullock ploughing and farm implements.

The Food Research Institute (FRI) is based in Accra. It undertakes research and offers advice on food technology, food industries and food marketing. It has offices, laboratories, stores and workshops and operates a pilot plant area. A total of 21 graduate staff plus technicians and general staff occupy the Accra site. Recent work has included studies and pilot projects on cowpea flour, tomato production and processing, gari processing, maize storage-loss assessment, and cassava storage. The present programme is constrained by lack of a budget for vehicles and research equipment; present budget allocations barely cover staff costs. The quality of work completed by FRI in the past has been good, and the Institute has staff capable of carrying out pilot programme work and investigatory studies, provided they receive programme operating funds.

Funding of Research. In 1986, agricultural research received a total of ₵ 2 155.8 million or 0.88 percent of Agricultural Gross Domestic Product (AGDP). In 1987, the corresponding figures were ₵ 2 768.6 million and 0.73 percent. In constant 1987 prices, the average for 1986/87 amounted to 0.80 percent of AGDP or US$ 0.72 per hectare of arable land. The proportion of agricultural research funds spent on major commodity groups is given in Table 6.1.

Cocoa received 45 percent of research funding although it contributed only 17 percent of AGDP. This does not diminish cocoa's

Table 6.1: Funding of Research by Commodity

	1986 (₵ million)	1987 (₵ million)	% Total	% Contribution to AGDP
Agriculture/livestock	1 438	1 492	50	71
Cocoa	1 452	1 141	45	17
Forestry	105	101	4	9
Fishing	23	35	1	3
Total	3 018	2 769	100	100

Source: MTADP, PPMED, 1989.

contribution to AGDP since the low figure could be explained by decreasing world prices. Agriculture and livestock received 50 percent of funding and contributed 71 percent of AGDP. The allocation of funds between different research institutes shows that in real terms all institutes received lower funding in 1987 than in 1974. Many scientists either spend time on secondary income-earning activities or move to more lucrative employment, but in the universities a nucleus of experienced scientists and support staff remains.

The main consideration is the strengthening of capacity at the national level to meet the research needs for agricultural development and growth. The present support for maize and cowpeas (through the Grains Development Project) should continue to provide useful results and the IFAD-supported National Root and Tuber Improvement Programme will give roots and tubers much needed support. The World Bank ASRP has a component for the review of agricultural research services and the preparation of a national master plan, which should identify priorities and strategies for the next 14-20 years. The review aims to suggest an appropriate institutional framework for coordinating research and improving links with extension and to quantify the manpower and budgetary needs of the system.

Two priority crops, cotton and rice, were identified within the ASRP as suitable for immediate support. Part of the strengthening of GIDA will include a component to develop and test simple, low-cost systems to control water in valley bottoms for the cultivation of swamp rice. Other research priorities identified for support under the ASRP were: farming systems research in the Upper East and Upper West Regions, which would build on the work started and centre on small ponds or reservoirs and the needs of village communities; continued support to ensure that the recently formed Agricultural Research Development and Advisory Committee which includes directors of research institutes, MOA departments and development agencies will continue to promote linkages between research and extension at national and field levels; and improved arrangements for the publishing and dissemination of recent research results, which would provide scientific and practical information for use by farmers and support agencies.

A medium-term to long-term strategy suitable for external assistance, which should be identified under ASRP funding, would include:

- strengthening of the reorganized research institutions, particularly those involved in research and adaptive trials;
- breeding, screening and selecting high-yielding varieties of food and industrial crops suitable for the different ecological zones;
- measurement of response of food and major industrial crops to fertilizer;
- regional soil fertility tests and measurement of soil fertility levels on an annual basis; and
- farming systems and mixed cropping research suitable for small farmers, including testing of improved technology, such as chemical use, bullock ploughing and soil moisture management and conservation.

Agricultural Extension

MOA is the principal agency responsible for extension but, as mentioned earlier, there is considerable duplication. A number of agencies, parastatals and NGOs have their own specialized extension services.

In the past, extension was primarily concerned with crop production activities and the distribution of inputs. Animal husbandry, fisheries and farm mechanization were not normally considered part of the national agricultural extension system. There are no exact estimates of extension staff, but a total of some 2 500 personnel were reported to be involved in extension activities. Their responsibilities were fairly wide and included: management and distribution of inputs; collection of cash from input sales; organizing group farms for joint activities; collection of rainfall records; undertaking market surveys; and establishing field demonstration plots.

Clearly MOA extension staff were involved in non-extension work and lacked logistical support, which further handicapped their ability to undertake normal extension work. As with other MOA staff, morale was low because of the absence of a clear mandate, low salaries, inadequate transportation, absence of materials, poor training and inadequate travel allowances. Moreover, linkages with research were poor and agricultural research was irrelevant because researchers did not know the needs of the farmers and there was a long time-lag between the creation of new technology and acquisition by the extension staff.

There has been a modest improvement in extension since the ERP was launched in 1983, when steps were initiated to overhaul the service, provide production incentives and make inputs more available to farmers. The result has been increased adoption of improved practices and a subsequent increase in crop yields, especially those of maize, cowpeas, sorghum and cotton. Under MOA's restructuring, extension has been reorganized under the Department of Extension Services to include crops and animal husbandry. The unified approach is aimed at addressing the peasant farmers' problems in an integrated manner, since they are seen to be primarily multi-commodity farmers who combine a host of enterprises involving crops and livestock alike.

Input Supply

Input supply is handled by both the public and private sector. During the early nineteen-sixties, the private sector was involved in distribution of fertilizer and other inputs. Developing shortages of foreign exchange and increasing subsidies on fertilizers shifted the responsibility to MOA, which became involved in the distribution and retailing of fertilizers throughout the country. The Ghana National Procurement Agency was responsible for importing fertilizers up to 1984; afterwards, the responsibility shifted to Crown Agents, the appointed procurement agent under the Reconstruction Import Credits financed by the World Bank. Some seeds have been produced by the Ghana Seed Company, Ltd. (now undergoing restructuring); and other inputs are largely imported or manufactured and distributed by the private sector or the Ghana National Trading Company, a State-owned retailing company. Such items include small implements (some of which are manufactured locally), agricultural machinery (mostly manufactured locally, with the exception of the motors), and agro-chemicals.

Under the various World Bank-financed Reconstruction Import Credits, the private sector's involvement in input supply has become stronger. Nevertheless, under present arrangements the major input items - fertilizers and seeds - are largely controlled by the public sector, and their supply has proved very unsatisfactory.

The failure of the public sector to provide these services is well recognized. Through the ERP and ASRP, the Government has committed itself to a phased programme privatizing fertilizer distribution over five years. The programme, initiated in 1988, is intended to bring the private sector first into retail and then into wholesale distribution and finally into importation. The fertilizer privatization programme started with a pilot retailing project in the Brong-Ahafo Region. Prospective retailers who responded to press advertisements by MOA were vetted to ensure that they had adequate storage facilities and capital. As of May 1989, there were 67 approved retailers in Brong-Ahafo who were registered with MOA. Of these, about 45 were operating in the sense that they were actually stocking fertilizer. The programme is subject to annual review. This being the case, MOA does not intend to withdraw abruptly from its role as wholesaler and retailer, but will continue in parallel with the private sector. If the private traders perform these functions efficiently, MOA will find itself saddled with unsold stocks and will then be able to withdraw. If they do not, MOA will continue to supply as before, thus providing some guarantee of continuity in fertilizer supply to farmers.

Chapter 7

Agricultural Credit

Since growth in agricultural production cannot occur without technological transformation, credit assumes an important role. The need for purchases of improved inputs creates a demand for production credit. Simultaneously, fluctuations in production and prices, as well as other uncertainties, create the need for consumption credit. The demand for credit becomes more pronounced as input prices start to increase. The following section highlights the role of the institutions that have evolved to satisfy the credit needs of smallholders and assesses the overall availability of credit to the rural sector.

Formal Credit System

The banking sector in Ghana comprises: the Bank of Ghana (BOG); three primary commercial banks - Ghana Commercial Bank (GCB), Barclays Bank of Ghana Ltd. and Standard Chartered Bank (Ghana) Ltd.; three secondary commercial banks - Social Security Bank, National Savings and Credit Bank and Bank of Credit and Commerce; and three development institutions - Agricultural Development Bank (ADB), National Investment Bank and Bank for Housing and Construction. In addition, there are the Merchant Bank, Ghana Cooperative Bank, and rural banks (RBs).

Judged by the banking network, Ghana is reasonably well covered. The various banks have a total of 319 branches. Moreover, there are 107 RBs.

Formal agricultural credit in Ghana is relatively better developed than in most African countries. Unlike those in most other countries, the commercial banks have actively tried to develop and promote credit, not only to the agricultural sector but to smallholders as well. All the banks in Ghana have provided credit to the agricultural sector. Between 1983 and 1986 total credit to the agricultural sector rose from ₡ 2.0 billion to ₡ 7.5 billion, or roughly 3.7 times in four years in nominal terms. In real terms over this period the increase was

94 percent or 25 percent per annum. On a proportional basis, however, the banks which provided 31 percent of total credit to the agricultural sector in 1983 decreased this percentage to 18 percent by the end of 1986. The decline was due partly to poor recovery of loans to agriculture, making the banks cautious, and partly to lower demand because of prevailing high interest rates.

Financing of Small Farmers

The total number of farmers is currently estimated at about 1.6 million; farmers with less than 1.6 ha (4 acres) number over 1.0 million. Owing to aggressive lending policies pursued by the banking system, over 400 000 small farmers (40 percent) have by now received institutional credit. This is a remarkable achievement. In contrast, in 1975 it was estimated that only about 7 percent of small farmers had access to institutional credit.

Over 60 000 small farmers (including fishermen) are provided with credit under the ADB scheme for production of food crops/fish. The progress made by the GCB in financing small farmers has been even more striking. Through its Commerbank Farmers' Associations, over 285 000 small farmers are provided with loans for food production. While Barclays Bank extends credit to small farmers through registered cooperative societies, the other commercial banks have adopted the group loan scheme. In addition, the rural banks established on the initiative of the BOG also lend to farmers.

This upsurge in the flow of institutional credit to small farmers is attributed, in part, to the positive response of the banking system to the credit guidelines issued by the BOG and, in part, to the dominance of agriculture in the Ghanaian economy, which forces banks to be actively involved. Initially, banks were cautious. Most banks participated in smallholder credit by forming small farmers' groups which were carefully selected. The loans were tightly supervised and constant contact was maintained with the communities. The farmers' response was encouraging, repayment rates were high and lending to the sector increased dramatically.

Since 1983, however, the lending experience has not been satisfactory. GCB, the largest group lender, and Standard Charted Bank have experienced recovery rates below 50 percent. Barclays have had a similar experience, while the Social Security Bank's recovery performance has reportedly varied around 30 percent. Not all banks have had a poor experience. ADB has reported recoveries of 85 percent while the Bank for Housing and Construction, which provides credit to groups through an NGO, experienced recoveries of over 90 percent in 1986. ADB's reported recovery rates are high because it does not factor overdue loans in calculating amounts due and, given a shortage of funds, it is only lending to farmers who have repaid. In other words, it has found good borrowers through the expensive process of eliminating non-repaying farmers.

A number of factors have contributed to this performance. Loan recoveries were adversely affected by the drought in 1983. Recoveries were also adversely affected by excess production and the collapse of prices in 1984. As banks became keen to lend to smallholders, loan officers, eager to meet targets, pushed credit. As a result, groups were loosely formed, often brought together with a promise of credit. Little focus was directed towards their cohesiveness. Banks would routinely finance groups without either maintaining direct contact with them or using existing resources to assist in doing so. All too often they would process loan applications without even verifying the acreages that the farmers intended to finance. All members would be given the same amount of loan (except the leaders who were given larger loans as incentives), regardless of the area developed. Moreover, since all banks are involved in group lending, they often form groups in the same community, and reportedly some groups formed by various banks have common members. At the same time, loan collections are seldom enforced. Banks rely on rejecting future applications as a means of enforcing recoveries rather than maintaining close contact with the communities. When input supplies have been late, credit has been diverted elsewhere.

Not excluded from the banks' calculations is the fact that smallholder credit is expensive. Constant contact with communities leads to expenses that, although lower on a group basis, are not covered by present margins. Despite this poor performance, banks are not considering an alternative approach to group credit. There is unanimity of opinion that group credit is the proper approach. Some modifications in present practices will have to be considered if credit is to succeed in achieving its objectives. For example, GCB plans to reregister the groups and form new ones, excluding the non-repaying members. It also plans to develop closer community contact.

From the point of view of smallholder credit the RBs and ADB are most important. In 1977, BOG took the initiative in organizing the RBs to develop banking facilities in rural areas. It has set up a separate department - the Rural Banking Department (RBD) - which is primarily responsible for developing RBs as sound financial institutions by provision of share capital, training and supervision.

In principle, rural banks are private banks organized in rural communities for mobilizing savings to extend credit to small farmers and other rural entrepreneurs. There are now 120 rural banks, up from 117 in 1987. An additional 38 are registered but not operating.

Rural banks are organized as joint stock companies with an authorized capital of ₵ 250 000, 50 percent of which is owned by BOG as non-voting stock (BOG has one seat on the Board). RBs are typically managed by 5-7 staff. The financial position as of December 1986 indicates that RBs had total resources of ₵ 2.5 billion (68 percent of these represented deposits). The number of depositors increased from 1 100 in 1976 to 452 000 in 1986. In nominal terms, the average deposit per borrower has similarly increased from ₵ 131 to ₵ 3 727 over the same period. Total loans at the same date stood at ₵ 709 million. Thus, while the RBs have been successful in mobilizing deposits, their lending activity has not been as strong. Total loans outstanding of ₵ 799 million are only 47 percent of deposits and 31 percent of resources. Their reluctance to make loans is partly affected by lack of investment opportunities in rural areas. Where demand exists, as in agriculture, for short-term loans, RBs have been affected by low recoveries, discouraging them from making loans to this sector. Because of the drought in 1983 and the decline in crop prices in 1984, recovery rates have declined significantly, from 90 percent in 1982 to 30 percent in 1984 and 1985.

Lacking lending opportunities, the RBs' intermediation costs are high. Savings deposit rates are only 12-13 percent while lending rates are 23 to 30 percent. Of 111 RBs, 6 are on the critical list, 60 are profitable and 45 are not. Major problems with RBs include a lack of qualified staff, untrained board members, and staff inadequately trained by BOG to inspect and control the banks. The Government has given priority to developing RBs to promote credit. Because of the difficulties outlined above, however, BOG has slowed down the expansion of RBs.

Informal Credit

In spite of a vast network of formal credit institutions, informal credit plays a significant role in Ghana. The role of informal credit in rural capital markets is not known, but in Ghana, as in other parts of West Africa, informal credit is well developed and meets critical needs during lean periods for consumption and production credit as well as for emergency and social needs such as funerals.

Such credit is available, in order of priority from the point of view of the borrower, from friends, relatives, landlords, traders or money-lenders. Friends and relatives usually do not charge interest. With the landlord, a loan can be interest-bearing or carry implicit transaction costs such as putting in free labour. Loans from other sources are generally interest-bearing. While interest rates are high and range between 50 percent and 100 percent per annum, the convenience of obtaining credit and the ease with which it is granted (no formal documentation) almost make the credit attractive to the borrower, particularly since it covers consumption needs. Formal credit, on the other hand, is seldom available on time and has a particularly high transaction cost to the borrower, who must frequently travel to the nearest branch to get a single loan approved.

Despite the relative attractiveness of an informal credit system there are some severe limitations. First, it is mostly short-term and the amount of funds available is limited. Second, interest rates often exceed the stated amounts because of invisible transaction costs; typically such arrangements include the sale of produce at harvest, often at below market rates. Third, informal credit at high interest rates can prevent farmers from developing an independent income resource base and, to some extent, impede development.

Agricultural Credit Policy

The report on the PIP in 1988 identified the major constraints to the long-term development of sustainable agriculture as:

- insufficient flow of institutional credit;
- inadequate supply and distribution of inputs;
- inadequate storage and marketing facilities; and
- ineffective or non-existent farmers' organizations at village level.

Policy measures and strategies proposed to remove these constraints included:

- encouraging and directing, through monetary policies, the flow of institutional credit to the agricultural sector in sufficient quantities;
- streamlining the procurement and distribution of agricultural inputs and, where desirable, privatizing them so as to ensure efficiency as well as accessibility to farmers;

- reducing post-harvest losses through the promotion and provision of improved on-farm storage facilities for small-scale farmers and improved processing of agricultural produce; and
- encouraging farmers at the village level to organize themselves into local cooperatives or other groups so as to gain formal recognition and access to institutional credit, input supply and extension services.

In 1988, the Government stated that its policy with respect to farm credit was: "To strengthen the institutional capability of rural banks and develop a manual for rural bank personnel. The Bank of Ghana will be required to assume a wider range of responsibility in the field of agricultural credit." The Government is also considering measures to promote savings and facilitate local resource mobilization. The Government's policy of maintaining real positive interest rates should improve the mobilization of rural savings and thus contribute to credit expansion.

There are four recent projects which should have considerable impact on the smallholder credit and input supply sector. The Financial Sector Adjustment Credit (FSAC), with IDA funding of over US$ 280 million and the participation of several other donors, provides funds for the financial and organizational restructuring of all the national banks, including ADB. The restructuring of ADB is receiving priority because of its importance to the Rural Finance Project, approved in 1989 to implement a financial restructuring programme for RBs and to strengthen credit unions. The objective is to enable them to become more efficient in mobilizing resources and credit delivery, especially to smallholders.

In 1987, the Government also prepared a Programme of Action to Mitigate the Social Costs of Adjustment (PAMSCAD) to address the needs of vulnerable groups in the short term. Several components are of relevance to smallholder financing. The first component seeks to generate and accelerate employment through small enterprises, the second to assist marginal and small-scale farmers to increase agricultural production and reduce post-harvest losses. Although funds are managed by appropriate banks, responsibility for approval and recovery rests with committees and agencies outside the banks.

Chapter 8

Agricultural Marketing

The structure of the marketing system is crucial in rural development as the transformation of agriculture away from subsistence creates increasing reliance by smallholders on markets both for the sale of output as well as for the provision of inputs. Markets function via institutions, formal or informal, public or private, that evolve to fulfil perceived needs or policies. The study of these institutions is as important as the analysis of prices, which are the ultimate result of the marketing environment.

Essentially five alternative marketing methods are recognizable in Ghana, viz. private enterprise, public or parastatal, cooperative, vertical integration and contracting. These have evolved to fulfil perceived needs and policies. In the food crop sector 95 percent of the trade is controlled by the private sector, whereas in the industrial and export crop sub-sector cocoa, coffee, oil-palm, rubber and shea-nuts are dominated by parastatals. There is a general belief, in some quarters, that the private marketing system functions well since, in the face of tremendous logistical constraints during the late nineteen-seventies and early nineteen-eighties, it managed to move goods from rural to urban areas. Much has also been stated about the relative efficiency of the private marketing system *vis-à-vis* the public system which, given the inherent institutional constraints and limitations of the latter (particularly the low salary structure), is hardly surprising. The central issue affecting the marketing system in Ghana, however, is not whether the private sector is more efficient than the public sector. The central issue is whether the marketing system as a whole is capable of providing the incentive framework to increase production, particularly from the smallholders' viewpoint, who account for over 80 percent of total farmers.

The private sector in food marketing comprises many petty traders, assemblers, forestallers, transporters, processors, commission agents, and space arbitrageurs. In the food crop sector *per se*, the itinerant traders and market-based wholesalers dominate the trade. The itinerant traders or forestallers procure the commodities, store them and transport them to the rural assembly markets or nearby roadsides before moving them to the urban markets. Sometimes some type of informal credit arrangement is made for the trader to provide production credit to the farmer during the production season. Buying and selling take place at the urban markets by the "market queens" who influence the conduct of the market to some extent. In some communities village assembly markets are organized on particular days of the week and farmers converge there with their produce either by headloading it or using a combination of alternative modes of transportation, viz. a tractor-trailer combination, bicycles, trucks, or oxen-drawn or donkey-drawn carts.

The private system has managed to provide uninterrupted services to the farmers despite all the logistical problems that plagued the Ghanaian economy in the late nineteen-seventies and during the first five years of the nineteen-eighties and are still prevalent today. Roads are still in poor condition, transport costs are high and the frequent shortage of vehicles, along with the limited supply of foreign exchange to purchase spare parts, have compounded the general problems of poor marketing infrastructure, lack of storage, high losses in storage and transport and poor communications. Despite these formidable constraints, a visit to the Ghanaian markets gives the widespread perception of vigour and cohesion. The retail markets, traditionally controlled by small private traders, are active and characterized by general availability of goods; the ERP, through currency realignment and general availability of foreign exchange, linked to import liberalization, has contributed to this general availability. A number of retailers operating on small margins, which are believed to be in the range of 10-20 percent, vie with each other for business. The general air of competitive retailing gives the impression of an adequate marketing system.

In Ghana, a number of public institutions have developed, at times duplicating each other's services. In agricultural marketing the following institutions have played the major role.

Ghana Cocoa Marketing Board (GCMB or COCOBOD) was established as a profit-making body to buy, process and market cocoa. Over time, COCOBOD has also been involved in exports of coffee and shea-nuts. Although established as a commercial body, COCOBOD operates more like a ministry with a total staff strength of some 62 000 as of April 1986, resulting in high marketing costs. In addition, some 20 000 employees work in its various subsidiaries. Essentially the Board undertakes a diverse range of activities both directly and through subsidiaries. Direct functions include supply of seeds and other inputs, quality control and extension. Cocoa production is undertaken through Plantation Ltd., its processing through the Cocoa Processing Company and sales through the Cocoa Marketing Company. Cocoa research is undertaken by the Cocoa Research Institute of Ghana, which also operates within the purview of COCOBOD.

Recently COCOBOD undertook a massive restructuring exercise to streamline its operations. Some 17 000 staff were retrenched and an additional 2 900 employees are to be laid off. This is expected to reduce the cost of COCOBOD's operations by reducing the staff expenses which amount to some 26 percent of sales. Staff salaries, estimated at ₵ 5.5 billion, accounted for some 50 percent of the 1985/86 budget. While recent salary increases will significantly offset the estimated savings, it is expected that the restructuring exercise will leave a leaner organization.

In spite of the reorganization, farmers continued to receive only 27 percent of COCOBOD's sales incomes. Approximately 26 percent of sales covered administrative expenses; 8 percent went directly towards special expenditures, including ₵ 1.9 billion for the feeder road programme in cocoa-growing areas; and the balance, a surplus of ₵ 17.1 billion (39 percent), was paid to the Government.

There is considerable controversy surrounding the role of COCOBOD. Prior to 1928, when COCOBOD was brought under state control, farmers' receipts averaged 81 percent of f.o.b. prices. COCOBOD involvement in development activities was indirect. As part of its mandate, the difference between the world market price and the producer price was kept as a "Stabilization Fund" to be used to top up the producer prices in order to maintain farmers' income and incentive in case the then volatile world cocoa price fell below the producer price. In course of time this Fund was cornered by the Government and became a regular input into the Government Development Expenditure Budget. However, one aspect of COCOBOD's role remains clear. As a government agency, it could not pay producer prices at anything but the official exchange rate. Considering the official rate was grossly overvalued (in 1983 the parallel rate reached ₵ 60 = US$ 1, when the official rate was only ₵ 2.75 = US$ 1) the terms of trade at the official price level at least moved in favour of domestic rather than export crops. Given these price distortions, it is not surprising that an active parallel market developed in cocoa. COCOBOD also handles the local purchase and export of shea-butter, kola and coffee. With the realignment of the cedi, a rekindled interest in coffee rehabilitation has been observed.

As part of its commitment to provide coffee for export, the Government has followed up its programme, stated in the 1987 Ghana Cocoa Board Corporate Plan (1987/88-1990/91), to encourage diversification with coffee, primarily for export. The announcement by Government in 1989 of a 48 percent increase in the coffee producer price is an important and positive step specifically designed to achieve this stated objective.

Ghana Food Distribution Corporation (GFDC). By its mandate GFDC was established to purchase, export and distribute foods, the last through a chain of grocery shops. In addition, it was also empowered to distribute inputs. At present, GFDC is primarily involved in food procurement and sale and also imports rice. Its role in other activities is limited. Export is relatively dormant because of limited opportunities, although in recent years attempts at export market penetration have been made successfully. Its main function today is the purchase of domestic crops, of which maize is the most important; the others are rice, plantain, yam, cocoyam and gari. Domestic purchases and sales account for some 67 percent of its trade, imports (rice) for 27 percent and inputs for 4 percent. GFDC, as a parastatal, also undertakes price support programmes for the Government. It acts as a last-resort buyer and sells food generally with a mark-up of 45 percent.

GFDC's role in the domestic price support programmes remains ineffective. Its maize purchases between 1982 and 1985 rose from 5 000 mt to 14 000 mt. This is only 2-4 percent of domestic maize production. GFDC claims that its market share in maize is some 16-18 percent of the marketed surplus and its objective is to reach a total volume of 20 percent of marketed surplus to provide an effective price support programme. In effect, the Corporation handles only about 5-10 percent of the food market in the country. The major food items it handles are cereals (maize, rice, sorghum and millet), legumes, cooking oil, plantain, yam, legumes (cowpeas) and gari. Since its main selling outlets are in the urban areas, the rural areas are not serviced by the Corporation and are thus left food-insecure. GFDC also regularly supplies food to government institutions like schools and prisons and operates a mill at Tamale.

In 1985, total maize production was estimated at 395 000 mt. If the 14 000 mt procured by GFDC were 10 percent of the marketed surplus, this would imply that the marketed maize surplus in 1985 was only 78 000 mt or some 20 percent of production. This is unlikely when one takes into account the consideration that in Brong-Ahafo and Ashanti, the major maize-producing regions, farmers market about

70-80 percent of their crop. GFDC's price support functions remain ineffective despite the fact that in many years the guaranteed minimum prices (GMP) are higher than harvest and farmgate market prices (Table 8.1). After 1984, when maize production increased sharply, GMP were 50 percent above farmgate prices. The reasons for this ineffectiveness are liquidity problems, poor management, lack of storage facilities and an inadequate transport system.

GFDC is also charged with the responsibility of maintaining buffer stocks and maintains a network of stores with a capacity of 150 000 mt in local assembly points, warehouses and collection points. Storage facilities are in poor condition and pest losses in some stores are reportedly high. As at December 1989, GFDC had storage capacity in silos of 9 600 mt and warehousing capacity in its own and rented property of 34 900 mt. However, GFDC, which has the largest amount of storage space, handles only 6-10 percent of the marketable surplus of grains and this demonstrates the problem of grain storage in Ghana. With such a low volume of operation by GFDC, grain storage in the country depends to a large extent on the private sector. Over the next five-year period, the Corporation has planned to triple its capacity to 150 000 mt. This will involve the conversion of its very large and abandoned concrete silos.

GFDC operates a GMP scheme for maize and rice on behalf of the Government. The GMP is fixed on a cost-plus basis, the average cost of production plus a reasonable margin. The GMP is an "adoption" price and acts as an incentive to farmers to use improved inputs such as fertilizers and agro-chemicals. GFDC's guaranteed price has been 10-20 percent higher than the market price at harvest time, but even then its volume of business has been limited by financial and logistical constraints. On the whole the price advantage which the Corporation has tends to be whittled away over time as the open market price rises. Thus, the cost-plus pricing neither benefits most of the producers nor GFDC in enabling it to buy maize and rice. For instance, during the 1988/89 season, GFDC could not sell most of the 20 000 mt of maize it purchased because for most of the time the domestic market price was lower than the cost build-up, which is made up mainly of the purchase price (GMP) and the cost of storage. The Corporation was thus left with large quantities of unsold stocks which had to be unloaded before the new season to clear its stores. In 1989, it did this by selling maize to WFP, Togo and EEC. Because the GMP is usually above the world market price, such exporting is done at a loss. Thus, GFDC, by operating the GMP, is working at a competitive disadvantage both on the domestic and international markets.

Table 8.1: Produce Prices for Maize and Rice, 1979-87 (cedis per mt)

Year	Maize Harvest Season				Rice Harvest Season			
	GMP [1]	Wholesale	Farmgate [2]	GMP as proportion of farmgate (%)	GMP [1]	Wholesale	Farmgate [2]	GMP as proportion of farmgate (%)
1979	80	170	102	78.4	120	282	169	71.0
1980	100	434	260	38.5	290	599	359	80.8
1981	165	606	363	45.5	420	1 593	955	44.0
1982	500	797	472	105.9	550	2 628	1 576	35.0
1983	1 800	2 294	1 377	130.7	1 000	6 480	3 888	25.7
1984	1 000	1 081	648	154.3	1 800	4 486	2 691	66.9
1985	2 000	1 750	1 050	190.5	2 000	5 273	3 163	63.2
1986	2 600	2 625	1 575	165.1	2 500	7 943	4 765	52.5
1987	4 200	NA	3 600	116.7	4 000	6 000	3 600	111.1

[1] Guaranteed Minimum Price.

[2] Assumed 60% of wholesale prices.

Source: Ministry of Agriculture and mission calculations.

However, the operation of the buffer stocks by means of the GMP is a social function which the Corporation must shoulder on behalf of the Government.

Grains Warehousing Company (GWC). GWC was originally formed to store cereals (maize, rice, wheat, sorghum) but it has also recently entered into grain purchasing. It now complements GFDC and offers the guaranteed minimum price. It procures grain directly or through cooperatives and buying agents. GWC has storage facilities of up to 20 000 mt in five warehouses and is planning to open silos in maize-growing areas in nine locations in the Ashanti and Brong-Ahafo Regions and in the Afram Plains (Eastern Region).

Ghana National Procurement Agency (GNPA). GNPA basically acts as an importer and wholesaler for a wide range of commodities including wheat, rice, sugar, maize and vegetable oils. Mark-ups are high, up to 35 percent of cost, insurance, freight (c.i.f.). GNPA is plagued by management problems. In addition, it imported some unwanted yellow maize which added to its financial woes. On account of these developments, the Bank of Ghana cancelled guarantees on GNPA's Letters of Credit in 1984. The agency, though still active, faces diminishing business prospects.

Meat Marketing Board (MMB). MMB is a government distributor of meat. MMB's annual sales declined from an average of 4 000 mt in 1974 to some 1 700 mt in 1984. Erratic supplies and high prices linked to poor management resulted in retailers seeking alternative sources of supply. MMB faces many institutional difficulties in meeting its mandate of importing and distributing meat. In 1986, cattle imports were discontinued and MMB had to reorient its operations to domestic trading. It also operates three ranches to augment its supplies. MMB's role in marketing is insignificant. Measured by numbers, it handled some 6 percent of pig production, 4 percent of cattle and 1 percent of smallstock. MMB's operations do not appear to yield any significant profits. In the second half of 1986 it reported total sales of ₡ 38.3 million, which yielded a gross margin of ₡ 15.7 million. The gross margin was below its salary and wage bill of ₡ 18 million. Total losses in the year amounted to ₡ 29 million. If its operations are to be continued, MMB needs to be dramatically reorganized.

Private Sector Marketing

The private sector is essentially more efficient than the public sector and dominates the marketing of food crops, meat and fish. In food crops, there are three main types of traders, namely itinerant, market-based, and food contractors. Itinerant traders operate in a geographical area by establishing contact and offering services to maintain this relationship. The market-based traders are wholesalers; by and large they have formed loosely based associations, led by "market queens" (the head of an association). Each "market queen" specializes in a commodity and, although linkages between "market queens" are not known to exist, she acts as an important link between wholesalers and retailers in an individual market. The last group, the food contractors, supply food to various institutions.

The marketing links vary from simple to complex, the simplest being from the producers to the rural consumer. The more complex marketing system leads to urban consumers through a network of intermediaries. Traditional linkages are believed to be strong and the itinerant traders operate on the basis of direct linkages by providing production or consumption credit. Itinerant traders buy, assemble and transport the produce to wholesalers at the consuming centres. At these points, the role of the "market queen" is quite critical. She reportedly regulates supply and demand to ensure certain price levels. Collusion has been indicated, and at times farmers and even itinerant traders have been prevented from free entry. Some surveys (Azinim 1980) indicate that between 47 percent and 52 percent of the traders themselves believe that "market queens" are price setters rather than price takers.

Regardless of the distribution efficiency of the various distribution systems (public or private) there is widespread concern that marketing costs are high, arising from a number of constraints which, *inter alia*, include poor transport facilities, poor roads, which lead to high transport costs, and poor storage.

Most farmers, lacking capital, dispose of their produce within a few months after harvest. Surveys indicate that 30 percent of the harvested surplus is sold within three months after harvest; within five months, some 80 percent is sold. It is believed that 96 percent of yam, 98 percent of maize and 95 percent of groundnuts are sold in farms or nearby rural markets. Estimates vary but farmers receive between 60 to 70 percent of wholesale prices. Although seasonal price fluctuations are significant, at times these vary between 100 and 200 percent.

Marketing System Performance

To analyse the performance of the marketing system one must examine its spatial and temporal dimensions, as well as the position of the smallholder *vis-à-vis* the opportunities offered to him. The analysis does not purport to pass judgement on private versus public marketing. It rather tries to bring out some salient features of the system as it currently operates.

Spatial Integration. If the marketing system operates efficiently then, subject to time delays due to transport, wholesale prices in various geographical regions should move in unison. In Ghana, the various markets are geographically quite close. Between the northern regions' markets and Accra the time it takes for produce to move (by truck or other means) is not more than a few days, even under the worst weather conditions. Hence, one would expect that prices in major marketing centres should not move independently.

To test this hypothesis the mission obtained monthly wholesale price data in several rural producing and urban consuming markets for 1982, 1983, 1985 and 1986 (data for 1984 could not be obtained) for maize, rice, yam, and cassava, the most widely consumed staples. Pairwise percentage differences between the prices of the various regions were computed. In other words, two regions and the monthly prices in each one of them were considered. Then the percentage difference between the price of one region and the price in the other, for each month for which data for both regions were available, was computed. If prices in different markets move in unison then the percentage differences of monthly prices across the regions should not vary too much and, therefore, the standard deviations of these differences should be small. Table 8.2 presents the mean, minimum and maximum values as well as the standard deviations of these percentage differences between major urban consuming centres and major rural producing areas. All these differences are expected to be positive on average as the commodities generally flow from rural to urban centres. Also the range between the minimum and maximum values should not be too large, and similarly the standard deviations should be small if there are continued flows from rural to urban areas.

The results, however, hold several surprises. For maize and the bulky products like yam and cassava, indeed, the average percentage difference between urban and rural prices is positive (except for cassava between Ashanti urban and Northern rural which, in any case, was computed for only five monthly comparisons. However, in almost all cases there are months in which the price relationship is severely

Table 8.2: Percentage Differences of Monthly Wholesale Prices Between Major Urban Consuming and Rural Producing Centres (1982-86)[1]

Crop	Accra Urban			Ashanti Urban		
	Ashanti Rural %	Brong-Ahafo Rural %	Northern Rural %	Ashanti Rural %	Brong-Ahafo Rural %	Northern Rural %
1. *Maize*						
Mean	21.3	26.8	35.1	6.9	15.2	19.9
Minimum value	-40.3	-75.0	-13.0	-65.5	-34.7	-25.9
Maximum value	51.0	59.0	73.9	38.1	55.4	62.3
Standard deviation	16.5	20.7	18.3	17.3	16.5	21.9
2. *Rice*						
Mean	9.8	11.6	11.1	-11.2	-22.3	-21.4
Minimum value	-102.4	-67.1	-54.5	-67.2	-99.0	-89.1
Maximum value	39.4	67.7	36.5	29.9	66.4	36.6
Standard deviation	28.1	31.1	23.1	31.1	41.1	37.5
3. *Yam*						
Mean	35.6	31.4	43.4	13.7	6.2	27.0
Minimum value	-113.4	-49.4	16.7	-168.5	-126.9	-24.0
Maximum value	73.9	71.4	66.8	64.2	66.2	64.2
Standard deviation	30.9	24.4	14.2	40.0	37.9	20.8

Table 8.2: Percentage Differences of Monthly Wholesale Prices Between Major Urban Consuming and Rural Producing Centres (1982-86)[1] (Cont'd)

Crop	Accra Urban			Ashanti Urban		
	Ashanti Rural %	Brong-Ahafo Rural %	Northern Rural %	Ashanti Rural %	Brong-Ahafo Rural %	Northern Rural %
4. *Cassava*						
Mean	44.9	45.9	8.3	15.5	10.1	-19.8
Minimum value	-67.7	-67.0	-45.5	-128.5	-149.2	-131.7
Maximum value	88.1	85.5	60.8	78.8	70.6	51.0
Standard deviation	32.2	38.6	38.3	50.5	67.5	57.0

[1] Except 1984. The statistics for each regional comparison are computed by considering the time series for which one typical element is the percentage difference between the price in one month in the urban centre shown in the top row and the price in the same month in the producing area indicated in the second row. If, for instance, there are 20 available monthly price data for Accra Urban and the exact same 20 monthly price data for the Ashanti Rural, then the statistics of the first column of the table are computed from a time series with 20 price differences.

Source: Computed from data provided by the Ministry of Agriculture.

reversed; the urban price being much lower than the rural price (this suggests a negative pairwise percentage difference for these months, which subsequently implies that the minimum value for all the computed percentage differences is negative). For rice, the relationship is even stranger. The average wholesale price of rice in urban Ashanti appears to be lower than in all the three major cereal producing centres. This can be explained by realizing that rice is the major staple cereal imported under food aid and is distributed mainly in urban areas. The ranges between the highest and lowest percent spatial price differences for a given product are enormous. For instance, the difference between the highest and lowest observed percentage price between the Ashanti urban and Ashanti rural areas is more than 100 percent. The standard deviation in the same case is about three times the value of the mean, implying very large variations in the monthly differences in prices between the two regions. If one restricts the analysis to the months just after or just before harvest (for maize and rice), then while the distributions (in terms of differences between maximum and minimum values) narrow, the general pattern of results stays the same. It thus appears from this analysis that markets for staple food crops are not very well integrated spatially.

Intra-seasonal Price Variation. Staple food markets in Ghana exhibit very substantial price variability within each marketing season. For the storable staple cereal crops (maize and rice) the prices in the lean season are usually much higher than at harvest time. Table 8.3 illustrates the national wholesale prices for maize and rice in the average harvest and lean season within each marketing year during the period 1975-86. The results indicate that for maize in most years the prices in the lean season are more than 100 percent higher than prices at harvest time. For rice, the pattern is less pronounced, and in one year (1978/79) the price in the lean season was below the price in the harvest season. Since the lean season usually coincides with the arrival of much of the food aid, it is likely that this could adversely influence intra-seasonal price patterns. The same, albeit on a reduced scale, can be observed for the 1983/84 season. In that year of extreme drought, food aid arrived in the middle of 1984 depressing national prices in the lean season (they were already quite high for the season as a whole).

Though no detailed analysis of storage costs was undertaken, from the above analysis it appears that, in almost all years, there is a price incentive to store cereal grains from harvest until the lean season. This incentive can be distorted by food aid or commercial imports, but it generally appears to be strong. For instance, if storage losses are

Table 8.3: Intra-seasonal Variation of Monthly National Wholesale Prices of Maize and Rice, 1975-86 (prices in cedis per bag)[1]

Year	Maize[2]				Rice[2]			
	% difference between min. & max. monthly prices within marketing year	Average price Sept.-Oct.	Average price June-July	% difference between late season and early season prices[3]	% difference between min. & max. monthly prices within marketing year	Average price Oct.-Nov.	Average price July-Aug.	% difference between late season and early season prices[3]
	(1)	(2)	(3)	(4)	(5)	(6)	(7)	(8)
1975/76	293.7	25.6	70.8	170.0	187.6	80.5	142.1	76.5
1976/77	248.0	57.9	169.5	192.8	67.4	164.3	226.0	37.6
1977/78	108.8	81.0	121.4	48.8	113.3	148.2	228.6	54.2
1978/79	151.0	96.1	201.9	110.0	84.6	273.8	229.7	-16.1
1979/80	340.6	170.7	605.6	254.7	301.4	282.1	795.8	182.1
1980/81	168.9	434.1	952.0	119.3	327.7	599.3	1 789.1	198.5
1981/82	100.6	606.3	974.4	60.6	268.4	1 593.5	3 231.8	102.8
1982/83	974.0	787.5	6 552.5	732.0	266.0	2 628.8	8 204.2	212.0
1983/84	79.5	2 294.4	2 627.9	14.5	45.3	6 480.6	7 329.1	13.0
1984/85	159.5	1 082.0	2 338.4	116.1	33.6	4 486.4	5 849.2	30.3
1985/86	167.9	1 750.8	4 054.0	131.6	90.2	5 273.2	6 921.2	31.3

[1] A bag of maize is 100 kg, a bag of rice in 93 kg.

[2] The marketing year for maize was assumed to be August-July, while that for rice was assumed to be October-September.

[3] (4) = [(3) - (2)] x 100/(2), similarly column (8) = [(7) - (6)] x 100/(6).

Source: Computed.

20 percent, interest rate is 20 percent and inflation 50 percent, then between the harvest and lean seasons a price difference of 100 percent would imply that a farmer who borrowed at 20 percent interest in order to store and not sell his crop until the lean time would make a reasonable real profit of 10 percent. The smallholders realize this and try to store for as long as possible. However, since they cannot obtain credit for storage, they have to sell early in the season to satisfy their cash needs. Projects that provide for this type of credit could substantially improve the earnings of smallholders.

Chapter 9

Grassroots Institutions and Non-governmental and Social Service Organizations

The difficulties experienced by the public institutions that have served the agricultural sector in Ghana over the last decade, and the attendant decline in the quantity and quality of services provided, have naturally led many smallholders to rely more on informal grassroots institutions as well as NGOs. It is thus important to assess the possibilities that these institutions offer for reaching rural smallholders. This chapter reviews the multitude of informal and NGO institutions in rural Ghana, analyses their mode of formation and operation, and in particular assesses their capabilities for being used as agents for the implementation of selected project components. Reliance on grassroots institutions and self-help schemes may prove even more necessary during the adjustment period, when the Government is pursuing a stringent budgetary policy.

Grassroots Institutions

Eleven types of grassroots organizations are found in Ghana. The organizations are roughly grouped into three categories: the first comprises four groupings which are relatively informal and socio-cultural; the second includes five further groupings which have arisen at the grassroots level as a more formal response to the organization of rural production; and finally, in the last category, are two relatively prominent examples of grassroots organizations developing from the activities of a multilateral agency.

Category 1

Susu Groups. *Susu* groups are informal savings groups which are very widespread. They operate on the familiar principle of each member of the group making a monthly payment to a group fund; one member of the group takes the monthly total as an investment sum for himself. The members take turns in receiving the monthly total. The system remains essentially informal and small-scale, though it would appear that "market queens" have a network of "*susu* agents" in urban areas.

Nnoboa. This is a traditional, labour-sharing scheme in which farmers supply group labour on each other's land in exchange for meals. Indications are that in recent years the custom has decreased, partly because farmers find it more rewarding to offer their labour against wage payment.

Socio-cultural Groups. There are an enormous range of socio-cultural groups concerned with entertainment, funerals and festivals. They are an important element in community life and a significant medium for the exchange of information.

Religious Congregations. Religious gatherings, whether Christian, Muslim or animist, are an important and virtually universal medium in which informal development, education and information exchange take place. The church and the mosque have been equally important elements in small-scale, local-level development.

Category 2

Community Growers' Associations. In a number of areas, commodity-specific associations have been formed for promotion and mutual aid among producers of a particular crop. There are, for example, pepper-grower associations, rice-farmer associations, vegetable-grower associations, etc. The character of these associations, in terms of scale, function and social orientation, is essentially determined by the scale of production and the commercial value of the particular crop. Members collaborate principally with respect to input supply and marketing.

Cooperatives. There is a tendency for cooperatives to deteriorate over the four or five years following their establishment into organizations run by a handful of relatively large-scale and locally influential farmers, principally for their own benefit. The majority of replies in a number of surveys indicate, not surprisingly, that in the future farmers would prefer to see the establishment of consumer cooperatives and a greatly expanded and simplified system of soft-term credit.

Abusa Groups.   In some of the cocoa-growing areas, *abusa* producers have organized themselves into mutual aid groups on a voluntary basis, which they refer to as "companies".   The purpose of the groups is to minimize the costs of labour while effectively carrying out farm operations by performing a variety of farm duties in turn, working the same number of hours on each of the farms operated by the members.   In cocoa-growing areas in Ashanti and Brong-Ahafo, this sort of group activity was widely practised and was invariably limited to weeding, harvesting of cocoa pods and headloading the beans to the nearest drying spot.   Along with such other factors as ready markets and credit from cocoa agents, this practice was uniquely responsible for the expansion of the cocoa industry in the two regions.

Tenants' Associations.   These have emerged in some areas where there are high concentrations of tenant farmers.   The associations tend to emphasize that their purpose is not political but rather to provide representation of the tenants' point of view with respect to local land use and administration issues.

Tribal Associations.   Tribal associations are quite often found among migrant groups.   The purpose of the associations is to make members feel at home; to defend their interests if necessary; to mediate occasionally between members and employees; to provide financial help to members; and to maintain ties with the home community.

Category 3

People's Participation Programme (PPP).   The FAO-supported PPP has two project areas in Ghana; one in the Wenchi area of Brong-Ahafo Region and one in the Begoro area of the Eastern Region.   PPP focuses on the rural poor by attempting to build a network of income-generating activities based on small homogeneous self-help groups and using resident group promoters usually recruited from outside the local beneficiary population.   Group saving is promoted and credit is extended on the basis of group liability.   The financial activities of the programme are backed by a guarantee-cum-risk fund.   Group networks are linked by the programme to government and NGO delivery systems.   It is perhaps important to note that the benefits of the programme have in the past been severely constrained by the long bureaucratic chain linking the grassroots activities with the Government and FAO headquarters in Rome.   In an attempt to ease financial administration problems, the relevant diocesan-level representatives of the Roman Catholic Church were recruited to exercise management of the component. In the PPP in Ghana, as elsewhere, the maintenance of group motivation is quite markedly strained by time-consuming decision making in the programme's support system.

Freedom from Hunger Campaign/Action for Development (FFHC/AD). FFHC/AD is another FAO-generated intervention in support of grassroots organizations. Funding is provided to producer groups on an *ad hoc* basis. Funding is less than US$ 25 000 per group and usually in the region of US$ 10 000. The duration of support is one year, occasionally two years. FFHC/AD reaches beyond NGOs to locale-specific groupings who have come together for the particular purpose of raising support for a single activity. The Ghana programme includes several groups engaged in small-scale farming: four in food processing; one in animal production (pigs); one in plant protection; one involved in a Resettlement Cooperative Farm; and five in fisheries. Four of the fishing groups and two of the food-processing groups are women's groups. Contact, formulation and delivery is usually through extension personnel of the MOA. As part of its support to the groups, FFHC/AD provides training in organization and management and promotes network formation.

It is immediately clear from this short review that grassroots institutional development pertinent to promoting the interests of smallholders is patchy and relatively weak. This situation is endemic to smallholder production everywhere since the only grassroots organization which has the longevity to be properly termed an institution is the family itself. The relatively informal arrangements, e.g., *susu* or *nnoboa* are, in effect, customs. The commodity-based associations and cooperatives are more suited to larger commercial types of production. With regard to the two attempts at externally promoted, local-level institution building, it is too early to say whether they will succeed in establishing long-term, self-sufficient grassroots organizations. What is clear is that Ghanaian smallholders are prepared to modify their fundamental individualism to a limited degree and undertake collective action when they have identified a clear, simple objective which can be achieved by group effort; when the task does not involve anything but the simplest managerial, administrative and financial arrangements; when there is a clearly perceived economic benefit; and when they are not constrained by the interests of those more powerful than themselves.

Smallholder development based on the external promotion of grassroots institutions must fulfil these conditions if it is to have any chance of success. It would seem, therefore, that when using such a development approach, grassroots organizations should focus on a specific production function. It should not, for example, be muddled up with community development as can often be the case. Supplementary human and material resources and training also have to be available to the organization on a timely basis until it has acquired the skills and capital to achieve the task by itself. There must be short-term economic benefits, not just medium-term or long-term returns. Finally, there must be a clear political commitment on the part of relevant authorities to the organizations' objectives.

Cooperatives

The history of the cooperative movement dates back to 1928 when cooperatives in Ghana were organized to market cocoa. The movement has had a chequered evolution and, as elaborated below, at one point over 8 000 societies were registered. As in other parts of Africa, however, it has not been able to gain a popular image because of its poor past performance. Though it is the declared policy of the Government that facilities and opportunities should be provided to establish multi-purpose cooperative associations to increase productivity and raise the quality of life, the policy is not matched by adequate efforts.

Currently, the Department of Cooperatives is responsible for the development of the cooperative movement. The Registrar of Cooperative Societies, who is the head of the Department, is responsible for registering the societies, auditing their accounts and supervising and inspecting them. The Department is unable to carry out its supervisory and statutory functions owing, *inter alia,* to lack of staff and budgetary constraints. The Department of Cooperatives, like other Departments, is understaffed in the professional and management cadres. As of 31 March 1987, there were 593 established positions, of which some 409 were filled. Lack of staff and funds and low salaries have led to deterioration in the service provided by a demoralized staff, as in the case of MOA. In some instances, even for the relatively few active societies, accounts have not been audited since 1984.

Cooperatives are organized on activity lines. As of 1986, there were about 8 406 registered cooperatives, of which agricultural societies numbered 3 995. Exact numbers are not known but some 30-40 percent of these societies are believed to be active. The financial condition of the cooperatives is not known but most societies are believed to be weak.

Data from a study (Brown 1984) indicate that some 20.7 percent of the population are members of cooperatives. Various replies to the study, from those who do not belong to cooperatives, indicate that the major reason for not belonging to a cooperative appears to be its non-existence in the local community. According to the same study, some 39 percent of those who were not members of a cooperative would like to join one. The main types of cooperative or self-help organization they wanted to join were: the consumer type (60 percent); farmers' organizations (18 percent); distillers' cooperatives (12 percent); bakers' associations (5 percent); marketing associations (1 percent); and food-processing associations (1 percent). Clearly, most respondents saw benefits from joining cooperatives to obtain supplies (86 percent). This is not surprising when one considers the serious problems of obtaining inputs on time.

Despite their perceived unpopularity, interest in cooperatives, particularly in rural areas, is not totally lacking in Ghana. With proper management, interest in cooperatives can be regenerated. The experience of a recent FAO pilot project in Sokyere and Ejura Districts seems to support this conclusion. The project has successfully demonstrated that, with proper management, cooperatives can supply the grassroots institutional framework to provide services to farmers. Cooperatives have become unpopular both with farmers and with the donors because of problems rising from outright interference and mismanagement. Donors have preferred to form informal groups as they are more likely to encourage participatory structures. While this is true, groups require significant managerial inputs to transform them into self-managing entities, with the added disadvantage that they neither have an institutional framework to ensure their continuity, nor a legal structure which can be sued in the event of default. Because of these limitations, granting of loan terms to groups has proved difficult. Cooperatives, however, which also require equally intensive support to assist them in becoming self-managing entities, overcome some of the above-mentioned limitations. There is no reason why one should be preferred over the other. Both face similar management problems and the choice should be left largely to the smallholders.

Non-governmental Organizations

Background. A very large and varied number of NGOs are currently working in Ghana: national and international, religious and secular, and also several volunteer agencies. A comprehensive survey of NGO activity in Ghana during the period 1985-86 was recently undertaken by Michelle Fruge for the Catholic Relief Services (Catholic Relief Services 1987). With respect to each NGO the report provides an overview of the organization's origins and purpose; the source and levels of its funding; its programme in Ghana and the location and sector of each of its projects; and its method of operation.

NGO Coverage. While most NGOs are limited in the scale of their operations and confined to one or two regions, there are a number with a presence in all regions. These are notably the major religious organizations and their affiliates, Canadian University Overseas (CUSO) and Voluntary Services Overseas (VSO). In effect, therefore, it is the main Christian churches and to a lesser extent the Ahmaddiya Muslim mission which provide the most widespread and deep-rooted NGO involvement in Ghana. Catholic Church development activities are coordinated by the apex organization of the National Catholic Secretariat's Socio-Economic Department and the equivalent body for the principal Protestant Churches is the Christian Services Committee of the Christian Council of Ghana. It appears that, while coverage is varied, the "outer" regions of Upper West, Upper East, Northern, Western and to a lesser extent Volta, have received rather more attention from NGOs than the other regions.

NGO Sectoral Involvement. The major involvement of NGOs in sectoral terms has been with health and agriculture. They have also been concerned to a lesser, but still substantial degree with water and sanitation, income generation through the development of small off-farm enterprises, skills training and non-formal education. A marked feature of the health and income-generating projects of NGOs has been their focus on rural women. The sectoral distribution of the NGOs' development activities reflects these organizations' traditional concern with improving and supplementing the provision of basic social services and augmenting the local employment and income-generating prospects of the "poorest of the poor".

Sasakawa - Global 2000 is a non-profit organization formed under the auspices of the ex-President Jimmy Carter of the USA and now receiving financial support from the Japanese Sasakawa Africa Association. It seeks to improve agricultural productivity by assisting the transfer of technology through a demonstration-diffusion system operating through the local MOA extension service, with a small number of qualified and highly motivated agronomists acting as catalysts and ensuring that inputs and credit are available, and that extension staff are motivated and mobile. Extension has been based on a lead farmer as the nucleus for a group of ten contact farmers, who agree to carry out a demonstration plot of at least one acre divided into half with improved technology and half with traditional technology. Global 2000 provides the inputs on seasonal credit. After one year the contact farmers become the lead farmers, enabling a rapid diffusion of improved technology through visible demonstration and comparison. Unlike a formal T&V approach, there are no regular contacts to follow through the development of the crop at intervals through the season and Global 2000's approach is essentially a one-shot operation at the start of the season to ensure that the farmer has the inputs and knows what to do. The demand for supervision inputs is consequently small, although the management of the demonstration crop may not be perfect. The Global 2000 agronomists' involvement is limited to designing the technology package with the Regional Agricultural Extension Officer; training the extension staff; arranging credit and inputs; ensuring the extension staff are mobile; and monitoring and evaluating the demonstration. The rate of development has been spectacular to date. From 40 demonstrations in 1986, the number of participants rose to about 1 600 in 1987 and an anticipated 18 000 in 1988. This rate of progress, however, could not be maintained with Global 2000's own resources.

Subsequently, Global 2000 modified its approach to enable the programme to be expanded to a target of 85 000 participants in 1989 and 320 000 in 1990. Groups of farmers called Farmers' Associations are formed spontaneously under the catalysis of MOA extension staff identified with Global 2000. Farmers' Associations are provided with inputs for a communal field of about 10-12 ha (4-5 acres) as a demonstration area. Inputs are also supplied on credit for the individual members to apply on their own fields. The association members are jointly and severally liable. At the end of the season when the maize is sold the association is responsible for collecting the credit repayment from its members and handing it to local extension agents to pass on to District Agricultural Extension Officers.

Although the Global 2000 achievement in animating a technically effective extension programme is commendable, the programme contains several weaknesses:

> It concentrates solely on maize (and sorghum in the north) because that was the available technology which had been developed; it ignores other crops and the intercrop farm systems.

- It encourages production without considering the need to address storage and marketing.
- It encourages a top-down extension approach which is not in line with MOA's policy objective of a flexible, multi-crop, farming systems orientation.
- It is reinvolving MOA in input distribution and credit allocation and recovery, at a time when MOA's stated policy is for extension staff to withdraw from these roles.
- It is not likely to be sustainable within existing credit ceilings. Achievement of the participant targets may require MOA to become involved in providing the necessary credit.
- It appears to ignore the declining profitability of intensive maize production at a time of rapidly rising fertilizer prices.

Technoserve is a private, non-profit organization which provides management, technical assistance and training to rural communities in order to assist and develop viable community-based enterprises. It has been operating in Ghana since 1972. Technoserve's strategy is to focus on selected commodity sectors, regions, and delivery systems in order to establish successful and replicable models. Oil-palm processing has been selected as a principal commodity sector in which cooperatives using appropriate technology can invigorate regional markets for palm oil, raising farmgate prices and increasing employment and income opportunities. Technoserve has also cooperated with Global 2000 in identifying maize-producing communities that can be assisted to develop cooperative enterprises for input supply, credit and marketing.

NGO Methods. A number of other NGOs play significant roles in agricultural development although their objectives, rather than being specifically agricultural, are oriented to self-help and community development. Despite their apparent diversity, NGOs have, by virtue of their concern with poverty alleviation and the provision of social services, combined with their limited organizational resources, evolved a relatively uniform *modus operandi*. The three elements which are most characteristic of the NGO approach are a high degree of community participation in the identification of needs and subsequent project components; an emphasis on the organization of beneficiaries into groups to encourage focusing of benefits and their equitable distribution among the target population, and also to maximize beneficiary rather than NGO responsibility for implementation; and the use of financial devices, such as revolving funds, in an attempt to reduce dependence on external resources while promoting project sustainability.

NGO Liaison with Other Development Agencies. In Ghana there has been a growing interest in determining how NGO work may be combined with the resources and interests of other types of agencies, in particular bilateral and multilateral development organizations. The principal examples of such cooperation are provided by UNICEF and the European Economic Community-European Non-Governmental Organization (EEC-NGO) co-financing scheme. UNICEF works mainly with the apex church organizations and their affiliates in the fields of primary health care, water, sanitation, nutrition and mother-child health, for which they have a common concern. The EEC scheme represents indirect cooperation in that EEC funds are drawn upon by European donor NGOs who then channel them either to their own operational personnel in Ghana or to cooperating national Ghanaian NGOs under the terms of a detailed code of practice.

Some NGOs in Ghana are able to draw funds from the small project-funding schemes administered by various diplomatic missions, though in other instances funds are only available by application through local government bodies.

NGO Issues, Problems and Opportunities. NGOs working in Ghana present the same advantages and disadvantages as such organizations everywhere. Their great strength is that they are innovative, flexible, sensitive to local micro-conditions, highly committed, low-cost and poverty-oriented, with an exceptional record of reaching the very poor. Their weaknesses, which can admittedly vary greatly from organization to organization, are that they may be quite limited in the scope of their activities and the range of their geographical coverage; there is high variability in their technical, managerial and administrative competence; they sometimes suffer from limited, uneven or unsustainable finance; and their motivation and idealism may perhaps be complemented by their placing quite a fierce emphasis on their independence, which circumscribes the possibilities of cooperation. It is not surprising, therefore, to find the church organizations and their affiliates pre-eminent in Ghana. Not only are they trusted by other agencies and by their beneficiaries (an important consideration, given some experiences of NGOs in Ghana), but they also enjoy an exceptional degree of institutional development and stability. This is a result of the vertical integration of their field-level development activities, through their diocesan and national bodies, with the activities of major church-based, fund-raising bodies in Europe and the United States. The secular equivalent is for national

NGOs to establish a long-term relationship, if they can, with international donor NGOs in order to assure financial stability.

With respect to NGO cooperation with non-NGO agencies, the issues reviewed above have occasionally been intensified. In particular there are problems of compatibility with respect to independence, scale and timing. The NGOs are particularly sensitive to the fact that their freedom of action may be reduced through cooperation with agencies which have greater financial resources and government contact than themselves. Secondly, both the NGOs and the cooperating agencies have experienced problems of reconciling scale. On occasion the NGOs have experienced difficulty in adequately recruiting competent staff for expansion of their operations. On the other hand, considerations of administrative costs, disbursement levels and programme impact have obliged non-NGO agencies to reconsider their cooperative arrangements with NGOs because of the difficulty of focusing-down to NGO levels of operation. Thirdly, a significant problem with timing has been that the benefits of beneficiary organization, using NGO personnel and skills, have sometimes been inaccessible to non-NGO agencies because they are institutionally geared to fixed-time projects with implementation deadlines. Since grassroots institution building can be a lengthy process even when not subject to delays or false starts, cooperation has proved difficult in this regard also.

With respect to such considerations, it is again not surprising that the churches in Ghana have emerged as probably the most viable of NGO cooperators. They are institutionally strong enough not to have qualms about the potential erosion of their independence; they operate at a scale which is relatively compatible with the size of intervention of multilateral agencies; and, while timing may in some particular cases still be problematic, they have the advantage of their long historical presence, having already provided the basis of local-level organization to some degree.

Social Service Organizations

Rural people have no form of social security available to them other than the support of kin or possibly the services of an NGO or church organization present in their locality. The national scheme for providing relief to people in need, be it a matter of sickness, old age, disability or economic distress, applies almost exclusively to the government sector and urban private enterprises of the larger kind. The scheme does not embrace, therefore, the self-employed, the underemployed and unemployed members of the community, most of whom are in rural areas. The smallholder has no insurance against the many forms of natural and economic disaster which can befall him, such as crop loss through fire or drought, or shortfall in income due to price fluctuations.

The main government department charged with the provision of social security is the Department of Social Welfare, which is part of the Ministry of Local Government and Rural Development. The Department's resources are extremely limited. The social service organizations are almost all local churches. The day-care centres are exclusively urban. In addition there is some limited liaison with NGOs. In 1987, the Department requested a budget of ₵ 194 052 900, of which ₵ 130 223 000 was approved. Budgetary control measures, however, reduced the approved figure by about 20 percent. The Department's principal responsibilities include managing regional vocational centres for young men and women (these were formerly correctional centres, in effect probation homes for delinquents, but they now also cater for non-delinquents); giving instruction in agriculture, basic artisanal skills and "home-building"; liaising with the probation services and providing hospital welfare services (its outreach capacity must be extraordinarily limited since according to the Director it has only one vehicle).

The Department also has responsibility for orphanages, social education services (primary health care, nutrition, sanitation and child immunization), and adoption and rehabilitation centres for the disabled. There is a school for the deaf, one for the blind and a number of sheltered workshops where the disabled are trained. No provision of tools is made at the completion of training, and workhouses where the disabled could formerly do piece-work have been closed. Equipment to help the disabled is virtually non-existent because of high costs. In conclusion, it is evident that the formal provisions of welfare are minimal, urban-centered and of doubtful relevance to the rural poor.

Linkages Between Grassroots and Other Institutions

There has been an increasing tendency among governments, multilateral agencies and NGOs, to view grassroots institutions as an organizational means to "reach the poorest of the poor". The approach is, more often than not, based upon a misconception of the character and function of these organizations. For example, government agencies in Ghana in the late nineteen-seventies conceived the *nnoboa* system as a basis for multipurpose cooperative development. To the development planners, *nnoboa* appeared to be a plausible candidate. It was useful in farming as a mutual labour exchange and in social projects such as feeder road and health post construction. Moreover, it had the capacity to mobilize labour quickly. The experiment, however, was unsuccessful. The reason was that *nnoboa* cannot be defined as a cooperative or even a pre-cooperative system in any meaningful way. In addition to the characteristics identified by the planners, *nnoboa* is also voluntary; it has no written rules; it is essentially informal; and it is temporary. The conventional cooperative, on the other hand, entails a long-term commitment; is a formal organization; has a set of rules often written out in a members' handbook; involves financial management and transactions; and requires an institutional and bureaucratic apparatus to support it. The *nnoboa* example typifies the difficulty of using a "piggy-back" approach to local-level institutional development in support of project components. The low level of formality, the simplicity of their tasks, the short-term operation and the lack of institutional linkages, which tend to be characteristic of grassroots organizations, are precisely a function and indicator of their management capacity. On the whole, therefore, it would seem more appropriate to approach the issues of local-level institution-building on the basis of the criteria outlined earlier. These issues are generally confused if it is suggested to beneficiaries that project interventions merely require the modification of grassroots organizations with which they are already familiar. In practice, these "modifications" invariably require a sufficient degree of change in organizational complexity and in levels of managerial and administrative competence; identifying them as an extension of existing practices is likely to become a source of unnecessary confusion.

Of the grassroots organizations reviewed, the churches would appear to be the only ones with a solid local-level presence and an institutional support system outside the Government. *Nnoboa* and *susu* are very limited in scope. Cooperatives are likely to raise problems of rehabilitation and reorientation, although their potential should not be underestimated. Tenants' and growers' associations are very localized and their relevance depends upon project and beneficiary identification. Local-level institutions with links to government structures are at present in the process of reorganization and redefinition. It is necessary to wait and see what their roles will be. In part this may depend upon a pilot programme being undertaken in two Eastern Region districts by the Ministry of Local Government and

Rural Development and UNDP. Part 1 of the programme is concerned with the establishment of a local-level planning system and Part 2 with the implementation of integrated rural development programmes for "buttressing" local development. The scheme is being carried out in connection with the Government's decentralization policies.

In conclusion, it should perhaps be restated that the issue is not so much whether grassroots institutions can be used for development purposes, but rather that great caution needs to be taken when matching their existing organizational capacity with proposed project interventions. Grassroots organizations are often ideal, for example, for the dissemination of information and hence serve a useful extension purpose. If, however, some change in the range and level of their activities is envisaged by a proposed project, then care is needed to ensure that these changes are simple, are clearly understood by the organization's members, and have been accepted as practicable by them. In addition, they need to accept and be clear about any additional responsibilities which may arise as a result of the proposed changes. From the project side, clear identification and timely availability of any supplementary resources (financial, managerial or technical) is essential for the implementation of the changes. If these conditions are met, then grassroots organizations can provide a useful foundation for poverty-oriented development.

Chapter 10

Initial Impact of Structural Adjustment on Smallholders and the Rural Poor

The Government's ERP, which started in 1983 and is currently being continued as a Structural Adjustment Programme (SAP), has involved major policy changes in the areas of international trade, exchange rate, fiscal and monetary policy, public investment, pricing and public sector management, as outlined in Chapter 1. The smallholder sector has been influenced by the SAP in several ways that can condition future agricultural growth and the strategies designed to achieve it. It is, therefore, crucial for future rural interventions to gauge the impact of the SAP. This chapter is devoted to an assessment of these initial effects.

The Setting Before and After the SAP

Agriculture and the rural smallholder sector are influenced by the programme to the extent that the pre-reform policies had affected their economic performance. Table 10.1 shows the evolution of some general economic indicators in the periods 1970-83 and 1984-86, the long period before the onset of the adjustment programme and the first three years of the ERP. By any standards, the difference in overall performance is substantial. The GDP and all its components, which (with the exception of the Government) had been declining in the period 1970-83, exhibited remarkable growth rates in the period 1984-86. Agriculture and services GDP, as well as total GDP, in 1986 stood well above 1970 figures, although GDP in industry in 1986, despite its recent growth, still stood at only 73 percent of its 1970 level.

The recent performance of agriculture and a comparison with earlier trends are shown in Annex A, Table A.7. In Ghana, yield figures are notoriously inaccurate so that area planted (for which

161

Table 10.1: Selected Economic Indicators Before and After the ERP

Indicator	1970-83 Average annual growth rate	1983	1984	1985	1986	1984/83	1985/84	1986/85
							Percent change	
National Accounts (℃ million at 1975 constant prices)								
GDP at market prices	-1.0	4 747	5 158	5 420	5 705[1]	8.7	5.1	5.3
GDP in agriculture	-0.6	2 534	2 780	2 802	2 951[1]	9.7	0.8	5.3
GDP in industry	-5.1	550	599	707	752[1]	8.9	18.0	6.4
GDP in services	1.7	1 798	1 917	2 064	2 154[1]	6.6	7.7	4.4
of which:								
Wholesale retail trade	-2.5	463	510	557	591	10.2	9.2	6.1
Government and other	5.6	728	737	774	800	1.2	5.0	3.4
Gross fixed capital formation as % of GDP at market prices		-9.2	3.8	6.8	8.8			
External Trade (US$ million)								
Merchandise exports (f.o.b)	-0.8	439	566	632	773[1]	28.9	11.7	22.3
Merchandise imports (c.i.f.)	1.5	539	681	727	780[1]	26.3	6.8	7.3
Balance on goods and non-factor services		-165	-206	-204	-137[1]			
Balance on current account		-230	-215	-283	-193[1]			
Prices (annual percentage change)								
Consumer prices	53.7	122.8	39.6	10.4	24.6			
Consumer food prices	33.5	144.8	11.0	-11.1	20.3			
Wholesale prices	26.2	128.9	81.5	56.3	30.2			

[1] Provisional.

Source: World Bank 1987b and World Bank 1985c.

statistics are probably not as unreliable as for yields) is a better indicator of farmer intentions and response to economic phenomena. It can be clearly seen from the table that the joint shock of the drought and the large influx of repatriated migrants in 1983 led to a sharp increase in area planted in 1984 in both cereals and starchy crops, which undoubtedly had very little to do with the ERP. The equally sharp fall in area planted in 1985 was probably the result of both low cereal and starchy staple prices in 1984, as well as a tendency of the repatriated and other drought-induced rural migrants to move to the urban areas after the shock of 1983 had subsided. The 1986-89 years show a generally positive overall picture. However, total area planted to both cereals as well as starchy crops in 1989 still has not reached 1970 levels despite the fact that both the total population as well as the number of holdings have increased substantially since then. Given the substantial shocks to the economy, it is difficult to indicate which part of the recent overall macro-economic improvement is due to the ERP.

Smallholder Linkages with the Money Economy

Macro-policies or sectoral policies affect smallholder producers through their links with the money economy in the following ways:

- by sale of marketable surplus which is directly affected by the general as well as relative prices of farm produce;
- by purchase of agricultural inputs, the availability and prices of which influence smallholder incomes;
- by incomes and remittances generated through the sale of labour to rural or urban areas;
- by purchase of consumer goods, the prices of which affect the overall purchasing power; and
- by availability of social services which in turn determines overall welfare and real incomes.

Devaluation

Perhaps the most significant policy reform under the ERP has been the drastic devaluation. Table 10.2 indicates the evolution of the official and parallel exchange rates from 1975 to 1989. It is clear that the distortion, as expressed for instance by the ratio of parallel to official rates, grew to very large amounts by 1983. With the onset of the ERP, distortion has gradually diminished. Despite the fact that with the establishment of the foreign exchange auction a rate is determined by

Table 10.2: Official and Parallel Exchange Rates, 1975-89 (cedis/US dollars)

Year (Nov.)	Official market rate (1)	Parallel market rate (2)	Ratio (2)/(1)
1975	1.15	1.99	1.73
1976	1.15	2.91	2.53
1977	1.15	9.20	8.00
1978	1.51	8.96	5.93
1979	2.75	15.56	5.66
1980	2.75	15.87	5.77
1981	2.75	26.25	9.55
1982	2.75	61.67	22.43
1983	3.45	76.58	22.20
1984	33.34	135.00	4.04
1985	60.00	160.00	2.67
1986	90.00	180.00	2.00
1987	167.00	250.00	1.50
1988	228.00	300.00	1.32
1989 (Nov.)	285.00	350.00	1.23

Source: Sallinger 1986, and mission estimates.

market forces, restrictions concerning the products that can be imported with the foreign exchange available to the auction, as well as the requirement for advance deposits, imply that the foreign exchange market is still not completely free although it is slowly moving in that direction.

Agricultural Price Changes

Devaluation has had some impact upon incentives to cocoa producers. Table 10.3 indicates the nominal prices offered by COCOBOD to cocoa producers and compares them with the world prices at official and parallel market rates. At the official exchange rate, the dollar equivalent of prices received by the cocoa farmers presents a distorted picture as it does not reflect the real purchasing power generated by the sale of cocoa to the official marketing channels. However, the cocoa producers were paid in cedis and most of the imported goods that they would have liked to purchase were only available in the parallel markets. Hence the real comparison must be between the prices transformed at parallel market rates with the world prices. As

Table 10.3: Incentives for Cocoa Farmers, 1975-89

Year	Official cocoa price (cedis/mt)	Cocoa producer price in US$/mt		World cocoa price (US$/mt)	Cocoa producer price as % of world market price	
		at official rates	at parallel rates		at official rates	at parallel rates
1975	602	523.5	302.5	1 245.4	42.0	24.3
1976	758	659.1	260.5	2 045.2	32.2	12.7
1977	1 333	1 159.1	144.9	3 788.4	30.6	3.8
1978	2 743	1 816.6	306.1	3 402.4	53.4	9.0
1979	4 000	1 454.5	257.1	3 292.0	44.2	7.8
1980	4 000	1 454.5	252.0	2 602.8	55.9	9.7
1981	12 000	4 363.6	457.1	2 076.8	210.1	22.0
1982	12 000	4 363.6	194.6	1 737.0	251.1	11.2
1983	20 000	5 797.1	261.2	2 118.0	273.7	12.3
1984	30 000	899.8	222.2	2 396.2	37.6	9.3
1985	56 600	943.3	353.8	2 254.0	41.9	15.7
1986	85 000	944.0	472.2	1 760.0[1]	53.7	26.8
1987	85 000	523.8	340.0	1 550.0	33.7	21.9
1988	150 000	741.2	500.0	1 140.0	65.02	43.9
1989	165 000	578.9	471.4	890.0	65.0	53.0

[1] World Bank price forecast.

Source: Ministry of Agriculture and FAO Commodity Review and Outlook, various issues.

the last column of the table indicates, however, the cocoa producer for all the period 1975-85 received less than 25 percent of the world price and in many years even less than 10 percent. It is no wonder that widespread smuggling of cocoa is reported to have taken place during this period (May: 1985). With the reforms in the cocoa sub-sector and the progressive devaluation of the cedi introduced by the Government in 1983, the producer price of cocoa increased from ₵ 12 000 per mt in 1982 to ₵ 165 000 in 1989. These increases in producer prices, together with improvements in the internal marketing of COCOBOD, have reduced smuggling and, combined with improved weather conditions, have resulted in an increase in cocoa production from 154 000 mt in 1983-84 to 165 000 mt in 1984-85 and 205 000 mt in 1985-86. In 1987-88, the production was 228 000 mt.

At parallel market exchange rates, maize and rice prices in Ghana could be considered, apart from fluctuations and transport costs, not widely different from world prices during the crisis period. This is because in Ghana staple food prices have never been effectively controlled and is one reason that devaluation did not cause "food riots" which have happened in other countries implementing stabilization programmes. If devaluation had any effect on food prices it would be between the prices of traded and non-traded food products, and possibly on the real prices as well. Table 10.4 shows the real wholesale prices of all the staple food crops in Ghana (deflated by the rural CPI). It can be noticed that real food prices experienced a peak in the mid-nineteen-seventies, then slumped through the late nineteen-seventies and early nineteen-eighties, jumped sharply in the drought year of 1983 and then sharply dropped the following year. From 1984 to 1986 real food prices have generally stayed at levels below those of the early nineteen-seventies.

Real cocoa prices in turn, after a brief increase in the early nineteen-seventies, almost constantly declined through the rest of the nineteen-seventies and early nineteen-eighties. It was only in the two years 1985-86 that real cocoa prices started to regain ground, although the real 1986 price was still only 80 percent of the real cocoa price of the early nineteen-seventies.

Table 10.5 illustrates the ratios of price indices for traded and non-traded staple foods and all food crops, as well as their ratio to the price of cocoa.

The results indicate that the prices of all food goods, traded or non-traded, followed a pattern according to which from 1970 until 1983 they increased considerably compared to cocoa. Since 1983, however, the pattern has been clearly reversed and food prices have been losing

Table 10.4: Index of Real Wholesale Prices of Major Food Crops and Cocoa, 1970-86 (1970=100)[1]

Year	Maize	Rice	Guinea Corn	Millet	Cassava	Yam	Cocoyam	Groundnut	Beans	Plantain	Tomato	All Food	Cocoa
1970	100.00	100.00	100.00	100.00	100.00	100.00	100.00	100.00	100.00	100.00	100.00	100.00	100.00
1971	93.79	94.78	96.78	98.65	120.23	109.87	119.96	90.30	104.04	135.32	91.02	106.54	92.44
1972	123.89	117.56	101.04	102.50	129.62	108.40	119.16	91.42	107.90	112.14	108.84	108.63	105.20
1973	112.93	120.00	120.80	112.55	112.43	112.92	136.58	108.43	109.20	142.01	134.84	115.68	105.17
1974	104.55	112.15	109.20	110.64	112.94	123.03	134.03	116.12	147.81	122.80	111.35	119.60	114.20
1975	101.98	120.76	87.60	85.68	135.77	132.07	126.38	109.01	120.42	124.12	114.09	122.70	96.24
1976	147.14	156.56	140.02	135.04	182.78	120.86	152.28	130.51	121.60	159.63	112.96	130.80	76.64
1977	140.97	101.71	142.33	137.16	212.66	115.39	182.31	114.91	113.85	218.66	97.50	128.99	61.88
1978	82.34	79.09	89.12	91.42	113.45	108.57	125.53	108.66	82.44	195.71	71.87	106.92	72.89
1979	72.28	56.54	67.59	68.87	83.08	84.56	97.54	100.83	98.92	42.98	83.88	83.05	66.75
1980	109.49	74.18	122.55	95.08	110.46	78.55	93.13	91.10	107.38	118.88	73.60	87.82	41.43
1981	97.87	65.43	82.03	80.47	129.35	66.21	92.79	93.68	126.27	87.80	65.93	77.64	59.36
1982	80.50	99.05	91.94	93.68	119.02	75.43	106.16	122.03	117.97	99.46	72.07	87.09	48.45
1983	365.96	274.02	401.75	311.34	427.86	225.58	484.08	279.64	311.12	389.61	147.03	275.44	74.18
1984	76.00	102.37	104.96	104.45	82.86	86.65	120.47	92.68	103.11	148.23	73.58	91.28	38.13
1985	60.89	73.01	59.04	64.03	71.54	68.96	56.53	86.44	87.52	119.87	96.26	72.19	66.12
1986	81.02	77.09	69.73	71.68	104.47	75.13	93.93	85.56	95.21	122.50	71.24	79.89	81.79

1 For cocoa the real producer price is indicated.

Source: Computed.

Table 10.5: Price Indices for Traded and Non-traded Staple Foods and Cocoa, 1970-86 (Index 1970=100)[1]

Year	Ratio of traded foods price to the cocoa price (1)	Ratio of non-traded foods price to the cocoa price (2)	Ratio of all food prices to cocoa price (3)	Ratio of traded to non-traded food prices (4)
1970	100.0	100.0	100.0	100.0
1971	101.7	116.2	115.3	87.6
1972	116.3	102.4	103.3	113.6
1973	109.1	110.1	110.0	99.1
1974	93.2	105.5	104.6	88.3
1975	110.8	128.7	122.5	86.2
1976	195.1	169.0	170.7	115.4
1977	212.0	208.4	208.5	101.7
1978	111.9	149.3	146.7	74.9
1979	103.5	125.8	124.4	82.3
1980	243.0	209.8	211.9	115.8
1981	151.2	129.3	130.8	116.9
1982	175.7	180.0	179.1	97.7
1983	462.4	364.8	371.8	126.7
1984	216.6	241.1	239.4	89.9
1985	96.7	110.2	109.2	87.8
1986	97.9	97.7	97.7	100.1

[1] The indices were constructed as follows: First the value of production (quantity produced times the wholesale price) for 1979 and 1980 was computed and summed for the two years for each product. Weights were then derived using the 1979-80 total production values. For the traded food index, maize and rice were considered, while the non-traded index included guinea corn, millet, cassava, yam, cocoyam, groundnuts, beans, plantain and vegetables. Vegetables included the quantities of tomatoes, pepper, garden eggs and okra, which are the most commonly produced and consumed. However, the price for tomatoes, as representative of all vegetables, was applied.

Source: Computed by Mission.

ground relative to cocoa. In 1986, the terms of trade between food and cocoa were very close to those in 1970. A very interesting result, however, can be observed by examining the terms of trade between traded and non-traded food crops. As is apparent from the last column of Table 10.5, there does not appear to be any major trend in the relative prices of traded versus non-traded staple food goods. The 1983 drought seems to have put a premium on traded staple crop prices but this trend was quickly reversed the following years despite the devaluation. In 1986, the relative prices between traded and non-traded food crops stood at an almost identical value to those in 1970.

The SAP gives strong emphasis to increasing the production of cocoa, the major export crop in Ghana. However, given the age structure of cocoa trees, it is doubtful whether this can be achieved quickly over the short to medium term. This is because more than 40 percent of the existing cocoa land is under cocoa trees of over 30 years of age and therefore declining in yield; on average about 20 000 ha per annum are going out of production. If all the old trees were replaced today it would take seven years for the new trees to reach fruition and another eight years for them to reach full maturity. Moreover, cocoa trees under seven years of age would only reach full production over the medium to long term. Therefore, the prospect for cocoa sector revitalization is more limited than may appear in the first instance since it depends on just over 50 percent of the land with cocoa trees between eight and thirty years of age, and not the entire cocoa sector.

The price trends noted above could have different impacts on smallholders, depending on their production and consumption patterns. By a procedure which is outlined in detail in Annex B, the typical staple food production and consumption patterns of a representative smallholder household for each of the ten regions of Ghana for 1986 were calculated. The procedure excluded the production of tree crops like cocoa, oil-palm and coconut. As was shown earlier (Chapter 3), tree crops, which are grown mostly in the south, are cultivated by larger, better-off farmers and not by the bulk of smallholders. Using these patterns, we computed a figure representative of the gross food-crop income and staple food expenditure of smallholders for each region and year.

Several caveats are in order before one proceeds to use the gross crop income and food expenditure figures. First, the analysis is based on production patterns for 1986 and consumption patterns of 1974. Clearly changes could have occurred in both of these patterns over time. However, rural consumption patterns are less likely to have changed since rural incomes did not increase drastically and relative prices did not undergo great changes. Rural production patterns changed somewhat between 1970 and 1984 in favour of staple food crops as indicated in Annex B. However, the changes, especially in the Northern and Upper Regions, do not appear to be significant enough to influence the overall results. The gross income figures to be examined do not account for variations in production due to weather-induced yield variations. These yield variations can be significant. In particular in 1983 crop yields declined by about 50 percent. This would imply that the computed gross income by the method used here, which uses constant yields, would be a gross over-estimate of true income in such years. Finally, the gross income figures, as well as the gross expenditure figures, do not account for regional variations in prices. This, however, is not expected to bias the analysis because regional prices were shown earlier to be not consistently related.

Table 10.6 indicates the indices of real smallholder gross income in all regions from 1970 to 1986. It can be seen that the real gross typical smallholder incomes in all regions rose in the mid-nineteen-seventies, then declined until 1982. In 1983, a smallholder who did not experience the yield declines due to the drought would have obtained very high gross income in all regions. However, the yield declines would probably have reduced gross real incomes by about 40-50 percent. Even then, however, real incomes would have been higher, compared to the pre-drought situation.

In the three years 1984-86, when yields had not experienced the sharp reduction of 1983, a traditional smallholder in all regions obtained gross real income of the same level as in the immediate pre-drought years which, however, was in all regions lower than that of the early and mid-nineteen-seventies. The reason for this result was price changes, since it is assumed that the crop patterns underlying the figures in Table 10.6 were the same throughout the period 1970-86.

With regard to regional differentiation, Table 10.7 illustrates the gross crop income per hectare of a representative smallholder, indexed so that in each year the Ghana average crop income per hectare is equal to 100. The table is meant to examine whether the crop price changes since 1970 have been such as to favour the crop patterns of certain regions. The first result that can be noticed is that the crop income per hectare of cultivated area was vastly different among regions. In the Upper East, for instance, 1 ha of land cultivated by traditional methods and with the average crop pattern in 1986, yielded only 21 percent of the gross income that 1 ha of similarly cultivated land yielded in Brong-Ahafo. This implies that in order for a

Table 10.6: Index of Typical Smallholder Gross Food Crop Income by Region, 1970-86 (1970=100)[1]

Region	1970	1971	1972	1973	1974	1975	1976	1977	1978	1979	1980	1981	1982	1983	1984	1985	1986
Western	100.0	110.6	115.7	119.0	118.3	126.6	141.4	148.0	110.0	80.3	91.8	86.1	89.0	304.9	90.5	74.5	86.3
Central	100.0	107.9	119.3	120.7	113.8	121.9	149.5	158.9	104.2	78.7	98.1	96.0	93.6	329.8	87.2	77.1	89.5
Greater Accra	100.0	96.7	114.4	127.8	110.9	116.5	130.0	123.8	81.1	82.3	84.9	81.3	81.7	226.6	75.9	87.0	78.5
Eastern	100.0	112.7	116.8	117.1	118.7	127.4	145.3	155.7	114.2	79.9	95.0	89.6	91.2	327.5	92.1	71.8	88.4
Volta	100.0	106.3	113.4	118.4	117.3	125.9	132.3	130.9	100.0	82.6	85.8	79.4	82.9	256.9	83.5	75.5	80.3
Ashanti	100.0	111.3	114.7	120.7	119.1	126.0	140.1	149.3	113.8	79.7	92.3	84.8	88.8	305.8	93.6	76.6	87.2
Brong-Ahafo	100.0	107.3	112.1	118.0	118.6	126.4	131.1	130.0	104.1	82.3	85.3	77.3	82.8	258.4	86.5	75.0	80.4
Northern	100.0	104.3	108.5	114.0	118.9	121.6	128.6	123.3	101.7	84.0	87.7	78.2	85.8	264.4	87.5	71.8	78.2
Upper West	100.0	103.2	106.9	113.0	120.2	118.6	128.2	120.7	100.5	83.5	90.1	79.6	88.5	274.5	90.9	70.9	78.0
Upper East	100.0	97.2	100.9	111.2	123.9	105.2	130.3	123.1	93.8	89.0	101.5	100.1	110.2	313.5	99.3	78.2	83.8
Ghana	100.0	106.7	111.6	116.7	118.8	123.3	134.0	134.0	104.6	82.4	89.7	82.2	87.7	281.1	89.1	74.0	82.0

[1] The figures were derived by first multiplying the production figures of Table B.4 in Annex B by the per unit national wholesale prices of the goods from Table A.12 in Annex A and then deflating the total gross income by the rural CPI and setting 1970 = 100.

Source: Computed.

Table 10.7: Index of Gross Food Crop Income per Hectare of a Representative Smallholder by Region, 1970-86 (Ghana=100)[1]

Region	1970	1971	1972	1973	1974	1975	1976	1977	1978	1979	1980	1981	1982	1983	1984	1985	1986
Western	53.8	55.8	55.9	54.9	53.6	55.3	56.8	59.6	56.6	52.5	55.1	56.4	54.7	58.4	54.7	54.2	56.7
Central	52.6	53.2	56.3	54.4	50.4	52.0	58.7	62.4	52.4	50.2	57.6	61.4	56.2	61.7	51.5	54.8	57.4
Greater Accra	65.2	59.1	66.9	71.4	60.9	61.6	63.3	60.2	50.6	65.1	61.7	64.5	60.8	52.6	55.6	76.6	62.4
Eastern	109.4	115.6	114.6	109.7	109.4	113.1	118.7	127.1	119.5	106.1	115.9	119.3	113.9	127.5	113.1	106.1	117.9
Volta	116.0	115.5	117.9	117.7	114.6	118.4	114.5	113.3	110.9	116.3	110.9	112.0	109.7	106.1	108.8	118.3	113.6
Ashanti	93.0	97.0	95.6	96.2	93.3	95.0	97.2	103.6	101.2	90.0	95.7	95.9	94.2	101.2	97.8	96.2	98.9
Brong-Ahafo	134.6	135.3	135.3	136.1	134.5	138.1	131.7	130.5	133.9	134.5	128.1	126.5	127.2	123.7	130.7	136.3	132.0
Northern	80.2	78.4	78.0	78.4	80.3	79.2	77.0	73.8	78.0	81.9	78.5	76.3	78.5	75.5	78.8	77.8	76.5
Upper West	77.7	75.1	74.4	75.2	78.6	74.7	74.3	70.0	74.6	78.8	78.0	75.2	78.4	75.9	79.3	74.4	73.9
Upper East	27.3	24.8	24.7	25.9	28.4	23.3	26.5	25.0	24.4	29.4	30.8	33.2	34.3	30.4	30.4	28.8	27.8
Ghana	100.0	100.0	100.0	100.0	100.0	100.0	100.0	100.0	100.0	100.0	100.0	100.0	100.0	100.0	100.0	100.0	100.0

[1] Gross crop income is obtained by multiplying the typical smallholder production of the various staples by the per unit wholesale prices in each year. By multiplying the same wholesale prices by the typical smallholder consumption pattern, a figure representing the typical smallholder staple food expenditure by region and year is obtained.

Source: Computed.

smallholder in the Upper East to enjoy roughly a similar crop income to that of a smallholder in Brong-Ahafo, he must cultivate five times as much land. This supports the general fact (manifested in the average size of holdings by region - see Table 3.5) that the size of holdings is larger in the northern regions of Ghana. It also supports the poverty analysis of Chapter 3 where it was shown that regions such as the Upper East have large numbers of poor smallholders. This is because, despite the fact that a holder needs five times as much land to obtain the same crop income as in Brong-Ahafo, the average smallholder size of holding is almost the same (see Table 3.2, Chapter 3). The crop pattern seems to be most advantageous in the Eastern, Volta, Ashanti and Brong-Ahafo Regions since one hectare of land there produces a crop income much higher than average. By comparison traditional producers in the Western and Central Regions must cultivate about twice as much land, and smallholders in the Northern and Upper West about 40 percent more in order to have an income comparable to that of the more favoured regions. If the regional income differential over time is examined, it appears that relative crop price changes have not tended to favour the crop pattern of one region versus another, and no major changes appear after 1983.

Input Costs

The ERP series of exchange rate alignments and subsidy removal have had a significant impact on input prices. Prices paid by farmers for compound fertilizer increased from ₵ 58/bag in 1983 to ₵ 3 600/bag in 1989. Sulphate of ammonia increased from ₵ 45/bag in 1983 to ₵ 2 350/bag in 1989. The price of other inputs mostly used by traditional farmers increased as illustrated in Table 10.8.

Purchased inputs for traditional technologies are mostly seed and hand tools, while for the more advanced technologies they include fertilizer, tractor or bullock-ploughing services, chemicals, etc. For all crops and technologies, the input price costs in the period 1981-87 increased by much more than the rural Consumer Price Index (CPI) (Table 10.9). For instance, the input costs for the traditional maize production technology increased by a factor of almost 19 from 1981 to 1987, while the rural CPI increased by a factor of 7. The increase has been particularly sharp between 1983 and 1987, especially for the improved and advanced techniques.

Table 10.8: Input Costs, 1983, 1987, 1989 (cedis)

Input	1983	1987	1989
Hoes	50	245	550
Cutlass	80	360	550
Sickle	60	160	200
Sacks	55	240	300
Seed (kg)	12	110	173

Source: Ministry of Agriculture.

Impact on Labour Markets

The ERP has also had a significant impact on both agricultural and non-agricultural labour markets. Given excessive civil service employment growth in the pre-ERP phase (14 percent annual average over 1975-82), the Government committed itself to retrenching the public service up to 5 percent annually (about 15 000 employees) during 1986-88. Most of the initial lay-offs in 1986 consisted of "ghost workers" and only a few dismissals. In 1987, the target of retrenchment was met mostly by the dismissal of identified excess staff. This was accompanied by raising civil servants' salaries and in particular those of higher-level staff. These changes are probably not too large to affect seriously rural labour markets, since only a fraction of the retrenched civil employees returned to the rural areas and then mostly to farm for themselves.

While real wages for both agriculture and non-agricultural employees declined substantially from 1970 to 1983, they have recovered somewhat in recent years (Table 10.10). A sharp increase in the real value of the GDP deflator for wholesale and retail trade in 1980-85 implies that rewards for trading activities were quite substantial. It appears from Table 10.10 that real rural wages for hired labour have gone from a peak in 1981 to a trough in 1984 (which is understandable given the massive repatriation in 1983), and then to have gradually risen. This development is consistent with the increased demand for rural labour by the cocoa sector, but it implies that smallholders using traditional technology and relying on hired labour for some farm operations are squeezed on that aspect of production cost.

Small farmers might be induced by this labour cost increase to substitute more family labour for hired labour if there is excess family labour. To obtain an idea of the potential impact on smallholders and other farmers of these developments, Table 10.11 indicates the returns

Table 10.9: Cost of Purchased Inputs for Staple Food Production, 1981-87 (cedis/ha)

Product	Maize			Rice		Forest	Sorghum/Combined Millet	Yam	Cassava (Sole Cropping)		Rural CPI
Region	All Ghana			Northern Region			Northern	Northern and Transitional	Transitional-Savannah		
Technology	Traditional	Improved	Advanced	Traditional	Improved	Valley Bottom	Traditional	Transitional	Traditional	Improved	
Year											
1981	118	833	1 289	379	1 333	463	109	1 642	92	261	100.0
1982	283	1 172	1 678	1 798	3 207	1 993	300	7 767	122	375	122.5
1983	420	1 584	2 090	1 798	3 207	1 993	350	7 768	157	975	281.3
1984	668	2 786	4 585	2 863	6 129	3 276	563	15 414	294	1 933	389.2
1985	1 145	4 531	7 897	3 800	13 240	4 945	670	19 267	440	3 700	423.4
1986	1 070	5 666	9 652	3 820	13 240	4 955	875	23 100	450	5 300	514.0
1987	2 193	9 503	17 133	4 043	13 523	5 208	1 073	23 378	703	7 503	694.0[1]

[1] Preliminary.

Source: Estimated Crop Budgets 1981-87.

Table 10.10: Trends in Nominal and Real Wages, 1970-87

Year	Minimum wage (₵/day) (1)	Average earnings of agricultural employees (₵/month) (2)	Average earnings of manufacturing employees (₵/month) (3)	National account deflator [1] (1975=100) (4)	Consumer Price Indices (1970=100)			Indices of Real Earnings (1970=100)				Wage for hired agricultural labour (₵/day) (12)	Real wages of (12) (1980=100) (12)/(5) (13)
					Rural (5)	Urban (6)	National (7)	Minimum (1)/(6) (8)	Agricultural (2)/(5) (9)	Manufacturing (3)/(6) (10)	Trade (4)/(7) (11)		
1970	.75	33.0	48.0	42	100.0	100.0	100.0	100.0	100.0	100.0	100.0	-	-
1971	.75	39.8	75.9	46	108.9	110.3	109.3	90.7	110.7	143.3	100.2	-	-
1972	1.00	39.8	84.6	51	118.9	123.0	120.3	108.4	101.4	143.3	100.9	-	-
1973	1.00	43.5	70.2	60	139.6	147.3	141.4	90.5	94.4	99.3	101.0	-	-
1974	2.00	59.6	104.0	76	164.3	177.7	167.4	150.1	109.9	121.9	108.1	-	-
1975	2.00	66.7	118.0	100	209.2	244.2	217.0	109.2	96.6	100.7	109.7	-	-
1976	2.00	71.5	125.0	144	330.8	368.1	339.3	72.4	65.5	70.7	101.1	-	-
1977	3.00	155.0	223.0	231	720.5	777.6	733.7	51.4	65.2	59.7	69.1	-	-
1978	4.00	172.0	306.0	474	1 258.6	1 333.6	1 270.0	40.0	41.4	47.8	88.8	-	-
1979	4.00	186.0	356.0	656	2 004.3	1 994.6	1 961.1	26.7	28.1	37.2	79.6	-	-
1980	5.33	329.0	552.0	1 318	3 229.1	2 822.7	2 943.5	25.2	30.9	40.7	106.6	-	-
1981	12.00	503.0	689.0	3 497	6 761.5	6 224.0	6 373.4	25.7	22.5	23.1	130.6	30	100.0
1982	12.00	559.0	787.0	4 695	8 283.1	7 601.9	7 794.6	21.0	20.5	21.6	143.4	60	163.3
1983	21.75	886.0	1 312.0	9 311	19 017.3	16 349.9	17 369.0	17.7	14.1	16.7	144.1	90	106.7
1984	32.50	2 322.0	2 812.0	15 006	26 314.1	23 014.8	24 242.1	18.8	26.7	25.5	148.8	100	85.7
1985	70.00	2 825.0	5 234.0	19 038	28 628.2	25 888.0	26 758.6	36.5	29.9	42.1	169.4	120	94.5
1986	90.00	-	-	-	34 757.2	33 142.3	33 331.6	36.2	-	-	-	150	97.3
1987	-	-	-	-	-	-	-	-	-	-	-	250	120.1 [2]

1 For wholesale and retail trade.

2 Assuming 35% rural inflation rate in 1987.

Sources: ILO 1985; World Bank 1987b; Republic of Ghana 1987f; Column (12) is from crop budget estimated by the Mission.

Table 10.11: Returns per Man-Day of Family Labour in Various Crops, 1981-87 (cedis/day)

Product Region Technology	Maize All Ghana			Rice Northern			Cassava Transitional Savannah		Agric. wage for hired labour
	Traditional	Improved	Advanced	Traditional	Improved	Forest Valley Bottom	Traditional	Improved	
Year									
1981	35.1	65.5	89.9	130.3	199.9	176.0	144.5	275.8	30
1982	-0.5	47.2	75.5	195.6	328.1	271.5	135.0	291.0	60
1983	325.9	493.0	648.3	310.1	517.2	425.6	565.0	1 043.8	90
1984	139.7	253.3	340.7	680.5	1 026.1	922.6	292.3	585.2	100
1985	59.3	157.1	216.9	417.3	588.1	564.5	240.7	501.3	120
1986	138.4	271.4	368.1	297.2	449.8	406.2	257.3	541.6	150
1987	130.5	331.5	451.0	290.0	537.9	402.3	214.2	554.7	250

Source: Mission estimates of crop budgets, 1981-87.

per man-day of family labour over 1981-87. The table is derived from crop budgets where the yields and technology are assumed not to vary over time. The results indicate that in many years, if yields are normal, the returns per man-day of family labour are larger than the rural wage. The realized returns, however, are bound to be smaller for most farmers since yield reductions due to weather can be substantial, and forced sales in the early harvest months reduce total returns. For instance, if it is assumed that maize yields were reduced by 60 percent in 1983 (the year of the severe drought), the per-day returns to family labour from maize production drop to ₵ 56.4, 146.5 and 210.6/day for the traditional, improved and advanced technologies, respectively. For rice a yield reduction of 50 percent in 1983 results in ₵ 79.4, 194.7 and 117.9/day for the three technologies indicated in the table.

Nevertheless, the results in Table 10.11 uniformly indicate that from 1984 to 1987 the *nominal* returns per man-day of family labour in all traditional technologies and all three products (maize, rice, cassava) declined. This was due to an increase in the cost of purchased inputs. In real terms, of course, the decline was much larger. The decline did not appear as pronounced in the non-traditional technologies and in some cases (e.g., maize) there was an increase. Given the concurrent increases of hired labour wages, the incentive appears to be strong to substitute family for hired labour, especially among growers using traditional technologies. The sharp decline in real returns to agricultural family labour, however, might also induce more people to migrate. This development could particularly impinge severely on female-headed rural households which do not have any spare family labour supply and must still rely on hired labour. The overall trend could further aggravate the process of marginalization, particularly among the lower strata of the smallholder community.

Consumer Goods

The devaluation of the cedi in the last few years has had two major effects on rural consumer goods. On the one hand, there seems to be an increased availability of consumer items in rural areas. Before the ERP, many consumer items and especially light consumer non-durables, were imported in the parallel markets. Since 1984, imports of consumer goods have been allowed officially under so-called Special Unnumbered Licenses. Under this scheme the foreign exchange is provided by the importer and no questions are asked as to its source. The foreign exchange available most probably comes from unofficial private remittances from abroad. In 1984, US$ 71.8 million of imports entered under this scheme. In 1985, the figure was US$ 51.7 million and in 1986 US$ 78.3 million (figures provided by the Bank of Ghana).

The second major effect of the devaluation and the ERP in general is on the prices of consumer items in the rural areas. Table 10.12 presents the indices for the various components of the rural CPI from 1978 to 1987. In the last column, the ratio of the rural food price index to the rural non-food price index has been computed. Since food production provides the main source of income for most of the rural smallholders, one could interpret this ratio as a proxy for the price terms of trade for rural food producers. It is evident from this ratio that the rural food terms of trade, which had improved substantially from 1978 to 1983, have constantly and dramatically declined since 1984. Currently the ratio of rural food to non-food prices stands at only 70 percent of its 1978 value. This development, mainly due to sharp increases in the prices of beverages, tobacco, clothing, footwear, fuel, power, furniture, and furnishings (which are mostly imported), can be largely attributed to the ERP.

Impact of Fiscal Restraint on Agriculture

The ERP has had a disproportionately harsh effect on public expenditure for agriculture. Table 10.13 illustrates actual public expenditure for agriculture from 1981 to 1985 and budgeted expenditure for 1986 and 1987. It is patently clear from the table that since 1983 expenditure on agriculture has suffered immensely. The share of agricultural expenditure in total public expenditures has declined from 10.4 percent in 1983 to a realized 4.2 percent in 1985, and a budgeted 3.5 percent in 1987. As a proportion of GDP, public expenditure on agriculture was trivial compared to the importance of the sector. Before 1983 it was about 1.1 percent, it declined to 0.5 percent in 1985 and is budgeted at 0.6 percent in 1987.

In terms of real purchasing values, total expenditure on agriculture declined from an index of 100 in 1981 to a low of 35.8 in 1984, 47.7 in 1985, and was not budgeted to go above 56.5 in 1987. It must be mentioned that, traditionally, the actual figures spent are lower than the budgeted figures. The index of real value of development expenditures on agriculture (mainly capital investment outlays) dropped from 100 in 1981 to 60.7 in 1984 before recovering to 95.1 in 1985. In 1986 the budgeted index stood at 136.9. While this is well above that of 1981, in 1987 it dropped in real terms to 83.7. Of the

Table 10.12: Rural Consumer Price Indices, 1978-87 (1977=100)

Weight	Combined 100.0	Food 49.8	Total non-food 50.2	Ratio of food to non-food indices (1978 = 100)
1978	174.7	155.0	194.6	100.0
1979	278.2	266.8	289.7	115.6
1980	448.2	442.7	453.7	122.5
1981	938.5	903.3	974.0	116.4
1982	1 149.7	1 212.8	1 086.1	140.2
1983	2 639.6	2 863.2	2 414.2	148.9
1984	3 652.4	3 178.4	4 130.2	96.6
1985	3 973.6	2 939.4	5 016.1	73.6
1986	4 824.3	3 537.4	6 121.5	72.6
1987[1]	6 040.8	4 359.9	7 735.2	70.8

[1] Average of first four months.
Source: Republic of Ghana 1987f.

₵ 983.8 million budgeted for development expenditures in 1987, ₵ 553.8 million or 56.3 percent was for construction work, and ₵ 156.4 million or 15.9 percent for plant, equipment, furniture and vehicles.

Table 10.14 shows the breakdown of the MOA recurrent expenditure budgets for 1987, 1988 and 1989. Of note are the extremely low shares spent on items 2 and 4: travel and transport, and maintenance and repairs. These small proportions, combined with the overall decline in real terms of the recurrent budget expenditures, imply that MOA cannot really perform its functions effectively. Also of note are the large shares in the total recurrent budget of MOA absorbed by the two large development projects, Upper Region Agricultural Development Project (URADEP) and Volta Region Agricultural Development Project (VORADEP) (included under subventions). These together absorbed 33.5 percent in 1987, and 31.3 percent in 1988. They declined to 14.4 percent in 1989. Given the high burden of recurrent expenditures that is imposed on MOA, it is no wonder that project performance was not as expected. The implications are that in order to enjoy sustained success, any future projects should minimize to the extent possible the recurrent cost implications for MOA.

Table 10.13: Public Expenditure on Agriculture, 1981-87 (₡ million, except where noted)[1]

Expenditures	1981	1982	1983	1984	1985	1986	1987
Agriculture total	969.4	962.5	1 536.6	1 320.6	1 940.0	3 354.0	3 870.1
Agriculture recurrent	803.0	827.6	1 389.3	936.3	1 276.0	2 163.0	2 886.3
Agriculture development	166.4	134.9	147.3	384.3	664.2	1 191.0	983.8
Agriculture expenditures as % of total public expenditure	11.0	9.8	10.4	4.9	4.2	4.6[2]	3.5[2]
Agriculture expenditures as % of GDP at market prices	1.3	1.1	0.8	0.5	0.5	0.7[2]	0.6[2]
Real value of total expenditures in agriculture (1981=100)[3]	100.0	81.2	58.2	35.8	47.7	66.2	56.5
Real value of development expenditures in agriculture (1981=100)[3]	100.0	66.3	32.5	60.7	95.1	136.9	83.7

[1] For 1981-85, figures are realized expenditures, for 1986-87 they are budgeted figures.

[2] Projected total expenditures from the World Bank 1987b were used to compute percent.

[3] Deflated by the national CPI.

Source: Republic of Ghana 1987f and Ministry of Finance.

Table 10.14: Components of the Recurrent Expenditure Budget of the Ministry of Agriculture

Item	Description	1987 (¢ million)	% of total	1988 (¢ million)	% of total	Change 1988/87 (%)	1989 (¢ million)	% of total	Change 1989/88 (%)
1	Personal emoluments	5 687	37.8	5 388	50.2	-5.2	5 823	37.4	8.1
2	Travel and transport	746	4.9	558	5.1	-25.2	1 371	8.8	145.6
3	General expenditures	277	1.8	232	2.6	-16.4	1 742	11.2	652.6
4	Maintenance & repairs	555	3.7	518	4.8	-6.7	264	1.6	-48.9
5	Supplies and stores	2 543	16.9	671	6.3	-73.6	2 244	144.0	234.5
6	Subventions	5 202	33.5	3 364	31.3	-35.3	4 115	144.0	22.3
Total (1-6)	All items	15 009	100.0	10 731	100.0	-23.0	15 559	100.0	184.0
Total (2-5)	Non-wage expenditure	4 121	27.5	1 979	18.4	-52.0	5 622	36.1	145.0

Source: Ministry of Finance and Economic Planning and Ministry of Agriculture's estimates, 1989.

Administrative and Institutional Reform and Farmer Services

Within the Ghanaian context it is difficult to assess whether structural adjustment has had a serious impact on institutions, particularly since such changes take time to implement and the budgets, though realigned in favour of supportive expenditure, still do not reach levels at which routine administration can proceed smoothly. There has been some readjustment of salaries but they are still not sufficient to sustain a moderate standard of living. The average civil servant still retains two to three ancillary occupations to make ends meet and cannot commit himself full-time to his job.

A number of implemented measures which, in the future, could prove beneficial include:

- *Reduction of staff:* Savings from salaries and wages of retrenched staff could be diverted towards increases in salaries or other administrative expenditures. The exact figures are not available but the total civil service strength is estimated at 300 000 and the Government has committed itself to reductions at the rate of 5 percent per annum between 1986 and 1988. Institutional reform is being implemented, albeit slowly; 11 000 staff were retrenched in 1986. The corresponding figure for 1987 was expected to be 15 000.
- *Salary increase and wage policy:* Some of these savings in salaries (¢ 1 billion) are being redirected towards salary increases, particularly to readjust them in favour of the higher-grade echelons. Such a step was needed. Although between 1984 and 1987 salary increases had been granted, in real terms the salary of a Principal Secretary in 1986 stood at 10 percent of the 1977 salary, and that of a messenger stood at half. The gap between the highest and the lowest grades stood at only 2.3:1 in 1985 and staff morale was low. Although with the increases the gap has widened to 5.7:1, staff are still not motivated because in a lay-off environment staff tend to be demoralized and because salaries in terms of real purchasing power still continue to be unattractive.
- *Realignment of the budget:* Between 1975 and 1982 the average real expenditure per civil service employee declined by about 85 percent. Although the Government has made efforts to improve this situation, owing to shortfalls in revenues in 1986 the real expenditure per civil service employee has remained at

10 percent of the 1975 level. The impact of this decline is visible in most offices (lack of paper, machines, transport, delay in payment of allowances, etc.). While measures are being taken to realign the budgets, the limited funds have to be directed towards readjusting salaries and related administrative budgets. The elimination of these disequilibria will take time to implement.

Private Sector Input Supply

The private sector is involved in manufacturing inputs (cutlasses, hoes, some agricultural processing machinery), and importing and distributing inputs to various points. Non-fertilizer inputs include over 30 items and cover agrochemicals, animal vaccines, Wellington boots, spare parts, farm tools and implements, fishing gear, nets, etc. Over 30 companies are involved in their distribution. Because of changes in the system of foreign exchange allocation, the private sector involvement in input distribution has varied.

Prior to the SAP, the private sector's participation in input supply was low. During this period the private sector competed for limited foreign exchange and there were wide margins for profit since foreign exchange was released at the official rate. In 1983, the rate was ₵ 2.75 = US$ 1, while the parallel market rate was ₵ 60 = US$ 1. The private sector's priorities were directed to commodities with high demand and most of the funds were used to finance non-priority imports. The parastatal sector was left to undertake distribution of agricultural inputs, used mostly in rural areas where distribution costs are high and the items move comparatively slowly.

Under Reconstruction Import Credits (RIC) I and II, imports of priority items, including agricultural inputs, were financed by officially released foreign exchange. MOA prepared the lists of items to be imported. They were procured by Crown Agents, the appointed procurement agency, and sold to private dealers. While under this procedure the demand was met, the private sector essentially became the distributor and importer of items whose quantity and quality were determined by civil servants. Some losses were registered.

Under the present arrangements, there is open licensing, and importers bid for foreign exchange under an auction system. Since the present licensing arrangement was introduced, some of the earlier deficiencies have been overcome, but only 5-6 percent of the allocations have been directed by the private sector towards agricultural imports. Some of these reflect the requirements of the tobacco and poultry industries. The import and distribution requirements of the food crop subsector have not been met for three reasons. First, there was some overstocking during the RIC programmes. Second, under the present procedure the private sector is required to put up the cedi equivalent of the purchased foreign exchange in advance. As there is usually a three- to four-month time lapse for imports and the interest rates are high (with all charges a borrower pays up to 30 percent), traders are not anxious to deal with items that are slow moving. And, third, there is a liquidity squeeze in rural areas because of rising prices, dampening demand for inputs.

Fertilizer Subsidies and Privatization

The issues of fertilizer subsidies and privatization of fertilizers are closely related. As long as there are subsidies, the private sector, aware of the Government's financial condition, will be reluctant to get involved in the fertilizer trade. As a first step towards privatization, the Government agreed to eliminate the subsidies by 1990. In the interim, fertilizer distribution remained ineffective. The problem still needs to be resolved and alternative solutions may have to be considered to address the issue.

Clearly, in this atmosphere, the current exercise to involve the private sector in distribution in rural areas does not appear to be strong. Most surprisingly, given such limited interest, some banks, ADB and GCB in particular, have attempted to fill the gap by arranging to procure and distribute inputs to meet the farmers' needs. Thus, while privatization of input distribution is a major policy objective under SAL/SAP, the prospects for complete privatization by the end of 1991, as envisaged, are remote, although MOA is moving according to the agreed implementation programme.

Prospects for Privatization of Fertilizer. If distribution of other agricultural inputs appears difficult to the private sector, fertilizer would appear even less attractive for the following reasons:

> Fertilizers are expensive and under the present licensing and foreign exchange arrangements would cost ₵118 million in interest charges. On the assumption of imports of 30 000 mt at US$ 150/mt, and with an exchange rate of ₵ 175 = US$ 1, the cost would be ₵ 787.5 million. On the assumption of six months' selling time, interest charges on the advance deposits would be ₵ 118 million.

- Fertilizers are bulky, require storage and a network of trained dealers to handle them.
- There is a risk element, as fertilizers have peak demand periods and any unsold stock is carried over for at least six months at high interest charges.
- It may take ₵ 1-2 billion for any company to develop the trade; from the traders' point of view, a decision to get into fertilizers would depend on opportunities in other sectors.

While privatization is a desirable objective, it could take a long time to fill the present gap. In the interim, farmers, small farmers in particular, continue to suffer. Farmers' Services Companies, or their equivalent, provided they are properly structured, could be the solution to meeting the input requirements of the small farmers.

Land Tenure

With respect to land tenure, the element of the SAP which is of immediate interest and concern is its remarkable emphasis on the revitalization of the cocoa industry. It seems most likely that this exceptional emphasis on a particular export cash crop will, with renewed vigour, precipitate the issues and aggravate the tensions of land pressure, land acquisition costs, socio-economic differentiation, and smallholder marginalization, which were associated with the original development of cocoa as an economic force in rural Ghana.

Interest Rates and Credit Demand

Structural adjustment, with its focus on positive and real interest rates, has given priority to resource mobilization. The impact of high interest rates on demand for medium- to long-term credit, so necessary for investment, does not seem to have been addressed. At present, with lending rates at 26 to 30 percent, few businesses can afford to borrow as financial costs are excessive. They must either put up greater equity capital or forego the investment. Consequently, resources are being mobilized at tremendous cost with few avenues for their investment. This contradiction is apparent in the banking system today. Despite the fact that their assets have declined by over 50 percent, as indeed have people's savings by the same amount, the banks remain liquid. Future SAPs will have to strike a more careful balance between resource mobilization and its utilization.

Social Services and the SAP

In view of the long period of economic decline preceding the introduction of the SAP, it is difficult to attribute current problems of poverty to the SAP. The problem is compounded by the breakdown of systematic socio-economic data collection.

Despite the lack of precise and reliable data to provide a quantitative analysis, the deleterious effect of the SAP on the social service provision, at least in the short term, is not in much doubt. The World Bank, with respect to health and education, has this to say (World Bank 1987b):

> Investments in health account for 3 percent of the total (public investment) programme. ... Resource and management constraints so far have prevented much progress towards reaching the target of providing (primary health care) to 80 percent of the population by 1990.

> The effects of cutbacks in other goods and services in health have severely constrained support to primary health care at the community level by restricting deliveries of essential supplies, mobile health units, and field supervision.

> In the area of cost recovery, the increase of hospital fees in 1985 has mobilized resources which are currently shared by the general budget (50 percent), the Ministry of Health (25 percent), and the hospitals (25 percent). Further increases are needed because fees are still below marginal costs, with a view to shifting the cost of curative health care to the user.

With respect to education, the World Bank states:

> The proportion of the education budget allocated to non-salary recurrent items has fallen from 19 percent in 1975 to 15 percent in 1984 and to only an estimated 6 percent in 1986, within a declining total.

> ... the boarding and meal subsidies for secondary schools are to be phased out ... This process (of lowering the share of salaries in recurrent expenditure) will be assisted by expanded cost recovery for building fees, exercise books and text books...

The current PNDC Government has recognized the need for urgent action on education and the budget has been increased. In addition, funds have been raised from various international development agency sources. About 40 percent of the budget is allocated to the rehabilitation of existing facilities, which have priority over new construction. The education component of the IDA-financed Health and Education Rehabilitation Programme was negotiated in December 1985, as part of the ERP. It is concerned primarily with the printing and distribution of text books, the provision of stationery and the improvement of educational management.

In addition to rehabilitation, the Government began to implement a major reform in the education sector in September 1987. The major structural element in the reforms is the reduction of the old statutory length of pre-university schooling from 12 to 7 years. In broad terms, the Government's policy is to increase greatly the proportion of children schooled up to the end of junior secondary level and to re-orient the curriculum away from "academic" specialization toward a content and method more "comprehensive" in style. This range of the educational system is now termed the Basic Education Programme (BEP). The Government argues that the new system will make limited resources more widely available and that educational content in the BEP will be more relevant. The Ministry of Education has estimated that the old system, in terms of the relevant age groups, catered to only 60 percent at primary, 28 percent at middle and a mere 7 percent at secondary levels. Under the new system, the intention is that all who enter primary level will proceed to junior secondary level: of these, 50 percent will go on to senior secondary level, of which 25 percent will proceed to tertiary education.

The reforms are now known as the Education Sector Adjustment Programme and come within the ERP (Phase II). Partial funding for them emerged from a Special Aid Consultative Group meeting, which was convened in September 1986.

The educational reforms excited a certain amount of opposition, although there was nothing especially new about them. Curricula in the Gold Coast and then Ghana have been repeatedly criticized as too academic, at least since 1950, and the structural changes are largely derived from proposals submitted by the Ministry of Education in 1972. The two main criticisms, standard with respect to educational reforms anywhere, are that educational standards will be lowered and that the 50 percent of pupils who end their education with graduation from junior secondary will be inadequately prepared for the insufficient number of jobs available to them. Whatever the validity of these general reactions, there are more specific reservations which are relevant to pupils drawn from rural areas. At present over 80 percent of secondary schools have boarding facilities, partly because their urban location prevents day attendance by rural pupils. Nevertheless, it is government policy, first, to reduce boarding facilities; second, where such facilities are retained, to phase out boarding and feeding subsidies; and third, to increase book cost at secondary and university levels. In theory, pupil/student access to essential textbooks will be enhanced and sustained by the establishment of revolving funds to help cover costs. Finally, the understandable concern of the Government with the formal sector has arguably led to insufficient consideration and commitment to non-formal education; i.e., dealing with the issue of illiteracy through mass campaigns, etc. On all four grounds, therefore, there is a *prima facie* case for anticipating that the rural poor in particular may be disadvantaged by current policies unless specific counter-measures are taken.

It should be recalled that these social service policies are being implemented in a country where 67 percent of rural smallholders are below the absolute poverty line. The negative impact of the SAP on the social sector has already been recognized by the Programme of Action to Mitigate the Social Costs of Adjustment (PAMSCAD). The PAMSCAD, arising from a multi-agency mission led by the World Bank and comprising IFAD, ILO, UNDP, UNICEF, World Food Programme (WFP), WHO and the United Kingdom's Overseas Development Administration, focusses on the SAP's social impact. There is a clear indication of these agencies' acceptance of the need perceived by the Government for supplementary programming in the social sectors. The interventions cover issues related to employment, agriculture and the small farmer by improving rural infrastructure, health provision and functional literacy; education; health; population and nutrition; shelter; and financial policies.

More particularly, in the employment sector, the package specifies placement and training of both retrenched and otherwise unemployed workers; in the public works sector of physical infrastructure, public housing and feeder roads; in the health and nutrition sector, the procurement and distribution of essential drugs and the expansion of supplementary feeding schemes; and in the education sector, rehabilitation of schools, teacher training, mass functional literacy, the establishment of a revolving fund for the bulk purchase of food for secondary schools, and income-generating activities for university students.

In conclusion, it should be stated that the documents on the SAP which are currently available are notably vague in their assessment of the medium- to long-term impact of the SAP on the quality of life of the rural poor in general and that of the smallholders in particular. The strong emphasis placed by the SAP on cost recovery and privatization is bound to increase the small rural producers' need for cash. Within current constraints this need can only be met through greater indebtedness to the informal credit system. It seems reasonable therefore to expect a marked intensification of dependency and marginalization. There are no reasons for supposing that the short-term, supplementary package supplied by the PAMSCAD for the social sector will not have to be renewed. This calls for addressing what are perceived as short-term problems in a long-term development perspective, one through which smallholders and the rural poor are assisted to realize their production potential.

Block Farming

MOA has identified the block farming concept as a possible means of first absorbing retrenched civil employees and also introducing new farm technologies to small-scale farmers operating on large, contiguous blocks of land. Under the scheme, a block of land is bulldozed clear of trees, ploughed, harrowed and then divided into farming units and allocated to small farmers for cultivation of particular crops. The concept is that modern and improved farming inputs such as seed, fertilizer and chemicals are procured in bulk and distributed to farmers, and agronomic and cultural practices which ensure high yields are prescribed for adoption. Credit is made available from the Agricultural Development Bank for input supply, labour, tractor mechanization use and construction of on-farm storage facilities. Marketing of produce is arranged with marketing institutions like the Ghana Food Distribution Corporation or farmers can sell their produce on the open market. The programme is being jointly managed by ADB, BOG, the National Investment Board and MOA.

A pilot scheme commenced in 1986 using redundant Food Production Corporation (FPC) workers on the Corporation's arable farmlands (formerly the State Farms). Other institutions included were the State Prison Farms, GIDA (on land at Asutsuare), the Federation of Ghana Business and Professional Women at Appollonia in the Greater Accra Region and at Lolobi in the Volta Region.

A total of 870 ha were cropped with maize, rice and vegetables, involving 1 156 farmers (of which only 131 were FPC workers) at a cost of ₵ 31.5 million. Of the total, ₵ 19.6 million was for the purchase of equipment, including 80 power tillers, 9 boomsprayers, 6 maize shellers and 10 wooden maize storage silos. The balance was spent on inputs such as fertilizer, weedicides, labour, seeds and fuel.

In 1987, the block farming project was expanded to include more Food Production workers and lands, and additional GIDA irrigation fields. Future plans are to establish plant and machinery pools at regional capitals which will clear land for block farming and recover the costs from the farmers over a reasonable length of time. The cost of this machinery alone is estimated to be US$ 19 million.

One such block farming project was started in Somanya in the Eastern Region. Crops grown there were maize, peppers and cowpeas. The local branch of ADB had provided credit for farm inputs at an average value of ₵ 81 500 per hectare. This, at 1987 maize prices of ₵ 4 200 per 100 kg, would require a yield of 19.5 bags to the hectare to repay the loan, exclusive of interest (presently 24.5 percent per annum). Yields of major season maize during 1987 were lower than expected and averaged 15 bags per hectare. This resulted in the farmers being in debt to ADB. At Appollonia, where rains had been erratic, yields of groundnuts, grown largely by women farmers, were much lower and the level of farmer indebtedness was higher.

It is apparent from these figures that the size of the loans advanced to the farmers was too high and even with the expected yield of 24 bags to the hectare (a very high yield), their returns would have been modest. An additional problem was that the costs of tractor mechanization (capital plus operating costs) do not appear to have been fully reflected in the tractor hire costs (ploughing is charged at ₵ 6 200 per ha) with the result that there was a subsidy element in the mechanization services.

Another problem being faced by the farmers is one of diminishing yields due to losses of soil fertility. As discussed in Chapter 2, clear felling of forest areas causes an irreversible change in soil structure and fertility which requires changes in the approach to farming systems if production is to be maintained. These changes have not yet been developed for Ghanaian farming conditions, with the inevitable result that yields will decrease and farmer enthusiasm will wane.

What the scheme does demonstrate is that, given access to inputs and credit, farmers will respond and adopt improved practices. If access to inputs and technology were combined with the shifting system of cultivation, yields and productivity would be higher.

Overall Impact on Smallholders and the Rural Poor

The picture that emerges from the analysis of this chapter is that smallholders are most likely not benefitting from the ERP in the short term. Devaluation and liberalization of the foreign exchange market, the hallmarks of the ERP, have turned the terms of trade against their products, and have drastically increased the cost of inputs as well as labour. On the positive side, it is likely that liberalization has somewhat improved the availability of inputs. The same observations also hold for rural consumer goods.

Cocoa is clearly favoured under the ERP compared to food crops, and the overall developments in food crop price seem to be leading to a slow decline in smallholders' real farm incomes. This process, however, has been going on for several years and cannot be attributed only to the ERP. In terms of regional differentiation, while the decline in real gross income of smallholders seems to be similar in all regions, farmers in the south tend to be larger users of purchased inputs. Hence, the negative impact is likely to be more severe for them.

The analysis has demonstrated that availability of both economic services as well as social services seems to have declined for the smallholder under the ERP. The MOA budget has seriously suffered under the ERP both in relative as well as real terms, thus crippling efforts to promote the government objective of increasing production of staple foods. On the other hand, reorganization of MOA will most likely streamline operations and improve efficiency in delivery of services. Finally, it appears that agricultural capital expenditures seem to be getting a boost under the ERP. This is a positive development; however, as with the reorganization of MOA, it will take time to take effect.

The analysis upon which these initial conclusions are based has also revealed some areas where more knowledge is needed in better assessing the impact on the rural poor. In particular it is felt that the situation in the rural labour markets, the shifting sources of income of rural smallholders, and substitutions in consumption and production patterns all deserve further study.

Chapter 11

Structural Problems and Constraints in Smallholder Development

The review and analysis of the smallholder sector in Ghana has revealed several obstacles to future development. The purpose of this chapter is to summarize and synthesize previous findings and suggest direct interventions. The incentive framework for agricultural production, crucial in guiding future decisions, is given special attention. There are other equally important institutional constraints that must also be assessed. The effort here will be to pinpoint the seriousness of the structural problems and constraints in order to help guide future development interventions.

Incentive Framework and Comparative Advantage

Agricultural development cannot proceed without financial incentives for producers. The major policy issues and questions that are of concern in this context are the following:

- Is the current mechanism of staple food price determination the most effective and sustainable for sending favourable price signals to agricultural producers? If not, what are the alternatives?
- How can vulnerable producer groups be protected from price plunges for food crops during periods of surplus?
- Will devaluation and trade liberalization under the ERP contribute towards an improved incentive framework for food producers?
- Does Ghana have comparative advantage in the production of staple food crops?

In the following paragraphs some answers to the above questions are suggested.

Food price determination. The food crop marketing system is basically in private hands but the various markets are only weakly connected. This implies, as already noted, substantial regional and local price variations around the national average.

The real wholesale prices of the various staple food crops, shown in Table 10.4, reflect substantial year-to-year variations (Table 11.1). The average absolute percentage change in year-to-year prices in the 1971-86 period ranges from 20.85 percent for groundnuts to 52.43 percent for plantain. Such price instability is very hard to cope with for producers who, in order to adopt improved practices, must be assured of some stability of return.

Further analysis indicates that the inferred price elasticity of demand for most food products is quite low (in the vicinity of -0.1). Values of this nature imply substantial price instability. They also mean that if a smallholder's crop production is correlated with aggregate crop production, then his income would fluctuate from year to year inversely with output, and by more than his crop output. In other words, a 10 percent decline (increase) in his crop production from normal values would imply more than a 10 percent increase (decline) in his crop income.

The situation for the smallholder, however, is much worse than this would indicate. Because of immediate cash needs after harvest, unless he has any credit to help him store the crops until the later part of the season when prices are usually much higher, he sells early in the season. To obtain an idea of the real situation facing him, computations have been made for each marketing year from 1981/82 to 1985/86, using national monthly wholesale price data, of the effective price a smallholder would obtain for maize and rice under traditional and improved technologies under different marketing strategies (Table 11.2).

The results of this analysis are quite striking in terms of return per family man-day of labour. A small increase in the average price that a farmer can get for his crop has much more than proportional impact on his return per man-day of family labour. In the 1985/86 crop year for instance, a farmer producing with traditional technology and selling early in the season in the way described above, would incur a negative return per man-day of family labour of -₵ 14.4.

It is thus clear that the current system of food marketing seriously impedes small food producers. The key conclusion that emerges is that, even within Ghana's system of imperfect and inefficient food markets, measures aimed at helping the farmer improve his marketing strategy could significantly improve his realized returns and income.

Table 11.1: Annual Changes in Real Wholesale Prices of Staple Food Crops, 1971-86 (figures are percent changes from previous years)

Year	Maize	Rice	Guinea Corn	Millet	Cassava	Yam	Cocoyam	Groundnut	Beans	Plantain	Tomatoes
1971	-6.21	-5.22	-3.22	-1.35	20.23	9.87	19.96	-9.70	4.04	35.32	-8.98
1972	32.09	24.04	4.40	3.90	7.82	-1.33	-0.67	1.24	3.71	-17.13	19.58
1973	-8.84	2.07	19.55	9.81	-13.26	4.17	14.62	18.61	1.20	26.64	23.89
1974	-7.43	-6.54	-9.60	-1.70	0.45	8.96	-1.87	7.10	35.36	-13.53	-17.42
1975	-2.45	7.68	-19.79	-22.56	20.21	7.35	-5.71	-6.13	-18.53	1.07	2.46
1976	44.28	29.65	59.84	57.61	34.63	-8.49	20.49	19.72	0.98	28.62	-0.99
1977	-4.20	-35.04	1.65	1.57	16.35	-4.53	19.72	-11.95	-6.37	36.98	-13.69
1978	-41.59	-22.24	-37.38	-33.35	-46.65	-5.91	-31.14	-5.44	-27.59	-10.50	-26.29
1979	-11.00	-28.51	-24.16	-24.67	-26.77	-22.11	-22.30	-7.21	20.00	-78.04	16.71
1980	49.41	31.21	81.31	38.07	32.95	-7.11	-4.52	-9.65	8.55	176.60	-12.25
1981	-10.61	-11.80	-33.06	-15.37	17.11	-15.71	-0.37	2.84	17.59	-26.14	-10.42
1982	-17.75	51.39	12.08	16.41	-7.99	13.94	14.41	30.26	-6.57	13.28	9.30
1983	354.59	176.64	336.96	232.36	259.47	199.04	355.98	129.16	163.73	291.72	104.02
1984	-79.23	-62.64	-73.87	-66.45	-80.63	-61.59	-75.11	-66.86	-66.86	-61.95	-49.96
1985	-19.87	-28.68	-43.75	-38.70	-13.67	-20.41	-53.07	-6.73	-15.12	-19.13	30.83
1986	33.04	5.59	18.11	11.95	46.04	8.95	66.16	-1.02	8.78	2.19	-26.00
Average value	19.01	7.97	18.07	10.47	16.64	6.57	19.79	5.26	7.68	24.12	2.55
Maximum value	354.59	176.64	336.96	232.36	259.47	199.04	355.98	129.16	163.73	291.72	104.02
Minimum value	-79.23	-62.64	-73.87	-66.45	-80.63	-61.59	-75.11	-66.86	-66.86	-78.04	-49.96
Mean absolute value [1]	45.16	33.06	48.67	35.99	40.26	24.97	44.13	20.85	25.31	52.43	23.30
Mean absolute value (excluding 1983-84)[1]	19.25	19.31	24.53	18.47	20.27	9.26	18.33	9.17	11.63	32.34	14.59

[1] This figure is the average of the absolute values of all percent changes exhibited in each column.

Source: Computed.

Table 11.2: Returns to Smallholders for Maize and Rice Production (Traditional and Improved Technologies) Under Alternative Marketing Strategies (cedis per man-day of family labour except as noted)

Marketing year	1981/82	1982/83	1983/84	1984/85	1985/86
Maize traditional					
Price A (¢/kg)[1]	4.14	7.39	16.33	7.30	13.69
Return per man-day of family labour	7.60	4.00	67.27 (47.00)[4]	-55.10	-14.40
Price B (¢/kg)[2]	4.37	18.95	17.55	9.73	17.81
Return per man-day of family labour	14.46	38.87	81.50 (-23.06)[4]	-26.78	33.53
Maize improved					
Price A[1]	4.14	7.39	16.33	7.30	13.69
Return per man-day of family labour	30.20	53.10	37.02 (13.50)[4]	2.80	62.50
Price B[2]	4.37	18.95	17.55	9.73	17.81
Return per man-day of family labour	33.58	226.48	155.13 (13.60)[4]	39.25	124.26
Rice traditional[3]					
Price A[1]	5.18	13.37	29.34	20.51	22.26
Return per man-day of family labour	13.50	41.80	187.20 (17.9)[4]	51.80	28.60
Price B[2]	7.43	21.74	30.06	21.42	25.04
Return per man-day of family labour	39.50	138.38	195.44 (18.47)[4]	62.29	60.08

Table 11.2: Returns to Smallholders for Maize and Rice Production (Traditional and Improved Technologies) Under Alternative Marketing Strategies (cedis per man-day of family labour except as noted) (Cont'd)

Marketing year	1981/82	1982/83	1983/84	1984/85	1985/86
Rice improved[3]					
Price A[1]	5.18	13.37	29.34	20.51	22.26
Return per man-day of family labour	36.70	113.10	345.40 (108.7)[4]	51.79	43.90
Price B[2]	7.43	21.74	30.06	21.42	25.04
Return per man-day of family labour	72.95	248.11	356.90 (114.48)[4]	161.95	88.71
Wage of hired labour	30.00	60.00	90.00	100.00	120.00

[1] This is the price assuming farmers sell all their produce in the first seven months of the marketing year.

[2] Price assuming produce is marketed evenly throughout the year, as explained in the text.

[3] Prices are for paddy rice.

[4] These figures assume yield reduction by 60% for maize and 50% for rice.

Source: Computed; the figures in the last row are taken from Table 10.10.

Price declines. In years such as 1984, prices for staple foods dropped precipitously after a good harvest on a substantially expanded staple food area. For instance, the returns per man-day of family labour from maize during the 1984/85 marketing year were negative, or very close to zero, for both traditional and improved technology. Clearly, incentives are very seriously impeded in such years and can contribute to farmers leaving their farms for better opportunities elsewhere.

The options for improving the price situation in such instances are really only two. Either incentives to store the crop (by private or public entities) until a subsequent year must be provided, or the crop could be exported if the marketing system can accommodate it and if the international market can absorb it. But in Ghana it does not appear that food surpluses are forthcoming in any except a most unusual year such as 1984. In fact, as shown in Chapter 1, the staple food situation is more likely to be a deficit one.

Apart from storing during the season from the post-harvest period to the lean months, the private sector is not likely to store substantial amounts of cereals across marketing years. This is because the risk is quite high and the expected private return will most likely not be high enough to justify it.

The only feasible solution, therefore, appears to be for the Government to store some grain in years of extreme surpluses for sale in years of shortage, especially in urban areas. The question is how much should be stored and how much investment in public storage infrastructure should be undertaken. As already mentioned, the Government aims to build storage facilities for 150 000 tons of cereal. At 1985-87 average production levels for rice and maize, this would be equivalent to about 28 percent of total production. When sorghum and millet are included, this capacity would still be 18 percent of national cereal production.

If farmers market on average as much as 60 percent of their total cereal output (a fairly high average proportion given that many cereal farmers, especially in the north, are subsistence farmers), then 150 000 tons amounts to 39 percent of marketed supply of all cereals or 46 percent of the marketed supply of maize and rice. It appears *a priori* that 150 000 tons is a very large amount of storage capacity in which to invest. It would take a highly improbable sequence of surplus and deficit years to make the investment pay, even by social profitability criteria. Nevertheless, some investment in public storage capacity could alleviate the precipitous declines in food prices in some years and the adverse price rises in years of shortage. The social profitability of such an investment, and the size and location of the storage capacity, should be the subject of a detailed study.

Devaluation and trade liberalization. Under the ERP it is unlikely that the price incentive structure for staple food producers will change. This is because there have been no significant public interventions, either before or after the ERP, in the marketing of staple foods, with the result that markets are relatively free. As was mentioned earlier, domestic maize and rice prices, when translated at parallel market rates, were comparable to world market prices. This implies that Ghanaian cereal markets have been integrated with the international markets (possibly through smuggling). It was also noted that the ratio of traded to non-traded food prices has not changed significantly after the ERP. This implies that perhaps even the so-called non-traded food crops are also integrated (directly by trade or indirectly through high substitutability with cereals) with the world food markets.

Comparative advantage. Comparative advantage calculations of staple and other food crops were undertaken by the World Bank in the context of their Agricultural Sector Review in 1985, and in the following year in the context of the appraisal of the ASRP (Sallinger 1986). The results of the two sets of calculations for staple foods are summarized in Table 11.3.

There is a wide difference between the two sets of indices of comparative advantage in Table 11.3, reflecting different assumptions about labour inputs to production. The mission assessment is that the technical assumptions behind the figures in column (1) are closer to reality. Hence, the figures in column (1) are a closer approximation to the true domestic resource costs. The tentative conclusion from this table is that, according to the best evidence available, all cereal products under traditional technology have comparative advantage in Ghana and could therefore be supported.

Food Aid and Disincentives

The total amount of cereal food aid for the last six years has not varied greatly (Table 11.4). It went from a low of 50 281 mt in 1982/83 (June-July) to a high of 94 247 mt in the drought year 1983/84. It has continued at slightly reduced levels since then, despite the fact that the food situation has improved enormously since 1983. The amount of non-emergency food aid declined dramatically in the worst drought year (1983/84) to only 29 757 mt while it increased to 76 734 mt in the large surplus year 1984/85. During the next two years non-emergency food aid stayed at roughly the same high levels of 1984/85. It appears

Table 11.3: Comparative Advantage in Staple Foods[1]

Crop/Technology	(1)[2]	(2)[3]
Maize		
Improved - draft	.18	1.27
Improved - mechanized	.18	1.39
Advanced - draft	.15	1.21
Advanced - mechanized	.15	1.32
Rice		
Traditional	.37	2.73
Improved	.32	4.05
Advanced	.11	8.75
Mechanized	.86	-0.72
Irrigated large-scale	.52	-0.72
Irrigated small-scale	.17	4.94
Sorghum/millet		
Traditional	.31	1.08
Semi-improved	.15	.79
Groundnuts		
Traditional	.69[4]	1.45
Improved - draft	.54[4]	1.00
Improved - mechanized	.50[4]	1.09

[1] Figures indicate the Domestic Resource Cost (DRC) coefficients. A value less than one indicates comparative advantage, a negative value indicates negative value added at world prices.

[2] Source: Sallinger 1986, using farmgate prices.

[3] Source: World Bank 1985a.

[4] Uses wholesale prices.

that the flows of food aid are reasonably constant and the donors just relabel certain amounts as emergency aid. The quantities imported under food aid constitute quite a large proportion of the country's total cereal supply. On the assumption that farmers market 60 percent of their total cereal output (a fairly large proportion) and if rice is converted to paddy equivalent, total food aid imports have amounted to about 20-30 percent of marketed maize and rice, or about 16 percent of total marketed cereals in normal years (excluding 1983/84) (Table 11.5).

The current WFP programme in Ghana consists of four food-for-work projects with a total commitment of US\$ 81 million. This is the largest WFP-assisted programme in West Africa, and is indicative of

Table 11.4: Food Aid Imports, 1981-87 (in metric tons)[1]

Year[2]	Cereals						Non-Cereals							
	Wheat[3]	Wheat Flour	Rice	Coarse Grain	Blended Foods	Total	Vegetable Oil	Butter Oil	Milk Powder	Other Milk Products	Meat & Meat Products	Fish & Fish Products	Pulses	Others
1981/82	39 034	-	17 850	3 000	8 524	68 408	1 814	630	586	-	-	386	-	-
1982/83	5 423	-	27 897	10 320	6 641	50 281	1 702	620	3 946	41	-	440	-	55
			(20 447)	(10 320)	(50)	(30 817)	(810)		(1 138)	(41)	-	-	-	(55)
1983/84	39 295	3 000	21 140	14 985	15 827	94 247	4 358	400	5 721	565	-	992	140	349
	(29 588)[1]	(3 000)	(1 090)	(14 985)	(15 827)	(64 490)	(2 531)	-	(2 393)	(565)		(625)	(14)	(250)
1984/85	33 988	4 759	23 630	3 614	20 645[4]	87 036	5 226	-	2 781	48	-	1 905	1 469	692
	(2 403)	(4 029)	(420)	(3 450)		(10 302)	(686)	-	(712)	-	-	(50)	(335)	(188)
1985/86	40 879	-	31 604	500	3 626	76 609	3 063	-	3 913	12	-	2 445	100	1 013
1986/87	23 709	1 095	36 437	420	20 286	81 947	8 356	-	2 509	-	-	2 568	-	1 148

[1] Figures in parentheses are amounts of the total which were delivered under emergency assistance.

[2] All figures refer to the June-July year.

[3] Includes Bulgur wheat.

[4] Some of this amount is under emergency assistance, but it was not reported by WFP.

Source: World Food Programme, Accra.

Table 11.5: Cereal Food Aid as Proportion of Domestic Cereal Marketed Production, 1981–86 (thousand metric tonnes)

	Cereal Production			Marketed Cereal[1]		Cereal Food Aid as % of Marketed Products	
	Maize & Rice[1]	Sorghum/Millet	All Cereals	Maize & Rice[2]	All Cereals	Maize & Rice[2]	All Cereals
1981/82	377.8	301.2	679.0	226.7	407.4	30.2	16.8
1982/83	301.4	246.3	547.7	180.8	328.6	27.8	15.3
1983/84	167.7	220.2	387.9	100.6	232.7	93.7	40.5
1984/85	650.4	315.0	965.4	390.2	579.2	23.0	16.4
1985/86	475.0	305.0	780.0	285.0	468.0	26.9	16.4
1986/87	638.7	298.0	936.7	383.2	562.0	21.4	14.6

[1] Assumed at 60% of production.
[2] Paddy rice.
Source: Computed.

the size of WFP's support to the Government's present policy reforms and efforts for structural adjustment. Food aid is being used as an incentive wage for workers to support the recovery of export sectors (timber and gold mining), transport infrastructure (railroads, ports, highways, feeder roads), oil-palm and rubber plantations and forestry. More recently, the petroleum refinery at Tema has been included under the WFP programme. Deductions are also being made of a small proportion of the value of the food from the wage of the workers and the proceeds placed in a government-held bank account to be used for financing social and economic development activities within the framework of the Government's public investment programme. These interventions are regarded as providing real incentives to the workers involved in the rehabilitation activities, and contributing significantly to maintaining labour employment, reducing absenteeism rates, and increasing workers' productivity, particularly in timber, gold mining, railroads, palm-oil and rubber plantations. On the other hand, it is clear from the profile of the smallholder that the wealthier producers are most likely to benefit from this implicit labour wage subsidy.

Given the improved general food situation in the country since the 1983 drought, WFP, in a review of its implementation experience, has tried to avoid having WFP-imported foods compete with locally produced foods, depressing local prices and creating a production disincentive. WFP is also aware of the importance of the selection of food baskets by placing emphasis on commodities which are normally in the import bills of the country such as rice, sugar, milk and fish products.

Part of the food aid is monetized (sold domestically at market prices). For example, in 1986/87, more than half (52.2 percent) of food aid in cereals by USAID, EEC, Canada, Japan and France was monetized at market prices through the Ghana Food Distribution Corporation. The profit on monetized food aid goes to the Government. The remaining 47.8 percent of the 1986/87 food aid in cereals by the above donors was given to NGOs and health care centres.

Technological Constraints

A mixed picture emerges with regard to technology. Proven packages of technology are available for maize, rice and root crops, but suitable technology for the drier Northern and Upper Regions is not available. For maize, improved planting material and field-tested packages are made available by the Grains and Legumes Development Board.

Similarly, improved varieties and a package of practices have been released for rice grown under irrigated conditions in the valley bottoms. For root crops, a selection of improved cassava cultivars have been introduced by IITA and are being tested by VORADEP. Similarly, the mini-sett technique is being tested by VORADEP for yams. Sweet potato varieties are also being introduced and tested. With the expected commencement of the IFAD-supported National Root and Tuber Research Programme, root crop technology should be further strengthened. Technology for the development of sorghum and millet is lacking, however, since improved planting materials for these important crops, which are staple food items in the Northern and Upper Regions, are not available. Equally inadequate attention has been given to developing soil and moisture conservation techniques. Consequently, yields are low and household and regional food security is a major issue in the food-impoverished north.

The only research institutes which have made a significant contribution during recent years have been those which have received donor support. Research on food crops has so far led to recommendations on improved technology for maize, rice and cowpeas only. For groundnuts, partial recommendations are available; for other food crops (cassava, yam, cocoyam, plantain and vegetables) improved technology is not available, although some breakthrough can be expected to result from the research presently under way.

Within the context of overall food security in Ghana, the technology to achieve food self-sufficiency and even food surpluses in selected crops exists. The major problems affecting promotion of technology are institutional (lack of finance, poor extension, and inadequate linkages between research and extension), lack of credit, untimely input supply, and poor infrastructure (in particular roads and marketing).

Institutional Weaknesses

Institutional weaknesses, arising from low morale, poor salaries and inadequate budgetary support, inhibit implementation of agricultural development projects. Moreover, MOA has been unable to fulfil its role of identifying priorities and formulating policies and plans for their implementation. Nor has it been able to deliver services to increase agricultural production. Research has been affected by lack of funds and poor pay scales leading to "brain drain". Inputs have seldom been provided on time. Pricing policy, critical for increasing production, has remained ineffective. Specific problems affecting MOA include inadequate professional staff and an excessive number of support staff. As a result most of the budget is consumed by salaries and wages, leaving few funds for supporting expenditure. MOA is also responsible for 18 parastatals, most of which incur losses. Action has already been initiated to divest or liquidate 14 of these institutions. Staff reduction under the SAP and a programme to strengthen MOA's policy planning capability under the ASRP are taking place.

Extension

One of the main reasons for the failure of the technology delivery system has been the weakness of the MOA extension staff in the field. Reasons for this are many and include low morale and low level of motivation of all MOA extension staff due to: absence of a clear and workable programme; low salaries; lack of transport; absence of extension materials; little in-service training; no access to technical literature; lack of updated messages for farmers; poor or non-existent linkages with research; absence of a formal, supervised work programme; and involvement in non-extension activities. Involvement in non-extension activities, combined with low salaries and lack of mobility, has resulted in an extension service which in effect is totally incapable of carrying out its mandate.

This breakdown of MOA extension services has hit the smallholder farmer particularly hard. When the service was operating, government emphasis on small farmer production ensured that a certain proportion of inputs, mainly fertilizer, hand tools and seeds, reached the subsistence farmer through the field extension staff.

As part of MOA's restructuring exercise, the World Bank under the ASRP has financed a study aimed at reorganizing the extension services at the national level. The results are being used to revitalize the extension service, with clearly defined priorities and close links with research, elimination of the problems of duplication of effort and involvement in non-extension activities. Consequently, input dispensing has been completely delinked from extension activities. Another improvement in extension is the creation of the Women Farmers' Extension Division in the Department of Extension Services to cater to the specific needs of women, such as food storage, processing and preservation, nutrition, child rearing, etc.

Road Communication System

The widespread deterioration of roads and communication systems has led to high transport costs. Transport problems inhibit distribution, both for inputs and produce, raising intermediation costs and contributing to price volatility. Ghana's extensive trunk road network (14 000 km of primary and secondary roads) is considered to be adequate but is in a poor state of repair. There is a clear indication that most of the 17 300 km of feeder roads remain largely unusable owing to severe maintenance neglect in the recent past. Under the ERP, considerable stress has been placed on road rehabilitation, and more than adequate funds have been pledged to undertake these activities. The World Bank's on-going Transport Rehabilitation Programmes are scheduled to be implemented to catch up with annual road deterioration and the accumulated maintenance backlog so that road conditions will improve from the present "30 percent good" to an estimated "70 percent good" by the year 1995. Given these commitments, the major constraint to implementing road rehabilitation and maintenance would be the ability of the Department of Feeder Roads to execute all these projects. The Government should consider feeder road and local road rehabilitation and maintenance as an important ingredient of the ERP as well as of any poverty alleviation and food security programmes.

Rural Credit

Ghana has a rich experience in agricultural credit. Almost every bank in Ghana is involved in it. Over the years, some 40 percent of the small farmers in the country have received credit. Credit in Ghana, however, is plagued by high intermediation costs and poor loan recoveries. Poor infrastructure has also contributed to the high cost of credit administration. Lack of general availability of transport has added to supervision difficulties and contributed to defaults. Similarly, price volatility has contributed to poor repayments. In 1983, farmers were unable to pay despite high prices because of the drought and resultant decrease in production. In 1984, the reverse situation inhibited loan repayments. Not surprisingly, intermediation margins in Ghana remain high.

The banking system is liquid but at the same time does not find a market for loans, partly owing to the high interest rate charges. The SAP seems to have hitherto concentrated on resource mobilization without looking at the effect of high interest rates on demand, leading to a situation of excess liquidity in the banking system. The excess liquidity has also arisen from banks being reluctant to lend to the agricultural sector on account of their recent experience.

With respect to demand for credit, an equally distorted picture emerges. ADB appears to have the demand but not the resources, while the other banks have the funds but not the demand. As part of the move to restructure the financial sector sponsored by several donors under the Financial Sector Adjustment Credit, banks are to undergo recapitalization and management reorganization, concentrating attention on their original mandates and reducing the weight of unproductive overhead costs. In addition, within the spirit of deregulation, sectoral allocations for lending are to be removed, interest rate restrictions having already been lifted. At the same time, within the framework of an anti-inflationary monetary policy, strict credit ceilings have been imposed on all banks by way of reserve requirements totalling 30 percent of assets, a policy that provides added benefit for bank restructuring by prompting more active recovery of outstanding loans. The impact of these policies on smallholder agricultural lendings is likely to be the withdrawal from the market of commercial banks and the two non-agricultural development banks (whose mandates are for housing and construction and medium-term investment lending). As a result, smallholder credit would become predominantly the responsibility of ADB and the small RBs. Given the current state of the financial sector generally, ADB and the RBs should promptly complete the organizational restructuring and recapitalization proposed under the Financial Sector Adjustment Credit. Both must take an active role in nationalizing the interest rate structure, which is no longer regulated by BOG, and their lending and loan disbursement procedures.

Input Supply

Owing to the transition stage reached between the former MOA extension-organized input supply and the present partially privatized system, farmers are suffering from lack of regular availability of the main inputs (fertilizer, seed and crop chemicals).

In the last two decades, the import and distribution of fertilizers, inputs to the cocoa sub-sector and seed production became government monopolies. Their timely delivery had suffered because of several constraints. Moreover, in the case of fertilizer, the right type had not been imported and, owing to foreign exchange scarcity and distribution problems, had not been available on time and in sufficient quantities.

Imports of other items are largely in private hands. Because of the switch to the automatic licensing system and the availability of foreign exchange, in theory, this should have led to a greater private sector involvement in imports. In reality, however, only 5-6 percent of the bids in the foreign exchange auction have been directed towards agricultural inputs. This is possibly because of the high transaction costs of imports, high distribution costs in rural areas, and also because of the slow turnover of these goods, particularly fertilizer. Under the ASRP, however, and with the substantially improved performance of MOA agencies for handling fertilizer importation and distribution, sufficient quantities of fertilizer, agrochemicals, veterinary drugs and vaccines, and fishing gear are now available through donor assistance from the EEC, CIDA, Kreditanstalt Fur Wiederaufbau, African Development Bank, IDA, etc.

The weakness of the Ghana Seed Company (GSC), which produces foundation and certified maize, rice and groundnut seed, and supplies sorghum, millet, onion and vegetable seed, is a further constraint on the input supply to farmers. GSC's main problems are related to financial management; the Company has difficulty in obtaining the requisite logistical support (transport) to ensure adequate supervision of seed production and to maintain seed processing and drying equipment. This has led to a decline in production of certified and, more seriously, foundation seed, which should be addressed if the needs of small-scale producers are to be met. Besides streamlining GSC to ensure adequate production, there is a need to organize contract seed growers to produce the certified seed. GSC would undertake the drying and cleaning and the subsequent distribution and sales. Well managed and supervised small-scale contract growers would produce better quality products than the present system. It will be prudent in the GSC restructuring to consider this. The future strategy for the revitalization of the seed industry in Ghana should be firmly based on the premise that production of certified seed and planting material for sale to farmers should be a private sector, commercial activity.

Chapter 12

A Framework for Agricultural Assistance to Rural Smallholders

This study is ultimately aimed at identifying the framework and type of possible external intervention in the rural smallholder sector of Ghana.   Projects to enhance smallholder development cannot be undertaken in the absence of an overall strategy.   The Government of Ghana has already outlined its priorities for agricultural policy and interventions must be in harmony with those overall objectives.   This chapter outlines an overall strategy for future assistance to Ghana. The strategy is aimed at alleviating some of the major constraints identified in the previous chapters.

Context in summary.   The problems associated with low production and poverty in the smallholder sector clearly predate the advent of structural adjustment.   Therefore, a strategy for future smallholder development must be conditioned by the declining trends that prevailed in the rural sector prior to the introduction of the ERP and the major policy changes since then.   As Ghana's rural poor are variously integrated within the money economy, they are not immune to changes in the macro-economic climate.   The challenge for rural development lies in the linkage between promoting macro-economic balance and securing the long-term development of the smallholder sector.

The starting point for viewing the recent past is the early nineteen-seventies.   This period marks the end of a long transition in the rural economy that saw massive migration from the rural north of the country to the rural south, in response to the increasing demand for labour by the cocoa industry.   Many of the migrant farmers established themselves as smallholders growing both cocoa and food.   The small scale of their operations quickly indebted many of these "stranger" farmers to larger farmers and traders, and increasingly marginalized them.

The onset of the oil boom in 1974 presented opportunities for many of these impoverished farmers in neighbouring countries, especially Nigeria. The pull from abroad was helped by a domestic push to migrate, characterized by low real cocoa prices and lack of alternative opportunities in the Ghanaian urban centres. The period from 1975 to 1983 is thus characterized by large outmigration mainly from the rural south to neighbouring countries. This development has had several consequences. Since many of the smallholders in the south had small cocoa plots, migration led to the abandonment of many cocoa farms and a decline in production. Since most of the migrants were male, many women-headed households were left in the rural south. Almost all of these women were engaged in food production. The decline in the availability of rural labour during this period, however, led to a decrease in the average size of cultivated farms, and to a reduction in the overall area planted to food crops. The decline in the marketed surplus in staple food crops, coupled with the general urban bias and the overvalued exchange rate during this period, led to massive cereal imports that most likely depressed overall cereal prices from the levels they would have attained in the absence of substantial imports.

The year 1983 marked another turning point because of the disastrous drought and the simultaneous repatriation of about 1.2 million Ghanaians from Nigeria. It also marks a drastic change in government policies resulting in the ERP. Most of the returnees from Nigeria settled in their original southern (and some northern) rural localities. This explains the huge increase in crop area planted in 1984, especially in the south, as well as the increase in the number of rural smallholdings observed in the 1984 census of agriculture. The influx of people to rural areas in the south and the drought dramatically shifted the cropping pattern in favour of food crops. The cropping patterns in the north, by contrast, remained largely unaltered.

Since 1984, the number of all holdings, as well as smallholdings, has declined substantially in the south, while in the north the decline is much smaller. In some northern regions there even appears to be a slight increase. This is consistent with the likely remigration of some of the rural males especially from the south, this time to urban centres within Ghana. It is also consistent with the recently observed decline in the area cultivated for food crops in the south. Price developments contributed to these trends since real food prices have declined. The recent shift in the terms of trade in favour of cocoa was also a contributing factor in this process. It created some pull of rural labour away from food production, increasing rural wage rates and costs of production for smallholders. The SAP appears to have affected the smallholder most seriously in this respect.

In this atmosphere of drastic economic change, a strategy for smallholder development must be considered in the context of an overall development strategy for agriculture. Agriculture has been largely neglected in the past as manifested by the low share of total investment allocated to this sector; smallholder agriculture has been neglected even more. The previous analysis of national food security (Chapter 1) points out that the food gap is growing and that, unless serious steps are taken, it will pose an increasing burden on the Ghanaian economy. Since, both on the export and the import-substituting front, emphasis should be on agriculture, the overall government policy in the medium term should give more attention to agriculture in general, and food production in particular.

Regional and National Food Security

The looming dangers posed by food insecurity influence the main thrust of the recommended strategy; this involves support for smallholder food production, and aims to enhance regional food security and to increase national marketed surplus of the main deficit cereal crops, maize and rice. The largest amount of marketed surplus in these staple crops comes from the south which, as indicated above, has undergone severe adverse changes and stresses.

A two-pronged strategy is recommended to increase food production. The first element relates to the enhancement of regional food security through assisting the drought-prone, resource-poor and poverty-stricken northern regions. The second element is to assist smallholders in the transitional zone of Ghana who provide the bulk of the national food requirements (the transitional zone cuts across Brong-Ahafo, Ashanti and Volta Regions, which together contain almost as many rural people below the poverty line in absolute terms as the northern regions). In addition, certain areas in the forest zone should be selected for assistance to smallholders engaged in traditional valley-bottom rice production.

The first major aspect of the proposed strategy involves strengthening food security and arresting environmental degradation in the north, the more remote and historically disadvantaged part of the country. It is inhabited mostly by poor, food-growing subsistence farmers and is particularly prone to weather-induced production fluctuations. Diseases and drought have led northern farmers to over-exploit the meagre resources of the region, which has resulted in adverse environmental consequences. This region is not expected to produce large food surpluses to enhance national food security. The low level of smallholder income, however, and increasing local food insecurity call for external assistance.

Smallholders in the south are the dominant food producers. They have rapidly increased, especially in the last few years. Generally, in the transitional zone, food production cereals are grown mainly for cash. These smallholders constitute the most promising group for increasing production and marketed surplus of maize. Support for smallholder food production in the south complements the World Bank and government strategy of export promotion of agricultural products, mainly cocoa, but also non-traditional crops like pineapples, shea-nut, ginger and others. Nevertheless, conflicts might arise because of the competition for hired labour by the export and food-producing sectors. Smallholder food production is labour-intensive and this technology is not likely to change rapidly or on a massive scale. Increased demand for rural labour is not likely, however, to pose a problem in the medium term. The SAP-induced retrenchment of civil employees will create unemployment in the urban areas. This development will slow down the rate of rural to urban migration, thus increasing the availability of rural labour.

Targetting the Smallholder

A common need under both elements of the strategy outlined above is ensuring that smallholders will be reached. The web of social and economic dependency that develops between smallholders and wealthier members of the farming and trading communities is a strong deterrent to smallholder development. This process results in socio-economic polarization and marginalization of the smaller farmers. The strength and stability of this process should not be underestimated. But unless this vicious cycle is broken, targetting the poor remains a major challenge.

The strategy proposed has two dimensions. First, the primary attention in any project should be upon income-generating activities, both farming and non-farming. Second, if the smallholder is to be able to resist the usurpation of his increased earnings by wealthier members of the farming community, he/she must be equipped with better bargaining power. The most time-tested method for ensuring this is through group activities and grassroots organizations. While informal group formation is the first step in a long process of organizing smallholders to improve their bargaining power and consolidate their economic gains, it should not be looked at as an end in itself. Informal groups are as easily dissolved as they are formed. The objective should be a gradual evolution from informal to more formal types of organizations (such as farmer-held companies or service centres, credit or input cooperatives, etc.) which have a better chance of long-term survival. For purposes of targetting, the inclusion of food processing in project proposals and related support activities as a measure to assist rural women is recommended.

It must be emphasized that Ghana is rich in traditional and spontaneously created grassroots institutions. Self-help schemes are reported to have increased in recent years. The trend has developed in response to reduced government services. Notable examples are road maintenance and development of social utilities in rural areas. Such revived initiatives should be capitalized on by both the Government and external donors. The Community Initiative Programme under the PAMSCAD, for example, is indeed a move in the right direction and deserves full support. Despite their perceived unpopularity, rural cooperatives, under appropriate conditions, can play an important role in this respect. With careful planning, interest in cooperatives can be regenerated as a form of grassroots institution building to provide services to farmers.

Collaboration with NGOs

Ghana is also very rich in a wide variety of national and international NGOs with religious affiliation or secular orientation. Owing to their past experience in rural development and recognized ability to deal with grassroots issues, a major element of any intervention strategy in Ghana should include close collaboration with rural NGOs. The major involvement of NGOs has been in health and agriculture. A marked feature of the health and income-generating projects of NGOs has been their focus on rural women. There would appear to be at least three optional models available from past experience which could be drawn upon in seeking NGO cooperation. First, a proportion of funds could be set aside for the use of NGOs, to be drawn on either directly or through the appropriate government department. Second, NGOs could be invited to participate in projects which have a grassroots organizational aspect to one or more of their components, both as local institution builders and as managers of the relevant finance. Third, volunteer agencies could be asked to supply personnel in technical assistance posts. The identification of which option and which NGO would be appropriate must, obviously, be decided in the early stages of the project cycle.

Support for Rural Women

In providing support for rural women, careful sequencing of assistance is required to improve the effectiveness of any project. Preparatory work with participating groups should begin well in advance of a potential project. Basic group formation and acquisition of skills should take place before new equipment is made available. Extensive consultations with women's groups should precede both their agreement to participate and the project's agreement to assist them. More attention should also be paid to increasing women's access to working capital. In this context, the PAMSCAD's programme of enhanced opportunities for rural women deserves full support. The scale of technology should be commensurate with raw material availability and managerial skills. Processing facilities should be installed close to the supply of raw material. Finally, it should be kept in mind that the introduction of income-generating activities *per se* does not solve all the problems of rural women. Maternal and child health and sanitation facilities are still urgently needed.

Flexibility Under a Changing Economic Environment

Developments in the Ghanaian economy over the last fifteen years have been significant, and often sudden and unexpected. The ongoing SAP is leading to substantial reorientation in many sectors and institutions of the economy, the outcome of which is not yet clear. Designing and implementing projects in such an atmosphere is not easy since the assumptions upon which decisions are made can change rapidly. Therefore, the following considerations must be taken into account, particularly during the transition period:

- Projects should not be complex in design; the number of components should be commensurate with managerial capabilities. Moreover, because of coordination problems, design should ensure that components outside the control of management should be kept to a minimum.
- With the present incentive and salary structure of the civil service, a simple design - with the shift of responsibility to farmers as soon as possible - would have more chances of success.

- Projects which have massive infrastructure development should be given more than five years for implementation.
- In the project design, availability of seeds should be closely scrutinized and, if necessary, they should be produced at the project level.
- Agricultural extension components should avoid a lopsided approach whereby only contact farmers are provided with extension advice.
- Storage facilities and the prerequisite support services, such as agricultural credit, should receive serious attention.
  With the successive devaluations of the cedi within the framework of the SAP, the relative cost of the factors of production has shifted in favour of labour-intensive undertakings. The design of future projects should unambiguously take this trend into account. For rural projects, adoption of labour-intensive techniques should be supplemented by other support measures to increase the productivity of land.
- Design should be flexible to respond to changing circumstances and farmers' feedback, and to allow for faster decision making in the field. Monitoring and evaluation with sufficient orientation in economic analysis should be provided in order to follow progress and to signal changes in economic conditions.

The SAP and the Policy Dialogue

It has been discussed at length and recognized by both the Government and the donors, that in addition to its positive effects, the SAP can have a negative social and economic impact on vulnerable groups, particularly in the urban areas. As this report substantiates (Chapter 10), however, the ERP has also probably had a severe adverse impact on the vast population of the rural smallholders, in particular those that are more fully integrated with the market, i.e., staple food crop producers. Several areas have been identified where enhanced policy dialogue with the Government could contribute toward better understanding of the changing nature of the constraints facing rural smallholders, as well as measures to improve rural production and well-being. Possible areas that offer themselves for policy dialogue through project assistance are: streamlining the institutional set-up for input supply and output marketing; smallholder credit; issues related to land tenure; and input and output price policies and rural food security.

The Response of the Government

The idea of developing a short-term action programme especially designed to tackle the immediate problems of the poor and disadvantaged during the implementation of the SAP was presented by the Government of Ghana at the May 1987 Consultative Group Meeting in Paris. When the donor community expressed interest in such a programme, the Government invited a mission led by the World Bank, with representatives of IFAD, ILO, UNDP, UNICEF, WFP, WHO and the UK Overseas Development Administration. The multi-agency mission visited Ghana in July 1987. Upon completion of its field work the mission prepared an *aide-mémoire* which contains the following section on smallholder producers:

> Immediate action could include replicating some components of the IFAD-assisted Smallholder Rehabilitation and Development Programme such as feeder road rehabilitation, village-level marketing and storage facilities, provision of credit for women's groups, etc. Moreover, efforts should be made to accelerate implementation of ongoing projects, particularly for those components which lend themselves to quick disbursement.

The work of the inter-agency mission led to the preparation of a document by the Government of Ghana entitled Programme of Action to Mitigate the Social Costs of Adjustment (PAMSCAD). It was presented to a donors' conference in February 1988, recommending the following criteria for the selection of projects:

(a) Projects should have a strong poverty focus, benefitting vulnerable/target groups.

(b) Projects should have high economic and social rates of return (for projects lending themselves to quantitative analysis).

(c) Projects should not strain present implementation capacity and should not divert financial and institutional resources away from ongoing projects. This may imply extending an ongoing project with a strong poverty focus.

(d) Projects should not create unsustainable future obligations for recurrent costs. This implies that interventions either be short-term (1-2 years), with costs being funded by additional donor support, or, if they are interventions which need to be sustained in the medium- to long-term, they should be sustained within projected levels of resource availability.

(e) Projects should not create distortions incompatible with the overall direction of the ERP.

(f) Projects should have political marketability and visibility in sensitive areas.

The General Nature of Proposals Under the PAMSCAD

Programmes under the PAMSCAD are defined in broad terms and generally fall within one or more of the following categories:

- Community Initiative Programmes, for which a list of projects will have to be prepared;
- Employment Generation Programmes: to include public works projects, credit schemes for small-scale enterprises and farmers, projects to enhance the economic opportunities for women and small-scale miners, and agricultural rehabilitation credit for peasant farmers; and
- projects designed to meet the basic needs of the vulnerable groups: water and sanitation, health, nutrition, shelter and education.

The issues of poverty alleviation and food security should be addressed within the context of balanced economic growth which effectively focusses on the structural problems prevailing in rural Ghana. The transition period under structural adjustment may last longer than expected. In the meantime, the Government cannot be expected to finance compensatory measures under a purely welfare approach. It is for these reasons that the inclusion of some of the rural-related proposals under the PAMSCAD as part of project components in future operations in Ghana is recommended. Among these proposals are community initiatives, agricultural rehabilitation credit for peasant farmers, and enhanced opportunities for women in development.

Annex A

Supplementary Tables

Table A.1: Balance of Payments as a Percentage of GDP, 1983-87 (percent)

	1983	1984	1985	1986	1987
Exports of goods (f.o.b.)	6.0	7.4	10.0	14.5	17.0
Cocoa	3.6	5.0	6.5	9.7	10.0
Gold	1.5	1.3	1.4	2.1	3.0
Diamonds	0.0	0.0	0.1	0.1	0.1
Manganese	0.0	0.1	0.1	0.2	0.2
Bauxite	0.0	0.0	0.0	0.1	0.1
Timber	0.2	0.3	0.4	0.9	1.9
Others	0.5	0.6	1.3	1.5	1.6
Imports of goods (c.i.f.)	-7.3	-8.7	-11.5	-15.6	-18.2
Oil	-2.0	2.1	-3.4	-2.4	-3.1
Non-oil	-5.3	-6.6	-8.2	-13.1	-15.1
Trade balances	-1.3	-1.4	-1.5	-1.1	-1.2
Services (net)	-2.1	-2.3	-3.1	-4.2	-4.8
Freight and insurance	0.2	0.2	0.2	0.3	0.3
Interest	-1.1	-1.3	-1.7	-2.0	-2.7
Other services	-1.1	-1.1	-1.7	-2.5	-2.4
Unrequited transfers (net)	1.2	2.7	2.2	3.7	3.8
Government	1.0	1.7	1.7	2.3	2.7
Private	0.2	1.0	0.5	1.4	1.1
Current account balance = foreign saving	-2.1	-1.0	-2.5	-1.6	-2.2
Capital account (net)	1.4	1.2	1.0	1.7	6.1
Long-term loans (net)	0.2	1.1	1.7	4.4	5.5
Medium-term loans (net)	0.2	1.4	-1.1	-1.7	-0.7
Trust fund	0.0	0.0	-0.1	-0.2	0.3
Private capital (net)	0.2	-0.1	0.1	0.5	0.7
Others	0.8	-1.1	0.4	-1.3	0.9
Errors and omissions	-2.5	0.3	0.6	-1.2	-0.6
Overall balance	-3.3	0.5	-0.9	-1.1	3.3

Source: Ministry of Finance and banking sources.

Table A.2: Central Government Operations and Financing, 1980-87 (₵ million)

	1980/81	1981/82	1982	1983	1984	1985	1986	1987
Total revenue and grants	4 397	5 253	3 502	10 241	22 641	40 311	73 627	111 046
Revenue	4 387	5 201	3 467	10 184	21 727	38 691	69 759	105 009
Taxes on income and property	1 039	1 506	1 004	1 780	4 125	7 993	14 121	24 087
Taxes on international transactions		788	525	4 990	8 242	15 764	28 467	44 644
Taxes on goods and services		2 147	1 431	1 689	5 562	8 373	19 621	26 167
Non-tax revenue (income and fees)	250	761	507	1 725	3798	6 562	7 551	10 111
Foreign grants	10	52	35	57	914	1 620	3 868	6 037
Total expenditure	5 999	9 220	6 147	15 175	27 485	47 891	73 328	106 987
Current expenditure	4 774	8 029	5 353	13 401	22 700	38 461	60 836	80 583
Wages and salaries				3 800	5 055	14 524	26 194	35 920
Interest	730			2 204	3 425	5 086	11 344	10 587
Other				7 397	14 220	18 852	23 298	34 076
Capital expenditure	1 226	1 191	794	1 774	4 785	9 430	12 492	26 404
Development expenditure	1 170	817	544	1 354	3 994	7 303	9 826	18 552
Net lending	56	374	249	420	791	2 127	2 666	4 852
Special efficiency	0	0	0	0	0	0	0	3 000
Surplus or deficit (-)	-1 602	-3 967	-2 645	-4 934	-4 844	-7 580	299	4 059

Table A.2: Central Government Operations and Financing, 1980-87 (₡ million) (Cont'd)

	1980/81	1981/82	1982	1983	1984	1985	1986	1987
Financing	1 602	3 967	2 645	4 934	4 844	7 580	-299	-4 059
Foreign (net)	430	215	143	970	1 816	3 522	-5 614	-1 180
Borrowing	0	0	0	0	5 073	9 562	13 412	23 654
Non-oil					5 073	9 562	5 193	
Oil							8 219	
Repayment	0	0	0	0	-3 257	-6 040	-19 026	-24 834
Non-Oil					-3 257	-6 040	-8 988	-14 817
Oil							-10 038	-10 017
Domestic (net)	1 172	3 752	2 501	3 964	3 028	4 058	5 315	-2 879
Banking system	650	1 190	793	2 145	3 106	3 011	2 471	-7 427
Social security	210	371	247	230	437	510	3 182	2 531
Other	312	2 191	1 461	1 589	-515	537	-338	2 017

Source: Ministry of Finance (Budget Division).

Table A.3:   Central Government Operations and Financing as Percentage of GDP, 1982-87 (percent)

	1982	1983	1984	1985	1986	1987
Total revenue and grants	4.1	5.6	8.4	11.8	13.4	14.7
Revenue	4.0	5.5	8.0	11.3	12.7	13.9
Taxes on income and property	1.2	1.0	1.5	2.3	2.6	3.2
Taxes on international transactions	0.6	2.7	3.0	4.6	5.2	5.9
Taxes on goods and services	1.7	0.9	2.1	2.4	3.6	3.5
Non-tax revenue (income & fees)	0.6	0.9	1.4	1.9	1.4	1.3
Foreign grants	0.0	0.0	0.3	0.5	0.7	0.8
Total expenditure	7.1	8.2	10.2	14.0	13.3	14.2
Recurrent expenditure	6.2	7.3	8.4	11.2	11.1	10.7
Wages and salaries	0.0	2.1	1.9	4.2	4.8	4.8
Interest	-	1.2	1.3	1.5	2.1	1.4
Other	0.0	4.0	5.3	5.5	4.2	4.5
Capital expenditure	0.9	1.0	1.8	2.7	2.3	3.5
Development expenditure	0.6	0.7	1.5	2.1	1.8	2.5
Net lending	0.3	0.2	0.3	0.6	0.5	0.6
Special efficiency	0.0	0.0	0.0	0.0	0.0	0.4
Surplus or deficit (-)	-3.1	-2.7	-1.8	-2.2	0.1	0.5
Financing	3.1	2.7	1.8	2.2	-0.1	-0.5
Foreign (net)	0.2	0.5	0.7	1.0	-1.0	-0.2
Borrowing	0.0	0.0	1.9	2.8	2.4	3.1
Non-oil	0.0	0.0	1.9	2.8	0.9	0.0
Oil	0.0	0.0	0.0	0.0	1.5	0.0
Repayment	0.0	0.0	-1.2	-1.8	-3.5	-3.3
Non-oil	0.0	0.0	-1.2	-1.8	-1.6	-2.0
Oil	0.0	0.0	0.0	0.0	-1.8	-1.3
Domestic (net)	2.9	2.2	1.1	1.2	1.0	-0.4
Banking system	0.9	1.2	1.1	0.9	0.4	-1.0
Social security	0.3	0.1	0.2	0.1	0.6	0.3
Other	1.7	0.9	-0.2	0.2	-0.1	0.3

Source: Ministry of Finance (Budget Division).

Table A.4: Public Investment Programme 1986-1988 - Public Development Expenditure (Project Aid, Grants and Budgetary Investments) (₵ million)

Sector summary exchange rate US$ 1.00= ₵ 150.00	Number of projects	1986 Total	1986 FC¹	1986 LC¹	1987 Total	1987 FC	1987 LC	1988 Total	1988 FC	1988 LC
Productive sectors	78	9 392	7 865	1 527	13 225.3	10 588	2 637.3	21 537	18 484.5	3 052.5
Agriculture	50	5 493	4 365	1 128	6 660.3	4 830	1 830.3	11 906	9 139.5	2 766.5
Industry	14	555	527	28	3 379	3 123	256	3 768	3 618	150
Mining and forestry	14	3 344	2 973	371	3 186	2 635	551	5 863	5 727	136
Economic/infrastructure sectors	96	25 331	16 874	8 457	34 100	23 711	10 389	68 951	55 589	13 362
Roads & highways	28	15 003	8 175	6 828	14 095	6 310	7 785	22 244	12 818	9 426
Transport and communications	38	6 749	5 839	910	9 620	8 147	1 473	19 304	18 390	914
Energy	21	1 120	795	325	6 144	5 670	474	20 180	19 018	1 162
Water supply	9	2 459	2 065	394	4 241	3 584	657	7 223	5 363	1 860
Social infrastructure sectors	27	1 325	650	675	5 382	1 904	3 478	5 667	3 380	2 287
Education	10	335	290	45	3 169	687	2 482	56	37	19
Health	17	990	360	630	2 213	1 217	996	5 611	3 343	2 268
Grand totals	201	36 048	25 389	10 659	52 707.3	36 203	16 504.3	96 155	77 453.5	18 701.5

¹ FC denotes foreign currency cost (translated to cedis) while LC denotes local currency costs.

Source: Ministry of Finance and Economic Planning (MFEP).

Table A.5: Imports of Cereals (thousand metric tons)

Year [1]	Domestic surplus + deficit -	Commercial Imports				Cereal imports under food aid
		Wheat	Maize	Rice	Total [2]	
	(1)	(2)	(3)	(4)	(5)	(6)
1975	-140.2	163.7	0.8	0.7	165.7	NA
1976	-134.7	89.0	10.6	4.1	106.4	NA
1977	-170.7	97.6	0.0	9.0	112.6	NA
1978	-221.4	169.6	0.0	45.4	245.6	NA
1979	-166.2	92.3	0.1	2.6	96.7	NA
1980	-151.4	31.7	12.6	65.9	154.1	NA
1981	-184.0	70.0	63.9	16.0	160.6	80.3
1982	-284.9	44.8	10.0	30.5	105.6	68.8
1983	-493.1	60.1	61.8	32.1	175.4	108.3
1984	-103.1	25.0	49.3	50.4	158.3	102.3
1985	-252.4	71.5	0.0	20.6	105.8	97.7
1986	-164.9	51.3	0.0	9.5 [3]	87.3	106.3
1987	-272.3	80.0 [4]	120.0 [4]	40.0 [4]	266.7 [4]	NA

[1] Rice has been converted to paddy equivalent. Figures reported for a year, e.g. 1981, refer to the 1981/82 (July-June) year. Figures before 1981 are not available.

[2] The rice quantities are divided by 0.6 to convert them to paddy equivalent in order to make the total comparable with column (1).

[3] Imports only up to June.

[4] Provisional, including government estimates. Actual figures will probably be lower.

Source: Column (1) from Table 1.4 in the text, Columns (2)-(4) for years 1975-80 from Sallinger 1986, 1981-87 from World Food Programme (WFP), Column (6) from WFP.

Table A.6: Arable Land and Cultivated Area in 1987 (ha)

Region	Geographical area	% of total	Arable area	Cultivated area	Surplus area
Greater Accra	324 500	1	243 375	106 998	136 377
Ashanti	2 438 900	10	1 463 340	1 181 788	281 552
Brong-Ahafo	3 955 700	17	2 373 420	974 585	1 398 835
Central	982 600	4	589 560	452 569	136 991
Eastern	1 932 300	8	1 159 380	873 405	285 975
Northern	7 038 400	30	3 519 200	1 417 356	2 101 841
Upper East	884 200	4	663 150	469 189	193 638
Upper West	1 837 600	7	918 800	439 189	479 611
Volta	2 057 000	9	1 028 500	295 123	733 377
Western	2 392 100	10	1 435 260	697 637	737 623
Total	23 843 300	100	13 577 745	6 908 162	6 485 823

Source: PPMED, Ministry of Agriculture, 1989.

Table A.7: Crop Area Planted and Production for Major Cereal and Starch Crops, 1977-89 (area in thousand ha, production in thousand metric tons)

		1977	1978	1979	1980	1981	1982	1983	1984	1985	1986	1987	1988[1]	1989[1]
Cereals	Area	773	704	834	822	804	788	743	1 275	964	881.2	1 126.9	1 046.0	1 166.1
	Production	648	588	679	711	679	548	388	965	780	866.7	1 056.4	1 146.0	1 217.3
Maize	Area	291	258	314	320	316	276	280	724	405	472.1	548.3	540.0	567.0
	Production	312	269	308	354	334	264	141	574	395	559.1	597.7	751.0	748.6
Rice	Area	61	59	61	65	46	44	37	69	87	76.1	72.0	51.8	71.6
	Production	63	61	63	64	44	37	27	76	80	69.6	80.7	95.0	73.7
Sorghum/millet	Area	421	388	459	438	443	468	427	482	472	333.0	506.6	454.2	528.0
	Production	273	258	307	293	301	246	230	315	305	238.0	378.0	300.0	395.0
Starch Crops	Area	609	673	664	796	767	658	603	2 838	837	963.3	960.2	782.5	1 003.0
	Production	4 025	4 434	4 353	5 199	4 991	3 879	3 097	10 094	5 385	6 012.0	6 000.6	618.5	6 208.4
Cassava	Area	257	283	280	386	337	275	242	814	356	387.2	389.5	353.5	415.0
	Production	2 119	2 334	2 320	2 896	2 721	1 986	1 375	4 065	3 075	2 876.2	2 725.8	3 300.0	3 327.2
Yam	Area	86	94	105	95	98	79	75	223	111	179.0	204.4	168.3	217.0
	Production	497	517	550	523	463	374	354	725	560	1 048.1	1 185.4	1 200.0	782.2
Cocoyam	Area	135	144	146	159	207	167	145	978	200	206.6	196.4	141.3	207.0
	Production	633	681	699	848	972	756	613	2 835	900	1 005.2	1 011.8	1 115.0	1 063.0
Plantain	Area	131	152	133	156	135	137	141	823	170	190.8	169.9	119.4	164.0
	Production	776	902	784	931	835	763	755	2 469	850	1 087.5	1 077.6	1 200.0	1 036.0

[1] 1988 and 1989 data are estimates.

Source: PPMED, Ministry of Agriculture, Accra.

Table A.8: Estimated Crop Yields Under Traditional, Improved and Advanced Cultivation Practices (kg/ha)

	Traditional	Improved [1]	Advanced [1]
Food crops [2]			
Maize [3]	700	1 200	1 800
Sorghum	300	600	-
Millet	300	500	-
Rice	600	1 000	1 200 [4]
Cassava	3 000	7 000	-
Yam	3 250	5 000	-
Groundnut	600	800	1 110
Cowpea	200	500	800
Industrial crops			
Cotton (seed) [2]	500	1 000	1 500 [4]
Tobacco (flue) [2]	250	750	-
Sugar-cane (tons/ha)	20	35	65 [4]
Oil-palm (oil) [5]	800	2 000	-
Export crops [5]			
Cocoa	250	500	-
Coffee	250	500	-
Rubber (dry)	400	1 000 (estate)	-
Coconut (copra)	600	900	-

[1] Anticipated yields for improved and advanced farming (and for estates) are mission estimates and, where possible, reflect experimental yields discounted by about 30%.

[2] Yields of annual crops refer to mono-cropping.

[3] Maize yields are for transitional and forest zones; yields for savannah areas would be 15-25% lower.

[4] Yields assume irrigation for rice, sugar-cane and cotton since these are the crops with the highest potential for irrigation.

[5] Yields of tree crops refer to non-estate crops, unless otherwise stated.

Source: Mission estimates computed from various sources including Ministry of Agriculture, World Bank and IFAD.

Table A.9: Livestock Population, 1977-87

Animal	1977	1978	1979	1980	1981	1982	1983	1984	1985	1986	1987
Cattle	823 661	35 912	857 004	876 841	903 724	1 215 059	1 002 015	1 077 843	1 064 778	1 134 870	116 977
Sheep	1 129 850	1 107 945	1 314 664	1 449 418	1 433 140	1 482 274	1 749 615	1 977 336	1 987 284	1 814 242	1 986 522
Goats	874 200	980 742	1 863 910	1 383 889	1 183 599	1 215 059	1 539 179	1 678 991	1 685 427	1 632 576	1 900 876
Pigs	151 007	165 959	185 421	224 407	259 899	169 945	316 626	487 893	413 112	468 653	398 949
Dogs	162 148	171 963	146 326	161 466	159 899	162 688	181 368	218 515	214 521	187 968	261 438
Cats	60 708	62 553	79 067	80 600	81 835	92 545	82 912	1 005 558	111 490	78 715	122 652
Poultry	4 580 089	6 281 967	7 269 567	7 532 544	6 056 017	4 874	5 949 491	5 893 123	10 024 496	6 418 709	8 214 086
Horses	2 990	2 309	2 451	2 578	2 559	2 490	2 741	2 176	2 514	2 211	2 136
Donkeys	6 341	6 823	4 844	5 017	6 320	7 380	6 746	9 366	10 814	13 182	13 595
Rabbits	-	-	-	-	51 939	60 551	45 277	47 150	85 987	90 607	82 569

Source: Department of Animal Health and Production, Ministry of Agriculture, 1987, and agricultural census, 1984.

Table A.10: Number of Holdings wth Different Number of Farms, 1986

Region	Total number of holdings	Number of holdings with									
		One farm		Two farms		Three farms		Four farms		Five farms	
		Number	%	Number	%	Number	%	Number	%	Number	%
Western	150 510	83 881	55.7	53 418	35.6	10 083	6.6	2 913	2	215	0.1
Central	146 497	95 618	65.3	39 779	27.1	9 804	6.7	1 144	0.8	152	0.1
Greater Accra	29 198	21 315	73.0	7 679	26.3	204	0.7	-	-	-	-
Eastern	197 810	133 577	67.6	53 874	27.4	8 565	4.3	1 146	0.6	648	0.3
Volta	147 177	85 811	58.3	47 032	32.0	11 479	7.8	2 128	1.4	727	0.5
Ashanti	264 909	130 051	49.1	103 192	39.0	28 596	10.8	2 949	1.1	121	0.1
Brong-Ahafo	168 104	85 811	51.0	62 943	37.4	17 004	10.2	2 222	1.3	124	0.1
Northern	116 304	44 246	38.0	56 193	48.3	5 658	4.8	4 223	3.6	5 984	5.3
Upper West	56 500	22 076	39.1	14 006	24.8	13 535	24.0	4 516	7.9	2 367	4.2
Upper East	154 864	39 570	25.6	58 194	37.6	42 434	27.4	12 423	8.0	2 243	1.4
Total	1 431 873	741 956	51.8	496 310	34.7	147 362	10.3	38 664	2.3	12 581	0.9

Source: Giri, Oku and Fukai 1987.

Table A.11: Extent of Production for Subsistence and Sale, 1986

Region	Total number of farms	Farms cultivated					
		For subsistence only		Mainly for subsistence		Mainly for cash	
		Number	%	Number	%	Number	%
Western	233 693	54 355	23.3	86 859	37.2	92 479	39.5
Central	209 924	12 946	6.2	153 609	73.2	43 369	20.6
Greater Accra	37 285	5 891	15.8	22 185	59.5	9 209	24.7
Eastern	274 844	57 681	21.0	142 542	51.9	74 621	27.1
Volta	226 459	78 215	34.5	119 533	52.8	28 711	12.7
Ashanti	434 624	85 486	19.7	288 169	66.3	60 969	14.0
Brong-Ahafo	272 217	36 947	13.6	145 941	53.6	89 329	32.8
Northern	220 418	86 379	32.8	111 275	59.1	22 764	8.1
Upper West	120 592	38 627	32.0	75 730	62.8	6 235	5.2
Upper East	344 167	171 162	49.7	136 684	39.7	36 321	10.6
Total	2 374 223	627 689	26.4	1 282 527	54.0	464 007	19.6

Source: Giri, Oku and Fukai 1987.

Table A.12: Wholesale Prices of Major Food Crops and Cocoa, 1970-86 (cedis per indicated weight)

Year	Maize (shelled) 100 kg	Rice (milled) 92.6 kg	Guinea corn 92.6 kg	Millet 92.6 kg	Cassava 90.7 kg	Yam[1] 100 kg	Cocoyam 90.7 kg	Groundnut 82 kg	Beans 109 kg	Plantain[2] 11.3 kg	Tomato 50.8 kg	Cocoa[3] ton	Rural CPI (1979 = 100)
1970	11.69	24.91	15.94	16.14	3.88	34.51	6.43	23.46	23.15	0.57	6.80	299	100.0
1971	11.94	25.71	16.80	17.34	5.08	41.29	8.40	23.07	26.23	0.84	6.74	301	108.9
1972	17.22	34.82	19.15	19.67	5.98	44.48	9.11	25.50	29.70	0.76	8.80	374	118.9
1973	18.43	41.73	26.88	25.36	6.09	54.40	12.26	35.51	35.29	1.13	12.80	439	139.6
1974	20.08	45.90	28.60	29.34	7.20	69.76	14.16	44.76	56.22	1.15	12.44	561	164.3
1975	24.94	62.93	29.21	28.93	11.02	95.35	17.00	53.50	58.32	1.48	16.23	602	209.2
1976	56.90	129.01	73.83	72.10	23.46	137.97	32.39	101.28	93.12	3.01	25.41	758	330.8
1977	118.73	182.54	163.46	159.50	59.45	286.90	84.46	194.24	189.90	8.98	47.77	1 333	720.5
1978	121.14	247.95	178.80	185.71	55.40	471.55	101.59	320.85	240.20	14.04	61.51	2 743	1 258.6
1979	171.70	282.28	215.95	222.78	64.61	584.90	125.70	474.10	459.00	4.91	114.32	4 000	2 004.3
1980	413.31	596.72	630.79	495.55	138.39	875.34	193.37	690.10	802.70	21.88	161.62	4 000	3 229.1
1981	773.59	1 102.01	884.12	878.16	339.35	1 544.87	403.41	1 486.00	1 976.50	33.84	303.15	12 000	6 761.5
1982	779.51	2 043.76	1 213.93	1 252.36	382.52	2 156.30	565.43	2 371.30	2 262.10	46.96	405.92	12 000	8 283.1
1983	3 857.59	6 154.98	5 774.41	4 531.19	1 496.91	7 019.50	2 806.70	5 915.60	6 494.50	200.25	901.55	20 000	9 017.1
1984	2 337.82	6 710.02	4 402.50	4 435.93	846.03	7 868.84	2 038.30	5 721.30	6 281.30	222.33	1 316.59	30 000	26 314.1
1985	2 037.91	5 206.69	2 694.10	2 958.41	794.61	6 813.21	1 040.60	5 805.40	5 800.40	195.61	1 873.99	56 600	28 628.2
1986	3 291.77	6 674.59	3 863.18	4 020.92	1 408.85	9 011.93	2 099.22	6 976.70	7 660.80	242.69	1 683.74	85 000	34 757.2

[1] MOA prices are given per 100 average tubers. It was assumed an average tuber weighs 1 kilo.

[2] Prices are given per average bunch. This was assumed to weigh 25 lb.

[3] COCOBOD price to producers.

Source: Ministry of Agriculture, Accra.

Table A.13: Regional Distribution of Physicians in Ghana (April 1984)

Region	Government	NGO	Private	Total	%
Greater Accra	197	-	144	341	41.5
Eastern	30	9	16	55	6.7
Central	22	4	13	39	4.8
Western	37	2	21	60	7.3
Volta	22	32	2	56	6.8
Ashanti	120	14	60	194	23.6
Brong-Ahafo	13	17	4	34	4.2
Northern	17	4	3	24	2.9
Upper East	6	3	2	11	1.3
Upper West	-	6	1	7	0.9
Total	464 (56.6%)	91 (11.1%)	266 (32.4%)	821 (100%)	100.0

Source: Ministry of Health.

Annex B

Smallholder Food Production and Consumption Patterns

The purpose of this annex is to describe the steps and the data used in arriving at the regional characterization of smallholder food production and consumption patterns. The resulting patterns were used to compute the evolution of smallholder gross income from food production as well as his food expenditures.

To compute average smallholder food production for 1984 the following procedure was used. First, on the basis of the census of agriculture, the total area cultivated in each region by all holders was computed. This was done by assuming a uniform distribution of holdings in each size class and taking the midpoint of each size class as the representative size for the class. For the class of holdings larger than 74 ha (30 acres) an average size equal to 123 ha (50 acres) was used in all regions. The next assumption was that smallholders do not have a crop pattern much different from that of all holders. This was suggested both by statisticians in Accra as well as by the fact that holdings in the two smallest size classes account for the bulk of all holdings. By dividing total area cultivated to a specific crop by the estimated total cultivated area, the area cultivated in each crop and region, per unit of total cultivated area, is obtained. Table B.1 indicates the estimated areas in food crops as well as the resulting region-specific cropping intensity for food crops. The table also indicates the total area cultivated in each region and the proportion of total area that is cultivated by smallholders. The typical size of a smallholder's holding in each region is found by a weighted average of the two smallest size classes for all regions and the three smallest size classes in the Northern Region (where because of ecological conditions the average holding must be larger).

The next step involved the estimation of the quantities produced by each typical smallholder in each region. This can be done by multiplying the per unit areas in Table B.1 by the average size of the holding (also indicated in Table B.1) and then for each crop by the

Table B.1: Crop Patterns of Smallholders - All Regions, 1984[1]

	Western	Central	Greater Accra	Eastern	Volta	Ashanti	Brong-Ahafo	Northern	Upper West	Upper East	Ghana
Maize	.446	.582	1.390	.627	.404	.283	.440	.317	.302	.025	.386
Rice	.082	.007	.012	.009	.035	.012	.035	.038	.080	.081	.038
Guinea corn	.000	.000	.000	.000	.041	.000	.008	.417	.468	.416	.134
Millet	.000	.000	.000	.000	.000	.000	.000	.338	.368	.553	.123
Cassava	.782	.582	.380	.755	.572	.471	.429	.252	.004	.000	.434
Yam	.106	.012	.000	.071	.113	.081	.232	.167	.204	.000	.119
Cocoyam	.368	.141	.000	.418	.123	.406	.321	.000	.000	.000	.211
Groundnuts	.000	.000	.000	.000	.077	.035	.064	.148	.136	.249	.080
Beans/Bambara beans	.000	.000	.000	.000	.000	.000	.000	.068	.457	.954	.107
Plantain	.411	.095	.000	.407	.059	.352	.217	.000	.000	.000	.178
Vegetables[2]	.153	.087	.498	.042	.079	.053	.147	.039	.025	.007	.083
Cropping intensity	2.349	1.506	2.280	2.329	1.503	1.693	1.893	1.784	2.044	2.285	1.893
Average size of holding of smallholder (ha)	.616	.514	.491	.498	.494	.518	.753	1.418	.684	.757	.581
Mean holding size for the region (ha)[3]	1.079	.635	.629	.560	.610	.999	1.350	2.707	1.047	1.366	1.045
Smallholder as proportion of all holders (%)	83.1	94.7	96.3	97.6	95.1	87.7	77.5	60.1	83.5	76.8	86.3
Total No. of smallholdings (thousands)	171	205.8	46.9	238.3	261.1	275.7	195.9	84.0	25.9	93.0	1 597.6
Total area under cultivation (thousand ha)	175.0	139.0	30.5	131.0	167.8	313.3	340.6	378.4	32.4	165.7	1 874.8
Percent of area cultivated by smallholders	60.2	76.4	75.0	90.8	76.8	45.5	43.2	31.5	54.9	42.5	52.3

[1] The figures denote the area cultivated in each crop per unit of total area cultivated.

[2] The area included was that for tomatoes, pepper, okra and garden eggs.

[3] Weighted average of all holding sizes.

Source: Computed from data in the 1984 census of agriculture.

yield of the traditional technology. These yields are given in Table B.2.

To obtain an idea of the potential changes from 1970 to 1984, Table B.3 reproduces the variables of Table B.1 for 1970. Several things are obvious by comparison of these two tables. First, the cropping intensity is substantially higher in 1984. In all regions, except Northern and Upper, the smaller cropping intensities indicated for 1970 could be due to the assumption that the average size of large holdings (larger than 20 ha) in 1970 is assumed equal to 60 ha while, for 1984, the average large holding is taken as 20 ha (these figures were suggested by MOA staff). However, this would not explain the stability of the cropping intensity in the Northern and Upper Regions. Noticeable also are the significant changes in the cropping pattern in 1984 in favour of staple foods in all regions except the Northern and Upper Regions, where the cropping patterns have remained largely unchanged. Also noticeable is the sharp increase in both the total as well as the proportion of smallholdings in all regions in 1984.

Table B.2: Yields of Food Crops by Traditional Producing Methods (kg/ha)

Maize	700	Yam	3 250
Rice	600	Cocoyam	900
Guinea corn	300	Groundnuts	600
Millet	300	Beans	300
Cassava	3 000	Plantain	1 725
		Vegetables	3 900

Source: Mission assessment of traditional smallholder yields.

The significant apparent change in cropping patterns between 1970 and 1984 could be due to the abnormal situation in 1983. To check this, the smallholder cropping pattern for 1986 was also computed on the basis of a smallholder survey carried out for 1986 (Giri, Oku and Fukai 1987). In that survey, the size classes were not as refined as in the 1970 or 1984 censuses (they were classified in classes of holdings less than 3 acres, 3-5 acres and larger than 5 acres). It was assumed that half of the holdings in the class 3-5 acres would be in the 3-4 acre category in order to conform to the 1984 classification (for the Northern Region all the holdings in the 3-5 acre category were included as it was impossible to isolate those among the large holdings (larger than 5 acres) that are between 5-6 acres). The 1986 survey revealed that very little of the area of smallholder plots was cultivated with cocoa, coconuts and oil-palm. This strengthens the validity of the

Table B.3: Cropping Pattern of Smallholders - All Regions, 1970[1]

	Western	Central	Eastern	Volta	Ashanti	Brong-Ahafo	Northern	Upper	Ghana
Maize	.118	.240	.223	.426	.058	.209	.415	.092	.160
Rice	.022	.005	.003	.038	.004	.015	.100	.047	.020
Guinea corn	-	-	-	.014	-	.007	.479	.466	.086
Millet	-	-	-	-	-	-	.295	.570	.088
Cassava	.171	.230	.260	.403	.054	.111	.036	.006	.124
Yam	.016	.038	.032	.086	.021	.120	.354	.057	.061
Cocoyam	.113	.105	.135	.055	.151	.181	-	-	.127
Groundnuts	-	-	-	.029	.002	.014	.145	.176	.035
Beans/Bambara beans	-	-	-	-	-	-	.061	.390	.053
Plantain	.214	.200	.219	.055	.303	.269	-	-	.204
Vegetables[2]	.014	.010	.036	.026	.009	.030	.070	.047	.025
Cropping intensity	.668	.828	.908	1.132	.602	.956	1.955	1.851	.983
Average size of holding of smallholder (ha)	.866	.696	.713	.677	.695	.802	1.130	.912	.762
Mean size of holding for the region[3] (ha)	3.769	2.129	2.575	1.579	1.579	6.683	4.964	2.195	2.911
Smallholder as proportion of all holders (%)	40.9	68.4	62.6	71.9	48.4	40.4	67.4	47.6	54.7
Total No. of smallholdings (thousands)	27.9	55.5	82.8	78.1	71.5	29.0	41.2	56.6	440.3
Total area under cultivation (thousand hectares)	257.6	170.5	378.0	170.0	987.7	353.3	145.4	361.7	2 824.2
Percent of area cultivated by smallholders	9.4	22.7	14.3	31.1	5.0	6.6	37.1	14.3	12.3

[1] The figures denote the area cultivated in each crop per unit of total area cultivated.

[2] Area included that of tomato, pepper and okra. In cases where area data was reported for two regions jointly it was apportioned on the basis of the 1984 shares of vegetable area in the regions.

[3] Weighted average of all holding sizes.

Source: Computed from data in the 1970 census of agriculture.

assumption that the smallholder crop pattern is largely determined by food crops. Table 3.5 in the text indicates the computed cropping pattern, and statistics similar to those of Tables B.1 and B.3. It is rather surprising that both the cropping pattern in 1986 in most regions (except Northern and Upper) as well as the cropping intensities are more similar to those computed for 1970 than those computed for 1984. This result reinforces the conclusion that 1984 was a rather unusual and transitional year and that the crop pattern of 1986 is closer to the traditional crop pattern of smallholders. For this reason the 1986 crop production pattern is used to compare production and consumption of smallholders. Table B.4 illustrates the quantities produced of the various staple crops by a representative smallholding in 1986 under normal weather conditions and traditional technologies in all regions in Ghana.

With regard to staple food consumption for 1984, the following procedure was used. The Summary Report on Household Economic Survey, 1974-75, reports quantities of consumed foods, self-produced as well as purchased. First, all consumed quantities of staple foods as well as processed staple foods (e.g. gari, kokonte) were converted to raw product equivalent. Then the total reported quantities consumed out of own production were apportioned to individual regions on the basis of quantity produced of the corresponding crop in each region in 1974. For lack of 1974 data vegetables were apportioned on the basis of area planted in 1984. Of the quantities consumed that were purchased, it was assumed that 25 percent were purchased by agricultural households. They were then apportioned to regions in proportion to their total agricultural population, which in turn was derived from the 1970 agricultural census by applying a uniform annual growth rate of 2.66 percent which was the annual growth rate for the total population during that period. This procedure gave total quantities consumed of all staple foods in 1974 by members of agricultural households only. Non-agricultural households were assumed to consume only purchased quantities. The per capita quantities consumed by farmers were found by dividing the totals by the number of individuals in farm households estimated for 1974, namely those that have own production. These per capita figures were then multiplied for each region by the average rural household size in 1984, which was obtained from the 1984 population census, to arrive at the average consumption per holding. Table B.5 indicates the estimated average quantities consumed by a typical rural agricultural household in the various regions, using 1984 rural household sizes. The indicated quantities are probably overestimates for two reasons.

Table B.4: Production of Food Crops by a Representative Smallholder - All Regions, 1986 (kg)

Region	Average size of holding (ha)	Maize	Rice paddy	Guinea corn	Millet	Cassava	Yam	Cocoyam	Groundnut	Beans	Plantain	Vegetables
Western	0.796	124.6	14.4	0.0	0.8	681.0	169.0	132.3	0.0	0.0	201.8	109.2
Central	0.696	208.6	9.0	0.0	0.0	831.0	39.0	76.5	3.0	0.3	174.2	171.6
Greater Accra	0.697	149.8	2.4	0.0	0.0	549.0	3.3	0.0	1.2	0.0	3.5	678.6
Eastern	0.677	277.2	13.2	0.0	0.0	1 272.0	295.8	242.1	2.4	0.0	374.3	0.0
Volta	0.663	169.4	11.4	0.0	0.0	894.0	347.8	30.6	0.6	0.9	65.5	401.7
Ashanti	0.714	169.4	3.6	0.0	0.0	771.0	237.3	251.1	7.8	1.8	452.0	171.6
Brong-Ahafo	0.791	254.8	33.6	0.0	0.0	1 116.0	692.3	139.5	27.0	0.0	277.7	522.6
Northern	0.909	373.1	15.6	147.6	88.2	537.0	786.5	0.0	183.0	64.8	0.0	210.6
Upper West	1.078	172.2	39.6	121.2	64.2	0.0	338.0	0.0	100.2	83.7	0.0	0.0
Upper East	0.809	21.7	0.0	62.4	96.9	0.0	0.0	0.0	100.8	128.4	0.0	0.0
Ghana	0.748	195.3	16.8	38.7	30.6	663.0	331.5	99.9	52.2	33.0	176.0	183.3

Source: Computed.

Table B.5: Average Smallholder Household Consumption of Basic Foods in 1984 (kg per annum)

	Western	Central	Greater Accra	Eastern	Volta	Ashanti	Brong-Ahafo	Northern	Upper West	Upper East	Ghana
Maize	168.0	204.0	132.9	156.5	228.9	259.2	408.5	362.5	263.1	232.4	234.5
Rice	25.5	20.2	23.6	27.8	27.6	25.5	29.1	138.1	48.1	42.5	43.7
Guinea corn	6.0	5.3	6.2	7.4	18.9	6.9	11.9	328.2	522.7	461.7	83.8
Millet	5.6	5.0	6.0	6.8	6.3	6.4	6.0	434.8	749.0	661.6	109.1
Cassava	2 648.2	2 029.9	1 416.5	1 667.4	2 815.4	2 008.0	3 692.7	226.2	213.3	188.4	1 932.5
Yam	85.1	73.3	120.9	142.3	367.6	206.8	1 372.2	1 349.7	339.1	299.5	370.5
Cocoyam	1 080.0	443.5	359.5	432.2	1 028.7	835.5	1 621.9	43.6	41.1	36.3	568.1
Groundnut	6.9	7.3	23.2	27.3	19.9	10.3	25.4	186.3	166.9	147.5	38.5
Beans	1.7	1.5	1.8	2.1	1.9	2.0	2.1	32.4	72.5	64.1	11.1
Plantain	1 045.4	626.1	548.6	645.8	195.5	1 879.6	1 475.0	151.0	142.5	125.8	837.4
Vegetables	144.3	66.9	76.3	89.8	74.7	70.6	255.0	175.2	72.5	64.1	100.7
Average 1984 rural household size per holding	4.32	3.82	4.46	5.25	4.85	4.90	5.19	9.27	8.74	7.72	5.27

Source: Computed.

First, the household size of smallholders is likely to be somewhat smaller than the average for all the rural population, because smallholders cannot afford large families. Second, the overall income deterioration since 1974 in Ghana has probably resulted in smaller per capita consumption of basic foods. Nevertheless, the figures are the best which can be derived from current data.

It must also be kept in mind that the estimated production figures are most likely overestimates of the quantities available for consumption because they neglect the post-harvest losses as well as the amounts retained for seed. On the other hand, many smallholders use improved varieties in at least a portion of their fields for maize, rice and cassava and this implies larger yields than the ones assumed above.

The potential 20-30 percent increase in average yields could, however, be counterbalanced by the post-harvest losses. For these reasons it is felt that the comparison between Tables B.4 and B.5 gives a reasonable approximation of current smallholder food production and consumption.

There are, of course, several caveats in the comparison of production and consumption patterns that come from completely independent sources. Given the unavailability of more detailed surveys, the derived patterns will be used to trace the general gross food income and gross food expenditure of smallholders.

Annex C

Methodology Note for Calculation of the Number of Smallholders Below the Poverty Line

To calculate the proportion and number of smallholders below the poverty line by region, one needs the following information: first, the empirical regional income distribution of rural smallholder farm households; second, the representative income of a smallholder's household by region; and third, the poverty line.

The rural smallholder income distribution is assumed to be proportional to the observed distribution of land holdings for the relevant year. This distribution is probably a very good approximation of income distribution in the Northern Region where farming is the major occupation and source of income. Since land is relatively freely available, more income can be obtained by cultivating more land, hence the size of holding is likely to represent the farm income-earning possibilities of the household. In the south, the true distribution is likely to be less skewed than the observed land distribution because smaller farmers tend to have proportionally more non-farm sources of income (however, not necessarily more income) in order to survive. The computed empirical probability distribution based on the distribution of land holdings is proportionally shifted for each year and region by the ratio of the adjusted mean smallholder household income (this is further discussed below) to the mean of the original land distribution. This process basically preserves the shape of the distribution (so that for instance both the mean and standard deviation of the new distribution are the same multiple of the original one) while stretching the axis.

The second step involves estimates of mean total income of smallholders by region. This was done by first computing the gross food crop income, which is likely to be all crop income, by multiplying the regionally observed crop patterns (which are given as proportions of total cultivated area planted to a specific crop) by the traditional yields and then by the average size of smallholding and finally by the national wholesale prices for the relevant products and year. The mean food crop income thus computed is an overestimate of true mean crop income for two reasons: first, the wholesale prices are higher than the prices the farmers receive at farmgate; and second, the farmer usually incurs some cash costs either for material inputs or labour and this lowers his net income. To get a better estimate of true crop income the following procedure was used. The census publishes tables which indicate the proportions of farms that are cultivated for subsistence only, mainly for subsistence, and for commercial sale (a farm refers to a parcel of land, while a holding can consist of more than one farm). (See Annex A, Table A.11 for a summary of these figures.) By assuming that the proportion marketed by subsistence farms is zero, by mainly subsistence farms 40 percent, and mainly commercial farms 80 percent, the average proportion of farm produce that is marketed is obtained for each region. Let that be "y" for some region. It is then assumed that farmers get on average 60 percent of the wholesale prices for the amount they sell. Then the farmer's effective crop income is (1-.4y) times the gross income computed above. This is so because for a proportion y of his crop the farmer gets .6p where p is the wholesale price, while for the remaining 1-y he in effect gets p (namely consumption out of own production is valued as income at full market prices). Hence if Q is the quantity of the produced crop, then his imputed crop income is:

$$.6pyQ+p(1-y)Q=(1-.4y)pQ$$

By computing y for each region the gross farmer income can be scaled to obtain a more realistic figure for his true farm income. This procedure still neglects the input costs and hence gives an overestimate of crop income.

Subsequently the crop income is adjusted upwards to account for non-crop sources of income. The figures obtained in the previous step are divided by the proportion of total income that is obtained from crops. This proportion is higher for non-fishing areas than for fishing areas and hence different proportions are used for each region. We use 0.44 for the Central and Greater Accra Regions, 0.6 for all other southern regions and 0.8 for regions in the north. (The number 0.44 was obtained from an ILO Study (ILO 1985), the other figures are mission estimates).

The above procedure gives a figure for the average adjusted total income of rural smallholders in each region. To obtain a distribution around this average, the distribution of land holdings in each region is used. The distribution of land holdings described earlier is shifted upwards so that its mean is equal to adjusted total income. The adjusted poverty level P (for the estimate of this see below) falls in one of the intervals of the distribution. The percent of households below poverty is computed by summing the empirical distribution for all the intervals below the one where the poverty level falls as well as the fraction of the density in the interval where the poverty line is: in other words, if the poverty line P falls within an interval (a, b) which empirically has density equal to y then the fraction (P-a)/(b-a) of y is added to the cumulative distribution below a.

The proportion of poor households thus estimated is likely to be an underestimate because input costs were neglected and subsequently total incomes tend to be on the high side. On the other hand, it could be an overestimate if the sources of income (especially non-farm) are underestimated.

Estimation of the Poverty Line

The purpose of this section is first to update previous estimates of the rural and urban poverty income levels and then to compare them with average observed earnings of smallholder households and various types of workers.

The starting point is the estimate made by the World Bank (World Bank 1985c) that absolute poverty income in the rural and urban areas is equal to US$ 150 and US$ 307 respectively. Absolute poverty income is described by Tabatabai (1986) as "that income level below which a minimal nutritionally adequate diet plus essential non-food requirements is not affordable." Tabatabai, through a series of steps, translated these figures to Basic Needs Income (BNI) per household and per working member of household for 1970 as illustrated in Table C.1.

These figures are within the range of ¢ 360-460 for annual household income adequate to cover basic needs in 1970, estimated independently by ILO (ILO/JASPA 1977). If one multiplies the urban, rural and national basic needs household income for 1970 as indicated in Table C.1 by the consumer price indices for later years, one arrives at the BNI for a household size of 5.27 for later years. The detailed time series for 1970-86 of this computation is given in Table C.2. For 1986 the national household BNI for a typical household is estimated at ¢ 130 660, while for the rural and urban areas this is estimated at ¢ 107 453 and ¢ 197 895 respectively.

Table C.1: Basic Needs Income, 1970 (cedis/year)

	Per household [1]	Per working member of household
Urban	597	309
Rural	309	160
National	392	203

[1] Average household size is 5.27, average number of working members per household is 1.93.

Source: Tabatabai 1986.

In 1970, the average household in Ghana had 1.93 working members while in 1984 the average household had 2.35 working members. Assuming a constant annual increase in the number of working members per household between these two points, the time series of basic needs household income can be converted to BNI per working member of a household. This is also exhibited in Table C.2. In 1986, the computations imply a BNI of ₵ 54 216 on a national scale, ₵ 44 586 for a rural, and ₵ 82 114 for an urban, working member of a household.

Table C.3 illustrates the ratio of three major reported earning series (adjusted on an annual basis) to the annual BNI per working member of household reported in Table C.2.

The table reveals that the average earnings of agricultural employees as a ratio of rural BNI, which fluctuated within the range of 2.4 to 2.9 for the first half of the nineteen-seventies, has almost steadily declined since then, to its lowest ratio of 0.42 in the drought year of 1983. It has subsequently recovered to 0.91, a level slightly above that of 1979-80. A similar pattern is observed for the average earnings of manufacturing employees when compared to the urban BNI. The improvement in average earnings has been faster in manufacturing than in agriculture for the 1983-85 period. In 1985, the average earnings of employees in agriculture were 9 percent below the rural BNI. By comparison, in 1974 these earnings were 188 percent above the estimated rural BNI.

If one uses the regionally computed food crop income for 1986 for a representative smallholder and adjusts it for household size and other sources of income, a figure for adjusted smallholder household income by region, that can be compared to the computed basic needs rural income, can be obtained. The estimated figure is likely to be an overestimate of true income because the gross crop income figure computed is an overestimate of true net crop income, as indicated in the previous section.

Table C.2: Basic Needs Income (BNI), 1970-86 (cedis per annum)[1]

Year	Average household BNI [1]			BNI per working member of household		
	National	Rural	Urban	National	Rural	Urban
1970	392	309	597	203	160	309
1971	428	337	659	218	172	336
1972	472	368	734	237	185	369
1973	554	432	880	274	214	436
1974	656	508	1 061	320	248	518
1975	851	647	1 458	409	311	701
1976	1 330	1 023	2 198	630	485	1 042
1977	2 876	2 227	4 643	1 344	1 041	2 170
1978	4 978	3 891	7 963	2 944	1 793	3 670
1979	7 688	6 196	11 910	3 495	2 816	5 413
1980	11 539	9 983	16 854	5 174	4 477	7 558
1981	24 984	20 903	37 164	11 055	9 249	16 444
1982	30 555	25 607	45 391	13 343	11 182	19 821
1983	68 086	58 793	97 626	29 347	25 342	42 080
1984	95 029	81 351	137 423	40 438	34 617	58 478
1985	104 894	88 505	154 579	44 073	37 187	64 949
1986	130 660	107 453	197 895	54 216	44 586	82 114

[1] Per average household size of 5.28.

Source: Computed by Mission by updating figures in Tabatabai 1986.

Table C.3: Average Earnings of Employees as a Ratio of BNI, 1970-86 (cedis per annum)

Year	Average earnings of all employees		Average earnings of agricultural employees [4]		Average earnings of manufacturing employees		Average earnings of employees in agriculture to those in manufacturing
	Cedis per annum	As ratio of BNI [1]	Cedis per annum	As ratio of RBNI [2]	Cedis per annum	As ratio of UBNI [3]	
1970	564	2.78	396	2.48	936	3.03	0.42
1971	606	2.78	448	2.78	911	2.71	0.49
1972	650	2.74	448	2.58	1 051	2.75	0.44
1973	751	2.74	516	2.41	842	1.93	0.61
1974	1 138	3.56	715	2.88	1 248	2.41	0.57
1975	1 224	2.99	800	2.57	1 416	2.02	0.56
1976	1 368	2.17	858	1.77	1 500	1.44	0.57
1977	2 580	1.92	1 860	1.79	2 676	1.23	0.70
1978	2 712	1.18	2 064	1.15	3 672	1.00	0.52
1979	3 432	0.98	2 232	0.79	4 272	0.79	0.52
1980	5 532	1.07	3 948	0.88	6 624	0.88	0.60
1981	-		6 036	0.65	8 268	0.50	0.73
1982	5 580	0.42	6 708	0.60	9 444	0.48	0.71
1983	13 320	0.45	10 632	0.42	15 744	0.37	0.68
1984	25 608	0.63	27 864	0.80	33 744	0.58	0.83
1985	40 164	0.91	33 900	0.91	62 808	0.97	0.54

[1] National BNI.

[2] Rural BNI.

[3] Urban BNI.

[4] Earnings of agricultural employees in establishments employing more than 10 workers.

Source: Computed.

Bibliography

Agricultural Development Bank of Ghana. 1987. "Small Scale Agricultural Producers and Women." Accra. Mimeographed.

Ahmed, Iftikhar. (ed.). 1985. *Technology and Rural Women.* Geneva: International Labour Organisation.

Amissah, S.B. 1985. "The Size of Holdings, Technology and Landlessness." Accra. Mimeographed.

Andah, K. 1978. "Ghanaian Women in Agriculture, The Case of Food Production." National Council on Women and Development Seminar. Mimeographed.

Ardayfio-Schandorf, Elizabeth. 1982. "Rural Development Strategies in Northern Ghana." Centre for Development Studies: Accra. Mimeographed.

——. 1984. "Urban Marketing System: An Analysis of Operational and Environmental Conditions of Marketing in Ghana." Accra. Mimeographed.

——. 1986. *The Rural Energy Crisis in Ghana: Its Implications for Women's Work and Household Survival.* (ILO) World Employment Research Working Paper WEP 10/WP.39.

Arhin, Kwame. 1985a. "The Expansion of Cocoa Production: The Working Condition of Migrant Cocoa Farmers in the Central and Western Regions." Accra. Mimeographed.

——. 1985b. "Land Acquisition, Land Dispute and Land Reform in Ghana: Tenancies and Security." Accra. Mimeographed.

Arthur, Kojo. 1985. "Ghana's Food Crisis: Alternative Perspectives." Trenton, New Jersey: Africa Research and Publications Project Inc.

Arwiman, Asante. 1984. "Ghana, Integrated Maize Processing and Storage, Land Use." Accra. Mimeographed.

Atsu, S.Y. 1980. Ashanti Farm Level Studies. Interim Report No. 1. Accra: Institute of Statistical, Social and Economic Research. Mimeographed.

Atta-Konadu, Y.K. 1967. "Comments on Polly Hill's Migrant Cocoa Farmer." Accra: Ministry of Agriculture. Mimeographed.

———. 1974. "Economic Optima in Resource Allocation for Smallholder Subsistence Farming in Ghana." Ph.D. Thesis, Michigan State University.

Azinim, A. 1980. "Maize Marketing in Ghana: Private Performance and Public Policy." M.S. Thesis. Legon: University of Ghana.

Benneh, George. 1985. "Dynamics of Land Tenure and Agrarian Systems in Africa: Ghana Case Study." Accra. Mimeographed.

Bequele, Assefa. 1983. "Stagnation and Inequality in Ghana." In Ghai, and Radwan. (eds.). 1983. Geneva: International Labour Organisation. 219-247.

Brainerd, T.R. 1984. "Lessons from Fisheries Development in West Africa." University of Rhode Island, International Center for Marine Resource Development. Mimeographed.

Breebaart, G. 1980. "Road Got No Mouth: Women in the Upper Region of Ghana as Participants in Their Own Development Process." Leiden University. Mimeographed.

Brown, C.K. 1984. *Social Structure and Poverty in Selected Rural Communities in Ghana.* Institute of Statistical, Social and Economic Research Poverty Series No. 6. Legon: Institute of Statistical, Social and Economic Research, University of Ghana.

Brown, C.K., and L.O. Gyekye. 1984. "Women in Cooperatives: A Pilot Study of Women's Economic Associations in Ghana." Legon: Institute of Statistical, Social and Economic Research, University of Ghana. Mimeographed.

Catholic Dioceses of Suyani, Ghana. 1973. "Report on Survey." Mimeographed.

Chambers, Robert, Richard Longhurst, and Arnold Pacey. 1981. *Seasonal Dimensions to Rural Poverty.* London: Frances Pinter Publishers Ltd.

Christian Service Committee and Volta Resettlement Committee. 1980. "Annual Report of the Christian Council of Ghana." Mimeographed.

Canadian International Development Agency (CIDA). 1986. "Shiriyan Aiyukan Maata-N-Tudo (The coming together of women of the north for prosperity and development): A Proposal for Women in Development Project for Northern Ghana." Mimeographed.

Crops Research Institute. 1983. "Programmes and Projects." Kwadaso: Crops Research Institute. Mimeographed.

Dadson, J.A. 1983. "People's Participation Project in Ghana: An Operational Manual (provisional)." Rome: Food and Agriculture Organization. Mimeographed.

Dapaah, S.K. 1984. "Effects of Relative Marketing Risks on Farmers' Acreage Allocation Between Export and Food Crops in West Africa: Empirical Evidence from Ghana." Paper presented at Institute of Statistical, Social and Economic Research Conference on Food Self-Sufficiency in West Africa. 1-3 May 1984. Mimeographed.

Ewusi, Kodwo. 1977. *The Socio-economic Determinants of Inter-regional Migration in Ghana.* Institute of Statistical, Social and Economic Research Discussion Paper No. 2. Accra.

—. 1983. "The Dynamics of Rural Poverty in Ghana and its Alleviation." WCARRD Follow-up Programme. In-depth studies series No. 8. Rome: Food and Agriculture Organization. Mimeographed.

—. 1984. *The Dimensions and Characteristics of Rural Poverty in Ghana.* Institute of Statistical, Social and Economic Research Technical Publication No. 43. Legon: University of Ghana.

—. 1986. "Economic Trends in Ghana 1984-85 and Prospects for 1986." Legon: Institute of Statistical, Social and Economic Research, University of Ghana. Mimeographed.

—. 1987a. *Improved Appropriate Technologies for Rural Women.* Accra: Adwinsa Publications.

—. 1987b. *Urbanization, Modernization and Employment of Women in Ghana.* Accra: Adwinsa Publications.

Ewusi, Kodwo, and Mabey. 1982. "Expenditure Patterns of Upper and Middle Income Groups in Ghana." Legon: Institute of Statistical, Social and Economic Research, University of Ghana. Mimeographed.

Food and Agriculture Organization (FAO). 1976. *A Framework for Land Evaluation.* FAO Soils Bulletin No. 32. Rome: Food and Agriculture Organization.

—. 1985a. "Report on FAO." Sponsored Seminar on Land Tenure and Agrarian Systems and Rural Development Held in Accra, 17-18 June 1985. Mimeographed.

—. 1985b. "Ghana, General Identification Mission." Vols. I and II. Report of the FAO/IFAD Cooperative Programme. Rome: Food and Agriculture Organization. Mimeographed.

—. 1985c. "Socio-Economic Base-line Survey of the Wenchi (PPP) Project Area." Rome: Food and Agriculture Organization. Mimeographed.

——. 1986. Freedom from Hunger Campaign/Action for Development. "1986 Projects." Rome: Food and Agriculture Organization. Mimeographed.

——. 1987. "Ghana Third Cocoa Project." FAO Investment Centre Preparation Mission Report. Doc. No. 108/86 CP-GHA.17. Rome: Food and Agriculture Organization. Mimeographed.

Food and Agriculture Organization/World Bank Cooperative Programme. 1987a. "Ghana Forestry Project." Report of Preparation Mission. Rome: Food and Agriculture Organization. Mimeographed.

——. 1987b. "Ghana Third Cocoa Project." Report of Preparation Mission. Rome: Food and Agriculture Organization. Mimeographed.

Food and Agriculture Organization/World Health Organization/Organization of African Unity/Regional Food and Nutrition Commission for Africa. 1983. "Food and Nutrition Development in the Northern Region of Ghana." Mimeographed.

Fruge, Michelle. 1987. "Survey of Organizations Involved in Development in Ghana, 1985-86." Accra: Catholic Relief Services. Mimeographed.

Gallin, R.S., and A. Spring. 1985. *Women Creating Wealth; Transforming Economic Development.* Association for Women in Development Conference. Mimeographed.

Ghai, Dharam, and Samir Radwan. (eds.). 1983. *Agrarian Policies and Rural Poverty in Africa.* Geneva: International Labour Organisation.

Ghana Grains Development Project. 1985. "6th Annual Report 1984." Accra: Ghana Grains Development Project. Mimeographed.

——. 1986. "7th Annual Report 1985." Accra: Ghana Grains Development Project. Mimeographed.

——. 1987. "8th Annual Report 1986." Accra: Ghana Grains Development Project. Mimeographed.

Ghedemah, C. 1978. "The Role of Women in Rice Production in Northern Ghana." Accra: National Council on Women and Development Seminar. Mimeographed.

Giri, R., S. Oku, and K. Fukai. 1987. "Agricultural Sector Survey 1986." Accra: Ministry of Agriculture. Mimeographed.

Goody, J. (ed.). 1975. *Changing Social Structure in Ghana.* London: International African Institute.

Government of The Netherlands. 1986. Technologies for Rural Women. First Progress Report. Mimeographed.

Green, Reginald H. 1987. "Ghana, Stabilization and Structural Shifts." Institute of Development Studies Workshop. Mimeographed.

Gyekye, L.O. 1986. "Women's Access to Land for Agricultural Production in Ghana." Legon: University of Ghana. Mimeographed.

Hansen, Emmanuel. 1984. "The Food Crisis in Ghana: National Policies and Organization." Trenton, New Jersey: African Research and Publications Project. Mimeographed.

Hart, David. 1980. *The Volta River Project: A Case Study, Politics and Technology*. Edinburgh: University Press.

Hill, Polly. 1958. "Migrant Cocoa Farmer in Southern Ghana: A Study of Rural Institutions." Mimeographed.

International Fund for Agricultural Development (IFAD). 1985. "Ghana Smallholder Rehabilitation Programme." Formulation Report. Rome: International Fund for Agricultural Development. Mimeographed.

——. 1986. "Smallholder Rehabilitation and Development Project." Appraisal Report, Vols. I and II. Rome: International Fund for Agricultural Development. Mimeographed.

International Labour Organisation (ILO). 1984. *Resources, Power and Women: Proceedings of the African and Asian Inter-Regional Workshop on Strategies for Improving the Employment Conditions of Rural Women, Arusha*. Geneva: International Labour Organisation.

——. 1985. *Labour Use and Productivity and Technological Change in African Smallholder Agriculture: A Case Study of Ghana*. Addis Ababa: International Labour Organisation, Jobs and Skills Programme for Africa (JASPA).

International Labour Organisation/Government of The Netherlands/National Council on Women and Development. 1985a. *Technologies for Rural Women - Ghana. Palm Oil Processing*. Technical Manual No. 1. Geneva: International Labour Organisation and Accra: National Council on Women and Development.

——. 1985b. *Technologies for Rural Women - Ghana. Soap Manufacturing*. Technical Manual No. 2. Geneva: International Labour Organisation and Accra: National Council on Women and Development.

——. 1985c. *Technologies for Rural Women - Ghana. Fish Smoking*. Technical Manual No. 3. Geneva: International Labour Organisation and Accra: National Council on Women and Development.

—. 1987a. *Technologies for Rural Women - Ghana. Gari Processing.* Technical Manual No. 4. Geneva: International Labour Organisation and Accra: National Council on Women and Development.

—. 1987b. *Technologies for Rural Women - Ghana. Coconut Oil Processing.* Technical Manual No. 5. Geneva: International Labour Organisation and Accra: National Council on Women and Development.

International Labour Organisation/Jobs and Skills Programme for Africa (JASPA). 1977. Employment Problems in the Rural and Informal Sectors in Ghana. Report to the Government of Ghana by an ILO/JASPA sectorial employment mission. Addis Ababa: International Labour Organisation. Mimeographed.

International Fertilizer Development Centre. 1986. "Ghana Fertilizer Privatization Study." Muscle Shoals, Alabama: International Fertilizer Development Centre. Mimeographed.

International Institute of Rural Reconstruction and Ghana Rural Reconstruction Movement. 1984. "An Experiment in Integrated Rural Development: The Mampong Valley Social Laboratory in Ghana." Mimeographed.

Konings, Piet, and James J. Rowell. (eds.). 1986. *The State and Rural Class Formation in Ghana: A Comparative Analysis.* London: Keagon Paul International.

Kwatia, Janet/United Nations Children's Fund/International Institute of Tropical Agriculture. 1986. "Rural Cassava Processing and Utilization Centre." Mimeographed.

Loutfi, Martha. 1980. *Rural Women: Unequal Partners in Development.* Geneva: International Labour Organisation.

May, Ernesto. 1984. *Exchange Controls and Parallel Market Economies in sub-Saharan Africa. Focus on Ghana.* Staff Working Paper No. 711. Washington, D.C.: World Bank.

Mensah, P. 1986. Farm Household Survey Vol. 1A (1984 Minor and 1985 Major Seasons). Field document of UNDP/FAO project GHA/85/011, "Pilot Project for Promotion of Integrated Agricultural Development in Sekyere District, Ashanti Region, Ghana". Mimeographed.

Mikell, Gwendolyn. 1984. "Filiation, Economic Crisis and the Status of Women in Rural Ghana." *Canadian Journal of African Studies.* 18 (1): 195-218.

Moffat, L., and F. Peters. 1984. "Data Gathering Mission, Women in Development, Northern, Upper East and Upper West Regions."

National Council on Women and Development and Canadian International Development Agency. Mimeographed.

National Council on Women and Development. various dates. *Annual Report*. 1980-1984. Accra: National Council on Women and Development.

Nettey, E., and G. Narty. 1983. Paper on "Government Consultation on the Role of Women in Food Production and Food Security." Accra. Mimeographed.

Okoso-Amaa, Kweku, M. Caurie, T.C. Lee, and C.O. Chichester. 1977. "Patterns of Production, Utilization and Consumption of Fish Along the Coast of Ghana." University of Rhode Island, International Center for Marine Resource Development. Mimeographed.

Oppong, C. 1978. "Links Between Women's Work Activity, Education and Motherhood in Developing Countries." National Council on Women and Development Seminar. Mimeographed.

Oppong C., and K. Abu. 1984. The Changing Maternal Role of Ghanaian Women: Impacts of Education, Migration and Employment. World Employment Programme Series. Geneva: International Labour Organisation.

Oteng, N.K. 1984. "Maize Marketing in a Rural Area and in Three Urban Centres." M.S. Thesis. Legon: University of Ghana.

Rabanal, Herminio R. "Brackishwater Aquaculture Development in the Volta Region." Report prepared for VORADEP. Ho, Ghana, and Manila, Philippines: Ministry of Agriculture. Mimeographed.

Republic of Ghana. 1970. *1970 Population Census of Ghana*. Accra: Central Bureau of Statistics.

——. 1972. "Report on Ghana Sample Census of Agriculture 1970". Vol. I. Accra: Ministry of Agriculture, Economics and Marketing Division. Mimeographed.

——. 1973. "Annual Report." Accra: Department of Social Welfare. Mimeographed.

——. 1974. "The New Structure and Content of Education for Ghana." Accra-Tema: Ministry of Education. Mimeographed.

——. 1975. "Report on Current Agricultural Statistics (1974)." Accra: Ministry of Agriculture. Mimeographed.

——. 1979. "Summary Report on Household Economic Survey, 1974-75." Accra: Central Bureau of Statistics.

——. 1984a. "Ghana Agricultural Policy: Actions, Plans and Strategies, 1984-86." Mimeographed.

—. 1984b. "External Trade Statistics 1983." Accra: Central Bureau of Statistics. Mimeographed.

—. 1984c. "1984 Population Census of Ghana: Preliminary Report." Accra: Central Bureau of Statistics. Mimeographed.

—. 1984d. "Draft National Food and Nutrition Policies and Programmes 1985-89." Accra: National Nutrition Coordination Committee and Joint FAO/WHO/OAU Regional Food and Nutrition Commission for Africa. Mimeographed.

—. 1985a. "Progress of the Economic Recovery Programme 1984-86 and Policy Framework 1986-88." Accra: Republic of Ghana. Mimeographed.

—. 1985b. "Quarterly Digest of Statistics." Accra: Statistical Service. Mimeographed.

—. 1985, 1986, 1987. "The PNDC Budget Statement and Economic Policy for 1985, 1986 and 1987." Mimeographed.

—. 1986a. "Ghana Agricultural Policy: Actions, Plans and Strategies, 1986-88." Mimeographed.

—. 1986b. "Report on Sample Census of Agriculture of Ghana: 1984." Vol. I. Accra: Ministry of Agriculture, Economic Research and Planning Service. Mimeographed.

—. 1986c. "Estimates of Area, Production and Yield of Principal Crops in Ghana: 1977-83." Published as Field Document No. 3 of UNDP/FAO Project GHA/84/003, "Improvement of Agricultural Statistics". Accra: Ministry of Agriculture, Economic Research and Planning Service. Mimeographed.

—. 1986d. "Five-Year Rehabilitation and Development Plan (1987-81) and Project Profiles." Accra: Ghana Water and Sewerage Corporation. Mimeographed.

—. 1986e. "The Search for Good Drinking Water from Hand-dug Wells for Small Rural Communities in Ghana (National Hand-dug Well Programme)." Accra: Ghana Water and Sewerage Corporation, Rural Water Development Division. Mimeographed.

—. 1986f. "Report on Home Extension Programme, Volta Region Agricultural Development Project." Mimeographed.

—. 1987a. "Programme of Actions to Mitigate the Social Costs of Adjustment." Report for Donor Conference. Mimeographed.

—. 1987b. "Problems of Small Scale Agriculture in Ghana." The Coordinating Committee of the Agricultural Sector. Mimeographed.

——. 1987c. "Performance of the Agricultural Sector: 1987." Accra: Ministry of Agriculture. Mimeographed.

——. 1987d. "Development Conditions in the Volta Region of Ghana." Ho: Ministry of Agriculture, Volta Region Agricultural Development Project (VORADEP). Mimeographed.

——. 1987e. "Public Investment Programme 1986-88." Accra: Ministry of Finance and Economic Planning. Mimeographed.

——. 1987f. "Quarterly Digest of Statistics (June 1987)." Accra: Central Bureau of Statistics. Mimeographed.

——. 1987g. "Water and Sanitation Conference Papers." Accra: Ministry of Public Works and Housing. Mimeographed.

——. 1987h. "Annual Sample Survey of Agriculture 1986." Accra: Ministry of Agriculture. Mimeographed.

Republic of Ghana/United Nations Development Programme. 1987. "Rural Water Supply and Sanitation Programme (1987-2001), Project GHA/82/004." Accra: Republic of Ghana/United Nations Development Programme. Mimeographed.

Republic of Ghana (MOA)/World Bank. 1989. "Medium Term Agricultural Development Plan (MTADP)." Various working papers. Mimeographed.

Sallinger, L. 1986. "Ghana Agricultural Sector Rehabilitation Project: Agricultural Pricing and Trade Policy Framework." Draft Working Paper No. 9, prepared for the World Bank/WAPAB. Mimeographed.

Sam, E. 1982. "Women's Access to Institutional Credit and Savings Facilities in a Selected Area in Ghana: A Case Study." Accra: Agricultural Development Bank. Mimeographed.

Seini, W. 1983. "Artisanal Fisheries." Legon: Institute of Statistical, Social and Economic Research, University of Ghana. Mimeographed.

——. 1984. "Conduct and Utility of Socio-economic Studies on the Fisheries of Ghana." Legon: Institute of Statistical, Social and Economic Research, University of Ghana. Mimeographed.

——. 1985. *Poverty of Resource Endowment and Use: Implication for the Production and Supply of Seed Cotton in Western Pagbong of Ghana.* Institute of Statistical, Social and Economic Research Technical Publication Series No. 47. Legon: Institute of Statistical, Social and Economic Research, University of Ghana.

Tabatabai, Hamid. 1986. *Economic Decline, Access to Food and Structural Adjustment in Ghana.* (ILO) World Employment

Programme Research, Working Papers . No. 80. Geneva: International Labour Organisation.

Technology Consultancy Centre. *Annual Review No. 11 (1982-83); No. 12 (1983-84); No. 13 (1984-85).* Kumasi: University of Science and Technology.

Tettey, E. 1983. "Towards Rural Women's Accessibility to Institutional Credit." Freetown: WACACT Seminar on Management Training and Agricultural Credit.

UN Regional Institute for Population Studies, Legon, Ghana, and International Labour Organisation. 1985. Proceedings of the Seminar on Women, Population and Development, Ghana. Mimeographed.

United Nations Children's Fund. 1984. "Ghana, Situation Analysis of Women and Children." Mimeographed.

——. 1986. "Services for Women and Children in Ghana (1986-1990)." Accra. Mimeographed.

United Nations Children's Fund/National Council on Women and Development/Food Research Institute. 1985. A Practical Guide to Improved Fish Smoking in West Africa.

United Nations Development Programme. 1987. "Development Cooperation - Ghana: 1986 Report." Mimeographed.

United Nations Development Programme/Food and Agriculture Organization. 1977. "Agricultural Statistics Support Project GHA/77/002." Field Document No. 4. Mimeographed.

University of Rhode Island. 1979. "Artisan Fishery Technology: Ghana, A Case Study of West African Fishery." Mimeographed.

Volta Region Agricultural Development Project Monitoring and Evaluation Unit. 1985a. "1984/1985 Baseline Survey." Mimeographed.

——. 1985b. "Contact Farmer Survey Report." Mimeographed.

World Health Organization. 1986. *Monitoring the Strategies for Health for All by the Year 2000.* Geneva: World Health Organization.

World Bank. 1976. "Appraisal of Upper Region Agricultural Development Project." Washington, D.C.: World Bank. Mimeographed.

——. 1984. "Ghana: Policies and Programmes for Adjustment." Vol. 1 (Main Report); Vol. 2 (Statistical Appendix). Report No. 4702-GH. Washington, D.C.: World Bank. Mimeographed.

——. 1985a. "Ghana Agricultural Sector Review." Report No. 5366-GH. Washington, D.C.: World Bank. Mimeographed.

——. 1985b. "Ghana Agricultural Sector Review." Background Papers to Report No. 5366-GH. Washington, D.C.: World Bank. Mimeographed.

——. 1985c. "Ghana: Towards Structural Adjustment." Report No. 5854-GH. Vol. I (Main Report); Vol. 2 (Statistical Appendixes). Washington, D.C.: World Bank. Mimeographed.

——. 1985d. "Upper Region Agricultural Development Project." Completion Report. Washington, D.C.: World Bank. Mimeographed.

——. 1986a. Consultative Group for Ghana. "Status Report." Prepared by the World Bank. Washington, D.C.: World Bank. Mimeographed.

——. 1986b. "Ghana Irrigation Sub-sector Review." Report No. 6173-GH. Mimeographed.

——. 1987a. "Ghana: Structural Adjustment Programme." (Report and Recommendations to the Executive Directors of the International Development Association). Report No. P-4493-GH. Washington, D.C.: World Bank. Mimeographed.

——. 1987b. "Ghana: Policies and Issues of Structural Adjustment." Report No. 6635-GH. Washington, D.C.: World Bank. Mimeographed.

——. 1987c. "Ghana: Agricultural Services Rehabilitation Project." Appraisal Report. Report No. 6645-GH. Washington, D.C.: World Bank. Mimeographed.

——. 1989. "Feeder Road Rehabilitation Project." Report on World Bank Preparation Mission. Washington, D.C.: World Bank. Mimeographed.

Index

"Abusa" groups, 149

African Development Bank, 208

Agricultural development, 77, 204-205

Agricultural Development Bank (ADB), 67, 127, 132

   Agrobusiness Individual Loans, 108, 191

   Commodity Credit Scheme, 108, 128

Agricultural gross domestic product, 20

Agricultural Research Development and Advisory Committee support needs, 123

Agricultural Services Rehabilitation Project (ASRP), 14, 30, 118, 119, 124, 126, 205, 208

Agriculture: exchange rate effects on prices, 20

   export diversification, 9, 20

   foreign exchange earnings (1987), 8

   government credit policies, 131, 132

   marketing, 133-134

   policies, 12-14

   role in economy, 20-21

Alley-cropping and soil fertility, 43

Animal draught power research, 122

Appropriate technology, 96, 105, 122

Artisanal. *see* Small-scale ...

Ashanti Region:

   cropping patterns, 27

   ecology and crops, 24, 26

Bank of Credit and Commerce, 127

Bank of Ghana, 7, 127, 129, 132, 190

Bank for Housing and Construction, 127, 128

Barclays Bank of Ghana, Ltd., 127, 128

Basic Education Programme, 188

Basic Needs Income (BNI), 62

Bauxite, 1987 earnings, 8

Block farming programme, 190-191

Brong-Ahafo Region:

   cropping patterns, 27

   ecology and crops, 24, 26

Bulk storage for grain, expansion under ERP, 33

Bush-fallow: in agricultural rotation, 26, 27

Cash crops (*see also* individual crops):

   effect on traditional land tenure, 73-75

Cassava: as a famine reserve, 28

   "gari" processing, 34, 104

   improved varieties from IITA, 45, 204

   policies for (1983-86), 13

   processing for storage, 34

   storage research, 122

   testing of new varieties (Volta Region), 45, 204

   where grown, 24, 26

Catholic Relief Services (CRS), 81

Central Bank [of Ghana] and liberalization of interest rates, 7

Cereals: imports (1975-87) 15

Charcoal: small-scale production by women's groups, 102

Children: health care, 82

"Chorker" fish smoking oven, 40, 102

Christian Council of Ghana, 80

Christian Services Committee, 153

Churches, in NGO activities, 157

CIDA:

   Grains Development Project, 29, 121

Input Supply, 208
Women in Development, 114, 117
CIMMYT and Grains Development
    Project, 121
Civil service reforms under ERP and SAP,
    6, 11, 183
Cocoa and cocoa industry:
    effects of government levies on, 91
    foreign exchange earnings (1987), 8
    Ghana Cocoa Marketing Board, 6, 7
    in-country migration, 51
    price reforms, 6
    real price trends, 166
    smuggling of, 91, 166
    effects of SAP on production, 169
    and traditional gender divisions, 94
    where grown, 24
Cocoyam, 12, 24, 26
Coffee: reform of farmers' price, 6
Colonial policies (history), 12
Commerbank Farmers' Associations and
    small farmer credit, 128
Commodity price collapse effects, 3
Community Development Department, 80
Consumer goods imports under Special
    Import Licences, 6
Consumer Price Index changes under ERP,
    173
Consultative Group for Ghana, 5, 216
Cooperatives, 128, 151-152, 158-159
Côte d'Ivoire: cocoa smuggling to, 91
Cotton: farmer price reforms, 6
    support priorities, 123
    where grown, 26
Council of Scientific and Industrial
    Research (CSIR), 118, 120
Cowpea: in Grains Development Project,
    43-44, 121, 122
Credit: formal sector, 127-130, 206, 207
    government policies (agriculture),
    131-132
    group lending, 108

informal sector, 109, 131
rural, experiences and plans, 108-109,
    206-207
Crops:
    production methods, 28-30
    regional patterns, 52-55
    rotations, 27-28
    yields, 31-32
Crops Research Institute (CRI):
    CIDA-supported Grains Development
        Project, 121
    IFAD-supported National Root and
        Tuber Research Programme, 45
    IFAD-supported Smallholder
        Rehabilitation and Development
        Programme, 42

DANIDA support for cereal storage under
    ERP, Ph. II, 34
Demography, 61-62
Department of Community Development:
    extension services for women, 109-110
    Home Science Extension Programme,
        110-111
Department of Cooperatives, 151
Department of Extension Services (of
    MOA):
    reorganization in ERP, 125
Department of Feeder Roads:
    constraints to effectiveness, 206
Department of Social Welfare, 81-155
Devaluation: effects, 6, 163-164, 178, 199
Development organizations for women,
    113, 114, 115, 116
Diamonds: foreign exchange earnings
    (1987), 8
District Land Allocation Committees:
    role and representation, 77
Drought (1982-83), 9, 12, 31, 42
Drugs, basic: supply constraints, 82

Eastern Region: ecology and crops, 24-26

EC: use of food aid from, 203
   donor aid for inputs, 208
Ecological zones, 24-26
Economic Recovery Programme (ERP):
   civil service reforms, 11
   consumer price index, 173
   education reforms in Phase II, 188
   exchange rate effects on inputs, 173
   extension improvements, 125
   fertilizer supply privatization, 126
   fiscal restraints impact on agriculture,
      179-180
   effect on labour markets, 174
   macro-economic performance, 8-11
   effect on MOA budget, 192
   policy instruments for, 5-6
   real wage trends, 174
   road rehabilitation, 206
   short-term effects on smallholders, 192
Economy and external debt burden, 9
Education, 82, 112, 188-189
Electrification, rural improvements, 8
Employment, patterns and changes, 62
Environmental Action Plan and the Mid-
      Term Agricultural Development
      Programme, 42
Environment, 21, 41-43
Erosion, sheet, 42
European Economic Community, 156
Exchange rate (*see also* Devaluation):
   effects on agricultural prices, 20
Exports: agricultural diversification, 9
   non-traditional commodities, 20
   in domestic price support, 198
Extended Fund Facility (of IMF), 5
   policy instruments in ERP, 6
   macro-economic targets, 6
Extension (general):
   activities of NGOs, etc., 124
Extension (MOA):
   Department of Extension Services, 125,
      150, 205

Extension services for women, 109-110
External debt, 3, 9

FAO: fish smoking improvements,
      102-103
   Freedom from Hunger Campaign, 150
   nutrition education, 80
   People's Participation Programme, 149
   strengthening of Post-Harvest Unit (of
      MOA), 33
Farm implements: appropriate technology
      research at Nyankpala, 122
Farm size and distribution, 27
Farmers' associations, and Sasakawa -
      Global 2000, 153
Farming systems, 27-28, 43-44, 123
Female-headed households, 31, 91, 93,
      109
Fertilizer, 29, 44, 185-186, 207-208
Financial Sector Adjustment Credit, 132,
      207
Fisheries, 38, 67-68
Fish smoking, 39, 102-103
Food: deficit growth, 15
   financing of imports, 15-18
   imports (1975-87), 15
   constraints to self-sufficiency, 204
   security, national, 14-18, 211-212
Food Aid, 199-203
Food-for-work schemes, 8, 200
Food Research Institute, Accra, 81, 122
Food Storage and Processing Project (of
      UNICEF), 117
Foreign exchange earnings, 8
Forestry, 40-41
France, use of food aid from, 203

GDP: growth under ERP, 8
Gender divisions, 94-96
Ghana Cocoa Marketing Board (Cocobod):
   price adjustments to farmers, 6
   and reform of SOEs, 7

Ghana Commercial Bank, 108, 128
Ghana Cooperative Bank, 127
Ghana Cotton Company, 119
Ghana Enterprise Development
  Commission (of the Min. of Finance
  and Economic Planning), 115
  support to small-scale manufacturing,
  115-116
Ghana Food Distribution Corporation, 13,
  119
  grain storage/handling in ERP Ph. I, 34
  and monetization of food aid, 203
Ghana Food Production Corporation, 7
Ghana Irrigation Development Authority
  (GIDA), 36-37, 119
Ghana National Procurement Agency, and
  fertilizer imports (pre-1984), 125
Ghana National Trading Company, and
  input procurement, 125
Ghana National Trading Corporation
  (GNTC) and fisheries inputs, 68
Ghana Seed Company, Ltd., 119, 125, 208
Ghana Timber Marketing Board, 40
Gold: foreign exchange earnings (1987), 8
Grains and Legumes Development Board
  (of MOA), 121, 203
Grains Development Project, 29-30,
  121-122
Grains storage/handling:
  improvements under ERP, 34
Grass-roots institutions, 147-151
  linkages with other agencies, 158-160
Greater Accra Region:
  large livestock farms, 52
Groundnut, 26, 43
Group formation, 68, 105-106
Group Lending Programme (of ADB), 108
Group Loan schemes, 128-129

Health and health services, 8, 79-80, 82, 86
Health and Education Rehabilitation
  Programme under ERP, 188-189

IDA, 40, 132, 208
IFAD: and crop improvement, 204
  framework for assistance, 209-217
  support to NCWD, 114
  National Root and Tuber Research
  Programme, 204
  Smallholder Rehabilitation and
  Development Programme, 42
  support to rural women, 216
IITA: and improved cassava varieties, 45
  and crop improvements, 204
  in Grains Development Project, 121
  and cowpea improvement, 121
  mini-sett technique for yam, 45
ILO: improved fish-smoking oven, 102
  support to NCWD, 114
  support to rural women, 216
IMF: Economic Recovery Programme
  (ERP), 5
  Extended Fund Facility, 5
Imports: data on cereals (1975-87), 15
Import substitution, 2, 9
Income: generation in social sector
  management, 8
  off-farm opportunities, 51
  sources for smallholders, 56-58
Industrialization policies (1966-81), 2, 12
Infrastructure:, 11, 203
Inheritance, 107-108
Inputs (agriculture, fisheries), 29, 125-126
  cost impact of devaluation, 173
  public procurement, 125, 207
  supply problems, 29, 68, 125, 207-208
  supply through donors, 208
  supply through private sector, 184-186
Integrated Community Actions for Women
  in Development (of UNDP), 116
Integrated pest management (IPM) in
  farming systems research, 42
Intercropping in farming systems, 27
Interest rates, 7, 131, 186

Investment: improvements under ERP, 8
Irrigation: sector development plans,
    35-37

Kenaf, 26
"Konkonte" and plantain storage, 34

Labour: family and rural wages, 178
    female and child in crop transport, 98
    numbers of, 56
    regional patterns, 56
    use (general), 31
    use by farmers, 56
Land: availability, 21
    distribution, 21, 46
    effects of SAP on, 185
    Land Allocation Committee, 77
    suitability assessments, 21
    security, 74
    tenure constraints, 69, 73-79
    types of tenure, 71-73
    use, 21
    women's access to, 107
Legal systems, customary and
    constitutional, 108
Legumes (*see also* Cowpea; Groundnut;
    Grains Development Project):
    trees and alley-cropping, 43
Livestock: main breeds, 37-38
    disease problems, 38
    imports of (1975-86), 15
    ownership patterns, 51
    sector contribution to AGDP (1977-87),
    37

Macro-economy: historical background, 1
    performance under ERP, 8
    post-independence strategies, 2
Maize: in Grains Development Project,
    121
    improved varieties, 29, 44
    mechanized mono-cropping, 28

policies for (1983-86), 13
production (1984-1985), 13
research at Nyankpala, 122
storage-loss research, 122
technology "packages", 29, 203
where grown, 26, 27, 28
Manganese: foreign exchange earnings
    (1987), 8
Marketing: and Cooperatives, 102, 133
Matrilineal systems and women's access to
    land, 107
Mechanization (*see also* Motorization):
    vs. labour-intensive development, 90
    in village-level processing, 103-104
Medium-Term Agricultural Development
    Plan (MTADP), 21, 43
Merchant Bank [of Ghana], 127
Migration: effect of cocoa decline, 51
    in-country, 21, 48-51, 62, 69
    in-migration, 1
    out-migration, 48, 91
    effect on population growth, 61
    repatriation from Nigeria (1983), 9, 12,
    31-32
Millet: improved technology needed, 204
    research at Nyankpala, 45
    traditional production, 27
    where grown, 26
Ministry of Agriculture (MOA). 118-120
    and agricultural policy (1983-86), 13
    analysis of budgets 1987-89, 180
    and block farming scheme, 190-191
    extension activities, 80, 109, 110, 125,
    205
    extension linkage with "Sasakawa-
    Global 2000", 153-154
    and input supply, 125-126
    institutional reform in, 120
    irrigation extension, 32
    irrigation targets, 36
    organization of, 119
    post-colonial changes, 12

responsibilities and staffing, 118-119
and State-Owned Enterprises (SOEs),
119-119
Ministry of Finance and Economic
Planning:
guidelines in PIP and SAP, 7
Ministry of Health (MOH), 80, 109
Ministry of Industries, Science and
Technology:
and agricultural research, 118
Ministry of Local Government and Rural
Development:
nutrition education, 80
and UNDP in local development, 159
Ministry of Youth and Rural Development:
extension for rural women, 109-112
Home Service Extension Programme,
110
Money supply under ERP, 8

National Council on Women and
Development (NCWD), 40
National Investment Board and block
farming scheme, 190
National Root and Tuber Research
Programme, 45, 123
National Savings and Credit Bank, 127
Netherlands, Government of the:
production of technical manuals, 116
support to NCWD, 114, 116
Nigeria: migration to (1970-82), 48, 91
repatriation from (1983), 9, 12, 31
NGOs: activities, 153-157
collaboration in IFAD plans, 213
coordination of activities, 117, 152
and food aid, 203
and health assistance, 80
liaison with other agencies, 156
methods of operation, 155
and nutritional rehabilitation centres, 80
sectoral involvement, 153
activities for women, 117

"Nnoboa", 148, 158
Northern Region: cattle, 51
ecology and crops, 26
plans for bulk storage (ERP Ph. III), 34
research on, at Nyankpala, 42
out-migration to Upper East Region, 21
sectoral support under SAP, 8
Nutrition, 8, 80-81, 158
Nyankpala Research Station, Tamale:
farming systems research (savannah), 42
Grains Development Project, 122
research activities, 122
and seed production, 122

Oil-palm: as a plantation crop, 27
small-scale processing, 103
where grown, 24

Parastatals. *see* State Owned Enterprises
(SOEs)
Pasturing: where important, 26
Patrilineal systems and women's access to
land, 107
Plantain:
where grown, 24, 26
Policy: government policies, 2, 12-14,
131-132
Population: structure and growth, 61
Post-harvest: lack of handling facilities, 13
handling and storage, 33-35
Post-Harvest Development Unit (of MOA):
strengthening by FAO, 33
Poverty: definition of absolute, 62
use of "Basic Needs Income": index, 62
effects and land tenure, 75-77
poverty line, 62-67
regional patterns, 66
Prices: food products demand elasticity,
195
marketing strategy need, 194
real, for producers, 2
real, variations in staples, 194

reform (administered), 6
Private sector effects of SAP, 184-185
Programme of Actions to Mitigate the
    Social Costs of Adjustment
    (PAMSCAD), 216-217
    and impact of SAP, 189
Provisional National Defence Council
    (PNDC):
    on Land Allocation Committees, 77
Public sector: finance charges since
    1983, 9
    reforms, 6
    wage reforms, 7
Public Investment Programme (PIP), 7,
    11-12, 82, 131

Rainfall and planting patterns, 44
Reconstruction Import Credits, 6, 125
Recovery rates of (loans):
    factors in commercial sector, 128-129
    under Small-Scale Loan Scheme, 115
Reforms:
    administrative, and farmer services,
        183-184
    in fiscal policy, 7
    institutional, under ERP, 180-184
    in MOA, 120
    of public sector, 6, 11, 184
    of SOEs, 119
Repatriation from Nigeria, 1983, 9, 12, 31
Research (Agriculture):
    adaptive, German aid for, 122
    commodity responsibilities, 121
    coordination, 120
    Council for Scientific and Industrial
        Research (CSIR), 118-119, 120
    Crops Research Institute (CRI), 121
    funding for, 122
    Grains Development Project, 29, 32, 43,
        121-124
    linkages with extension, 125

National Root and Tuber Research
    Programme, 45, 123
    needs, 123
    Nyankpala Research Station, 42, 122
    organization of, 120, 125
    plans (long-term), 123
Resource base for agriculture, 23-26
Rice: imported varieties, 45
    improved practices for valley bottoms,
        204
    large farm mono-cropping, 28
    research at Nyankpala, 122
    research priorities for swamp, 123
    where grown, 24-26
Root crops: National Root and Tuber
    Research Programme, 204
    research on, 42
Rubber, 24, 26
Rural Banks (RBs), 108, 127-130, 132
Rural incomes and assets, 46-51
Rural poverty estimates, 62-67

Sanitation: improvement, 8, 85
    rural coverage, 85, 86
Savings: improvements under ERP, 8
Sector rehabilitation and PIP, 8
Seeds: foundation, at Nyankpala, 122
    improved varieties of maize, 44
    Ghana Seed Company, Ltd., 125, 208
    supply plans, 208
Share-cropping tenure, 74
Shea-butter: small-scale production by
    women's groups, 102, 103, 104
Shifting cultivation and environment, 41
Smallholders: cropping patterns, 52-55
    consumption and expenditure patterns,
        59-61
    credit under PAMSCAD, 132
    government policy impact (pre-1980),
        90
    income sources, 56-58
    linkages with money economy, 163

short-term effects of ERP, 192
in social sector management, 8
structural constraints to development,
    193-208
targetting in IFAD plans, 212, 213
and tree crops, 52
Smallholder Rehabilitation and
    Development Programme, 42
Small-scale fisheries, 67-68
Small-Scale Loan Scheme (of Ghana
    Enterprises Development
    Commission), 115
Small-scale production by women's
    groups, 102-104
Smoking, of fish, 39, 102
Smuggling: of cocoa out, 3, 91, 166
of timber, out, 40
Social security: Department of Social
    Welfare, 158
Social Security Bank, 127
loan recovery rates, 128
Social services:
    organizations, 158
    under SAP, 187-190
Socio-economic differentiation, 86-91
Soil: conservation research needs, 204
    fertility and alley-cropping, 43
    fertility losses, 191
    fertility maintenance, 43
    fertility research, Nyankpala, 122
Sorghum: improved technology needs,
    204
    "pito" brewing, 104
    replacement by maize, 45
    research at Nyankpala, 45, 122
    traditional production, 28
    where grown, 26
Staple crops: comparative advantages, 199
    policies for (1983-86), 12
State-Owned Enterprises (SOEs), 2, 7,
    118-119

Storage:
    bulk, capacity increases under ERP, 34
    government policies, 198-199
    price incentives, 144, 198
Structural Adjustment Programme (SAP):
    administrative reforms in, 183-184
    circumstances leading to, 1-4
    and Economic Recovery Programme
        (ERP), 4-8
    effects on private sector, 184
    fiscal policy in, 7, 179-180
    focus on cocoa increase, 169
    institutional reforms in, 183-184
    macro-economic performance in, 8-11
    privatization target, 185
    and civil service reforms, 183
    and smallholders, 161-192
Sugar-cane, 26
Sweet potato: testing improved varieties,
    45, 204

Taxes: effect on cocoa industry, 91
    on non-food crops, 2
Technology in crop production, 28-30,
    44-45
Tobacco: reforms of farmers' prices, 6
    where grown, 26
Togo: cocoa smuggling to, 91
Trade: barriers, 2
    effect on food prices, 199
    policy reform under ERP, 5
Traders, role and importance of women,
    98-99
Transport:
    Department of Feeder Roads, 206
    general problems, 8, 206
    infrastructure rehabilitation using food
        aid, 203
    railways rehabilitation, 8
Transport Rehabilitation Programme, 206

UNDP: and education reform
(ERP Ph. II), 188
Integrated Community Actions for
Women in Development, 116
and local development, 159
support to rural women, 116
UNICEF: Food Storage and Processing
Project, 117
improved fish-smoking oven
("Chorker"), 40, 102, 117
and NGO liaison, 156
and nutrition education, 81
support to NCWD, 114
support to rural women, 116
support to small-scale processing, 117
United Kingdom, Government of:
credit for forestry sector, 40
and education reform (ERP Ph. II), 188
support for bulk storage (ERP Ph. I), 34
Upper East Region: bulk storage plans, 33
cattle, 51
cropping patterns, 27
ecology and crops, 26
Upper Region Agricultural Development
Project (URADEP), 180
Upper West Region: bulk storage plans,
34
cattle, 51
cropping patterns, 27
Urbanization, 8, 61
USAID: support to NCWD, 114
use of food aid from, 203

Volta Region: crops grown, 26
ecology of, 26
Volta Region Agricultural Development
Project (VORADEP), 180
Voluntary Service Overseas (VSO), 153

Wages: civil service reforms, 7
real, trends under ERP, 174

Water: assistance for well-drilling, 85
rural access to, 85
regional variations, 85
-related diseases, 86
supply improvements, 8
Watson Commission Report (1948), 12
Western Region: bulk storage installed
(ERP Ph. I), 34
crops grown, 24
ecology of, 24
WHO and nutrition education, 81
Women (*see also* Development;
Extension; Female-headed
households):
and access to credit, 108-109
and access to land, 107
appropriate technology needed for, 96
education levels/literacy, 112
and extension services, 109-112
farmers and new maize technology, 29
"gari" processing, 104
and Ghana Enterprises Development
Commission, 115
group formation benefits, 105-106
and hired labour, 99
as labour in transport of crops, 98
NGO activities for, 117
and off-farm activities, 100-106
productivity constraints, 99
and rural development role in
agriculture, 96-99
rural, targetted in IFAD plans, 213-214
and social sector management, 8
support from international agencies, 116
31st December Women's Movement,
115-116
traders in crops, 98-99
workload and responsibilities, 94-100
World Bank:
and ERP, 5
Reconstruction Import Credit Facilities,
6

and SAP, 5
and restructuring of SOEs, 7
World Food Programme (WFP), and food-
    for-work projects, 200

Yam: as a cash crop, 28
    mini-sett technique, 45, 204
    where grown, 26

A Note on the Authors

Alexander Sarris is currently Professor of Economics at the University of Athens, Greece. He received his Ph.D. in economics from the Massachusetts Institute of Technology and has taught at the University of California at Berkeley.

Hadi Shams, who served as the Senior Economist for the Africa Region in the Policy and Planning Division and as a Project Controller for the Africa Division at IFAD, received his Ph.D. degree from Cambridge University and has lectured on agricultural planning and development management at universities in Iran. He is currently on secondment to UNDP/Office of Project Services.

ıe